Emerging Patterns
in American Higher Education

EMERGING
PATTERNS
IN AMERICAN
HIGHER
EDUCATION

edited by LOGAN WILSON

AMERICAN COUNCIL ON EDUCATION · WASHINGTON, D.C.

© 1965 BY AMERICAN COUNCIL ON EDUCATION
One Dupont Circle
Washington, D.C. 20036

Second impression, January 1966
Third impression, July 1966
Fourth impression, February 1968
Fifth impression, January 1971

Library of Congress Catalog Card Number 65-19783

ISBN 0-8268-1274-0

PRINTED IN THE UNITED STATES OF AMERICA

Contributing Authors

JAMES E. ALLEN, JR.
State Commissioner of Education, New York

ROBERT C. ANDERSON
Executive Vice-President, Auburn University

JOSEPH AXELROD
Dean, School of Humanities and Fine Arts, California State College
at Palos Verdes

LOUIS T. BENEZET
President, Claremont Graduate School and University Center

MARY WOODS BENNETT
Dean of the Faculty, Mills College

EDMUND G. BROWN
Governor of the State of California

JOHN T. CALDWELL
Chancellor, North Carolina State of the University of North Carolina at Raleigh

THEODORE A. DISTLER
President Emeritus, Association of American Colleges

ELMER ELLIS
President, University of Missouri

HAROLD L. ENARSON
Academic Vice-President, University of New Mexico

JOHN T. FEY
President, University of Wyoming

WILLIAM P. FIDLER
General Secretary, American Association of University Professors

JOHN W. GARDNER
President, Carnegie Corporation of New York

MILLARD E. GLADFELTER
President, Temple University

RIXFORD K. SNYDER
Director of Admissions, Stanford University

BLAIR STEWART
President, Associated Colleges of the Midwest

RUSSELL I. THACKREY
Executive Secretary, National Association of State Universities and Land-Grant Colleges

STANLEY J. WENBERG
Vice-President for Educational Relationships and Development, University of Minnesota

LOGAN WILSON
President, American Council on Education

Preface

ALTHOUGH modifications in the structure of higher education still lag behind changes in the function it is called upon to perform, new patterns of organization and administration are emerging at a rate faster than many persons—including educators—are aware. These new forms are developing in the relationships *among* colleges and universities as well as those *within* them. *Emerging Patterns in American Higher Education* should heighten the general awareness of what is happening and increase the readiness to meet the enormous pressures our system of higher education will be subject to in the years ahead.

Most of the papers included in this volume were first prepared for the annual meeting of the American Council on Education in San Francisco on October 1–2, 1964, but the presentation here is not simply a set of proceedings. Five of the papers (those by Joseph Axelrod, Lyman A. Glenny, James C. Messersmith, Robert H. Kroepsch and M. Stephen Kaplan, and Russell I. Thackrey) were published prior to the conference and given limited circulation to members of the Council as background material for the discussions to follow. My own commentaries originally appeared elsewhere and are included because of their relevance to the theme of this book. ("American Higher Education Confronts Its Future" is based on a manuscript for a North German Radio broadcast in 1963; "Myths and Realities of Institutional Independence" appeared in *Graduate Comment,* April 1964; "Form and Function in American Higher Education" is reprinted from the *Educational Record,* Summer 1964; "Basic Premises for a National Policy in Higher Education" was given as a lecture at Harvard University during the summer of 1962; "A Better Partnership for the Federal Government and Higher Education" was first published in the *Educational Record,* April 1963.

"Autonomy and Interdependence: Emerging Systems in Higher Education" was the theme of the Council's 1964 meeting. Some of the presentations made on that occasion were not entirely relevant to the reorganized treatment in this volume, but twenty-seven of them proved to be highly appropriate and these have been revised for present purposes. Most of the authors are well-known educational leaders who are also recognized authorities on their various subjects. Personally and for the Council I want to express appreciation for their contributions. I also want to thank Mrs. Carla Sykes, staff assistant, for her editorial services in reviewing all of the manuscripts.

January 1965   LOGAN WILSON

ix

Contents

American Higher Education
Confronts Its Future

LOGAN WILSON

RECENTLY IN educational circles the "explosion of population" and the "explosion of knowledge" have been talked about to the point of becoming clichés. Much less attention has been given, however, to other circumstances which affect the nation's colleges and universities. Is the broad pattern of American higher education an appropriate one for our present and future needs? What new systems of organization and administration are emerging? Can further changes be anticipated?

The various contributors to this book address themselves to these and other important questions having to do with the structure and function of higher education. Many of them touch upon conflicts between the concepts of "autonomy" and "interdependence," and show the varying influences brought to bear by centripetal and centrifugal forces.

The American System of Higher Education

As background for the commentaries to follow, it should be noted here that there is really no formalized, national system of education in the United States. On the primary and secondary level, according to one source, there are approximately 48,000 basic administrative units, each with a large measure of independent control of schools. On the upper reaches, the autonomy of units on the same campus is suggested in somebody's description of the large American university as an agglomeration of entities connected only by a common plumbing system. Moreover, not even this connection exists among the separate campuses of the more than 2,000 colleges and universities which comprise American higher education.

If educational adequacy is to be judged solely by the number and variety of institutions, then perhaps there is no cause for worry. Counting only institutions listed in the *U.S. Office of Education Directory*, there are 644 of the junior college type, 792 four-year institutions, 455 which offer work through the master's level, 223 which grant the doctorate, and 25 unclassified. Of these, there are 12 under Federal control, 405 under state control, 357 under local

1

government units, 507 private and nondenominational, 483 Protestant, 361 Roman Catholic, and eight Jewish.

No other nation even approaches us in the number and diversity of institutions of higher education. They range in size from those including mere dozens of students to those enrolling more than 45,000. Some admit only the few of top ability and clearly defined interests, whereas others accept any high school graduate and offer credit courses in everything from needlecraft to nuclear physics. As one study notes, the kinds of student cultures found on American campuses vary from the so-called collegiate, or "rah rah," to the predominantly vocational, academic, and noncomformist. Among these institutions, one sees the whole spectrum of contrasts between a community of individuals and a bureaucratic collectivity of trainees.

In general, our colleges and universities are more affected by outside social forces than they once were. Some are autonomously apart from their immediate environment, but most are caught up by it and cannot escape popular conceptions about what they ought to be. Their curricula are heavily influenced by changing occupational requirements; their size, by the rise of large-scale enterprise; their structure, by the growth of bureaucracy; their expansion, by the sharp population rise; and even their aims, by requirements which the larger society imposes.

To be sure, in few places have we gone as far as the Russians in merely professing broad aims while actually training specialists to meet political and economic requirements. Regardless of trends toward uniformity, nonetheless, the varied totality represented by our system of higher education still comes close to that supposedly impossible ideal of being all things to all men.

American colleges and universities continue to be characterized by localized independence in decision making. Causally viewed, their institutional freedom is related to the fact that they have never been subjected to the control of any political, religious, or other centralized agency. We take justifiable pride in a system which is characterized by diversification, decentralization, local autonomy, and free competition.

Strengths and Weaknesses of the System

The strengths of such a system, however, should not blind us to its weaknesses. That it has been on the whole well adapted to the demands of the past is no evidence for its being equally well adapted to the needs of the foreseeable future.

I am not about to suggest that we suppress the real values of academic freedom or that we abandon the utility of institutional diversity. Higher education's dispersed support and control, its free interplay of competition and cooperation have in general served us well. Even our disagreements about the means and ends of education are very often the manifestations of a healthy condition. Unplanned diversification, nonetheless, is not to be equated with the best interest of any particular college or university, much less that of our entire educational structure. One commentator has observed that we have in this country a congeries of institutions varying greatly in governance, size, atmosphere, programs, faculty quality, student characteristics, and intellectual standards.

In many states regulations are so lax that diploma mills are allowed to get away with open fraud. Certain regions have altogether too many indiscriminately established and inadequately maintained institutions. In other sections, there is a dearth of colleges and universities. Almost everywhere there is little evidence of a logical and carefully evolved division of labor. Candor should impel us to acknowledge, therefore, that the "rich diversity" of our educational ideal can become in reality little more than a poor divisiveness.

The virtues of decentralization also carry their attendant defects. Mere arithmetic addition of disparate educational enterprises may not produce a total endeavor sufficient for our national needs. Warranted fear of any arrangement resembling a Procrustean bed seems to be accompanied by an unwarranted disregard for the fact that decentralization per se affords no built-in protections against outside imposition. Furthermore, in an era of increased interdependence, decentralization leads to an unevenness of educational opportunity which limits the entire nation's manpower potential. Although no sensible person would advocate having our military manpower needs handled separately by private and public agencies in the fifty states of the Union, this is in effect what some believe to be the only proper educational approach to broader and more complicated manpower requirements.

Like diversification and decentralization, local autonomy is a widely cherished aspect of the American system of higher education. Its usefulness to the advancement of learning should not be underestimated, and even the provincial standards it has sometimes fostered have not been entirely lacking in utility. Today, nonetheless, the important denominators of intellectual achievement are universal and long since ceased to be matters for local determination.

The Costs of Unilateral Action

As it has become more important to the general welfare, higher education has also become more complicated, expensive, and interrelated. Entrenched views of institutional autonomy not only increase unnecessarily the price we must pay for an adequate educational system but also decrease both its efficiency and effectiveness as a coordinated instrumentality serving the best interests of the nation as a whole. These observations are not intended to imply that education at any level should be subservient to political needs, and I wish to go further and stress my view that the body politic, like the institutions it contains, should be regarded as a service agency to individuals. But in a free society important forms of competition must be regulated if chaos is to be avoided. Is there a valid reason for exempting educational institutions from this common requirement?

Although we like to think of educational changes as reflecting an orderly growth, the actual process, we must acknowledge, has often been quite different. For all the instances where interinstitutional competition has strengthened the rivals involved, there are at least as many where wasteful duplication and proliferation of mediocrity have ensued. Attitudes of educators as well as laymen impede a sensible division of responsibilities and an appropriate set of relations within and between institutions. Much lip service is given to the concept of diversity, but in practice there is an indiscriminate tendency to imitate the prestigious model of the university. Popular pressures build up to convert junior colleges into senior colleges, to have four-year institutions add graduate-level work, and to expand universities endlessly in horizontal directions. In the scramble, of course, unit costs rise unnecessarily, quality gets diluted, and shared objectives are forgotten.

Not only do state and regional needs tend to be neglected amid narrowly partisan efforts, but also national objectives are often omitted from consideration. Piecemeal incentives have been devised on the Federal level to offset the fortuitous circumstance that most of our institutions were not established and are not maintained primarily to serve national objectives. As these financial measures become more conspicuous, they do produce a changing pattern, but responses to them are sometimes slow and reluctant.

Some Federal measures are indeed ill-conceived, to be sure, and it is to be expected that their institutional implementation is not always enthusiastic. In view of the status of centralized coordination and planning under voluntary and strictly educational auspices, however, the legislative and executive branches of the Federal Government can hardly be blamed for moving into a vacuum which must be filled.

Paradoxes of Organization

My remarks up to this point may have given the impression that little, if any, coordination exists among our educational institutions. Actually, of course, American higher education does have a complex scheme of over-all organization. Numerous associations, mostly voluntary in membership, have evolved to promote varied but common ends. Perhaps because it is loosely rather than tightly articulated, higher education in the United States has spawned a large number and almost bewildering variety of groupings.

However, I doubt that any American educator could name more than a fraction of the 549 regional and national education associations, or the 148 college professional fraternities, honor and recognition societies, or the 480 state education associations, the 58 religious education associations, or the 15 international education associations which total more than twelve hundred organizations—nearly all voluntary in nature—having to do in one way or another with American education.

Beyond the associations consisting mainly of educators, still other individuals and groups are involved in the total organization of American higher education. For instance, there are lay boards of trustees and visitors, legislatures, governors, state budget officers, state-wide commissions and "super boards," semipolitical regional agencies and compacts, cooperative interinstitutional arrangements for mutual developments, more than forty executive agencies of the Federal Government, the Congress itself, and so on. For institutions as well as individuals, these frequently impose mandatory rather than merely permissive relationships.

In brief, although the 2,000 and more American colleges and universities may be inclined to go their separate ways, there is certainly no lack of agencies and associations intended to promote many kinds of unified effort. The sheer number and multifarious functions of these aggregations create further problems in themselves, however, so that paradoxically the whole of American higher education is both underorganized and overorganized.

It is still difficult for many persons to think of education in national terms. Even educational leaders are prone to behave as if the most pressing problems were confined to their particular specialties, campuses, or constituencies. This attitude persists despite the increased mutuality of disciplines, the expanded interconnections of institutions, and the growing interdependence of nations. Instead of a united effort to resolve the basic educational issues confronting the nation, accordingly, our collective endeavor is being confused and weakened by vested-interest group pressures, splinter movements, and fragmented approaches.

Whether voluntary enterprise is capable of achieving the long-range as well as the immediate objectives required of American higher education, if our nation is to survive and flourish, remains to be seen. In any event, more concerted effort is necessary, and we no longer have any option between disjointed *laissez faire* enterprise on the one hand and planned, integrated activity on the other. The only real choice remaining for institutional and associational leaders is whether they will get together to exercise major initiative in the reorganization of higher education, or stand aside while others assume this role.

1

The Changing Environment
of Higher Education

The New Conditions of Autonomy

JAMES A. PERKINS

THE IDEA OF university autonomy—of the sanctity of academic pursuits—is as old as the idea of the university itself. From the very beginning, this idea has been the doctrinal shield protecting the university from the state. More subtly, its quiet but persistent influence has helped to attenuate the relations of the university and the church. It has been the conceptual guardian of academic freedom, the moat around the city of the intellect whose drawbridge will lower only in response to internal signals.

These somewhat medieval figures of speech come naturally to the pen because the modern university was born in those middle centuries when autonomy was a necessity for survival. It is clear that the idea of the autonomous university was both in origin and usage a defensive term, a protection against both bishops and kings, a barrier to make secure those who would pursue rational studies in an irrational world, a doctrine calculated to keep the inquiring mind removed from the corrosive influence of mundane affairs.

But the medieval city has long since given way to the metropolis, the monastery to the mission and the modern knight is most probably a colonel with a Ph.D. in physics. The academic man has also "suffered a sea change." He has emerged from laboratory or library into the world of affairs. Consultant, entrepreneur, global traveler, and global investigator, he has left his restricted world to tender his advice, solicited or otherwise; to secure support for his projects; to organize his profession; to help make the world safe for the intellect; and, at the same time, to contribute that intellect to the world.

In this new posture, he has found himself among friends and admirers in both industry and government, many of whom have had very similar training. From this joining of hands of state, corporation, and university, some of the most dynamic and powerful forces of our era have emerged. New ideas generated on the campus have led to new business ventures and new public responsibilities. These ventures and these responsibilities have established requirements for new academic disciplines, new research directions, and new research tools. And these new university requirements have been financed in turn by the state and the corporation, and thus the modern, dynamic spiral has been put in motion.

8

Any university with a college of agriculture knows that the application of university-spawned technology to farming has made it possible to feed the starving in many parts of the world. We also know that it is the success of this mission that has led to ever-increasing budgets for even more spectacular research. And, surely, university-based research on nuclear structure led to the discovery of atomic energy with its large public applications, both military and civil. And these public programs are, in turn, the source of even greater demands on universities for further research.

We are only beginning to understand the enormous, even revolutionary power that has been created by this combination of interests. It has contributed to the evolution of the service state; to the idea of the private corporation with public concerns; and to the development of the modern university itself, which is responsible for much of the vitality of both. Now that these new relations have become stable features of the modern world, it is necessary for us to understand their impact on the university and especially to understand the profound changes which these new and close working relationships have brought to the very conditions of university autonomy.

Growth and Specialization

Caryl Haskins has provided a useful model for the study of organisms and organizations. He shows how growth leads to complexity, complexity to specialization, and specialization to a dynamic interplay of independence and integration. I think this model applies particularly to the development of higher education and, I believe, helps illuminate the new conditions of university autonomy. In explaining how I believe this to be so, I will first say something about the internal working of the university, then about the growth of external structures concerned with education, and then about the organizational hierarchy that is emerging. In all of this we should look for the great social imperatives that determine where in this hierarchy decisions must be made. From our analysis, perhaps we will have a better picture of the future of the two ideas of autonomy and interdependence.

First, with respect to the functioning of the university itself: How have its internal workings been affected by the new relationships it has established with government and business? Clearly it has, more than anything else, grown larger. In general, universities have become bigger rather than more numerous. And with this growth, the universities surely have become more complex; they have spawned an increasing array of colleges, schools, divisions, and departments to take care of the new groups as they emerge from the generality of study into the specificity of new disciplines and professional societies.

With specialization, the university internally has become caught in the eternal tension and counterplay of autonomy and interdependence. The more specialized the individual activity, the more difficult the job of supervision by university leaders and the greater must be the degree of decentralization that is both demanded and granted. In this case, internal autonomies are achieved just because the problem of supervision is intellectually most difficult. I might pause to observe that it takes a courageous dean and fearless president to deal firmly with budgetary requests from a specialty they can neither pronounce nor spell. And when they dare to intervene, they must rely heavily on past training in the proper interpretation of voice inflection and iris dilation as useful guides for executive decision making. But, of course, this is the stock in trade of all administrators, be they deans, presidents, company officers, or public officials.

Decentralization of decision making within the university is a reality reasonably familiar to most university presidents, though perhaps less well understood by the many publics whose frequent expectations for presidential decisiveness are, with almost equal frequency, disappointed. It is, however, with respect to the companion process of integration that the university does not follow the laws of other organisms.

Decentralization and Specialization

In the biological world, for example, increased specialization in the various parts of those wonderful sea creatures, the siphonophorans, has led to a tighter and tighter integration of the whole structure. Similarly, the specialization of tasks among the Incas led to a highly integrated society. But specialization within the university has not, on the whole, led to internal integration; it has, instead, tended to give impetus to the process of decentralization. The reason for this can be found in the same connections between the university and the outside world that led to specialization in the first place.

Stated differently, the impulse among these university specialties to communicate has led to strengthened outside relations rather than inside relations. Specialist has called to like-minded specialist, and together they have found their long-run interests better satisfied in larger organizations elsewhere than in the university which is their home base. The scale of activity, the cost of apparatus, the concern for large applications beyond the reach of the single university have led specialists, be they demographers or high energy physicists, to find a more natural and certainly rewarding headquarters in the regional laboratory or large foundation. In short, the refinement in specialization is almost reason enough for intellectual traffic to run on extra- rather than intra-university lines. But the cost of the enterprise and its new scale and scope have added new impetus to the desire and need for integrating these relations through larger nonuniversity structures.

Faculty and Administration

Before we proceed to an examination of these new external organizations, there is a special feature of the university landscape that must be noted as bearing further on the tendency for external integration. I refer to the pattern of administrative and faculty relationships in our large universities. This is too large a topic to deal with adequately and fully at this time. However, I advance the general proposition that, where administrative officers have not been able to involve themselves directly in the central academic business of the university, conditions work in favor of the external, rather than internal, forms of integration. Where the administrator has not had the background, ability, or desire to exert educational leadership, few large faculties have been able to provide that leadership for themselves. The result almost necessarily must be a diffusion of decision making. In short, where administrators are picked for their political or military experience rather than for their academic interests, or where faculties believe that administrators should be excluded from their counsels, the stage has been set to rob that university community of its prospects for internal cohesion. Without internal cohesion, the prospects for external integration are enormously increased. And with external integration, the prospects for university autonomy are reduced.

This is the real point of Harold Dodds's book on the university presidency—that the administration and faculty must learn that they have at least one overlapping mission, which is the internal integrity of the university—and the president and the faculty that forget this mission will see their university become a gigantic intellectual mobile—put in motion only by the chance currents of air generated by the opening and closing of distant doors.

State, Regional, and National Organizations

Let us turn now to the world of organizations concerned with higher education outside the university, a world which has been subjected to the same forces of growth, complexity, specialization, and integration as has the university itself. Just as growth within the university had led to complex internal arrangements, so has growth of higher education led to complex arrangements on the state, regional, and national scene. Just as new departments, schools, and divisions have arisen within a university to take care of new and special developments, so have special types and kinds of structures arisen to reflect various types of special interests in higher education. Specialization has really had a field day at the university level: two-year and four-year colleges; simple and complex universities; technical institutes and teachers colleges; men's, women's, and coeducational; religious and secular; public and private. Indeed, the process of specialization within the university looks like a very well ordered business compared to the process of specialization as it has affected the growth of our colleges and universities themselves. And this was inevitably so because there was no authority that could exert control over the development of these institutions in the same way that a university can exercise moderate control over the development of its own specializations.

And just as within the university, specialization has led to the need for and the demand for new integration, so has specialization in institutions of higher education themselves inevitably led to demands for integration. And these, too, have taken a bewildering variety of forms at all levels—state, regional, national, and worldwide. For our purpose here, it is fortunately not necessary to describe or review the various education-oriented organizations that have developed at all geographic levels, public and private, professional and institutional. I shall be content to confine this discussion to the effects this whole off-campus process has on university autonomy.

At the state and regional levels, efforts have been made to coordinate educational activities. These systems of coordination have been, in the main, systems applying to universities themselves. Coordination on the basis of subject matter is rare, but general institutional matters such as budget, personnel, or purchases are far more typical areas of state-wide activity. Thus at these levels, and particularly at the state level, the problem of autonomy is to maintain freedom from general executive controls.

The response at the national level, however, has been different, for until very recently the Federal Government in Washington has not had an educational mission as such. Educational activity there has been a by-product of other Federal programs that use various university specialties. It is not unnatural, therefore, that within the Federal Government organizations such as the National Institutes of Health have arisen to plan and coordinate Federal activities on the one hand and the national interests of particular specialties on the other. Although this Federal coordination is most advanced in the sciences and technology, the legislative hoppers are full of bills to establish similar organizations for the humanities, the arts, and the social sciences.

But, where the states have established organizations to coordinate the activities of universities as a whole, at the Federal level the coordination is solely with respect to subject matter. This presents an entirely different set of problems for those concerned with university autonomy. As national coordination of academic disciplines advances, without any counteractivity at the university level, the autonomy of the university will not be violated. It will simply be by-passed. And someday a series of Federal programs and organizations that have effectively mastered the appropriate coordination of individual disciplines may face the necessity of keeping these programs in some higher balance and focus. I suspect we are about to begin an important public discussion about the nature of the national organizations, both public and private, that can best contribute to this need for balance and focus.

There are at the national level, however, a variety of private institutions that have operated in this relative vacuum of Federal responsibility. The great national foundations have been hospitable to those who think and work on nationwide problems. They have, also, necessarily evolved some assumptions of their own about educational priorities, both here and abroad, and have gauged their responses so as to give affirmative replies to those whose projects coincided with these assumptions. Libraries, area programs, and medical studies have all been supported by foundations because of their views of national requirements. And here, just as in the case of Federal agencies, it is subject-matter specialties within universities that are the direct concern of foundations—not, generally speaking, the universities themselves.

International Agencies

It is, also, necessary to mention the recent establishment of international agencies to promote worldwide concerns as they emerge and are identified. On the public level, Unesco is becoming increasingly visible and, in partnership with the U.N. and its specialized and regional agencies, is exercising increasing influence with respect to strategy for educational development, particularly in the less well developed parts of the world. And, in the private sector, we have also seen the creation of regional and universal agencies in the same bewildering array that characterizes the national scene. Almost inevitably, these will grow stronger and more powerful.

The Hierarchy of Structures

Looking back over this pattern, one can picture a discontinuous hierarchy of organizations ranging upward from department through college, to university, state coordinating body, regional compact, national institution, and international body. With such a hierarchy, the autonomy of the university is just one autonomy with which higher education is concerned. And we have seen that these autonomous units interact and interconnect. As departmental autonomy within universities increases, the forces working toward external integration will meet less resistance. And since these external lines run to state and Federal agencies, their power and influence relative to the university will be increased.

Now that we have described the profound forces that suggest a re-examination of the idea of university autonomy, and now that we see that the university is only one level of organization in a hierarchy of structures, we can determine the considerations that make university autonomy both a problem and a precious asset. We turn, therefore, to the great social imperatives placed on education and ask whether the idea of autonomy serves the great requirements of academic freedom, innovation, and planning.

Academic freedom is the university's contribution to society's real and pervasive interest in the free and inquiring mind. Whatever reservations are invoked under the stress of short-run fears, there is a visceral belief that this freedom is the necessary condition of both our democratic society and technological progress. And academic freedom has been of special concern because of the university's delicate responsibilities for training the young, for maintaining and passing on our democratic values, and for demonstrating how change and stability can be kept in balance. These most sensitive tasks have required extra protections, and it is at the university level that they are uniquely provided.

The triad of university faculty, administration, and lay board of trustees representing the public interest represents a powerful and leathery combination that has provided a remarkably tough and durable buffer between the individual faculty member and those who would prevent his freedom of speech or word. As a matter of fact, we too little appreciate the enormous contribution of the lay trustee as a decisive link in this chain. We need only talk to our fellow educators in other parts of the world where the lay trustee is unknown to realize how our academic communities would otherwise be exposed to the hot pokers of special interest. The informed lay trustee who says, "Stop, it is I who represents the public's interest in this matter," is perhaps one of the greatest contributors to our free academic communities.

Clearly, no other level in the hierarchy really shares this mission, although the A.A.U.P. has been a potent champion of faculty interests in academic freedom. But, with this exception, no other organization exerts real influence: not department, state authority, regional council, national agency, public institution, or private philanthropy. Autonomy for the university surely has its strongest case in its role as the great protector of intellectual freedom. To reduce that autonomy in favor of public authority would represent a danger not to be taken lightly.

Our next test of "whose autonomy for what" lies in the need for innovation and change, and here the case for the unique contributions and responsibilities of the university is less clear. Although it is true that many educational ventures have been originated and carried out within the single university, it is equally true that other organizations, some of them designed and established by the universities themselves, are increasingly the source of important ideas for educational improvement. The new mathematics, for instance, was sponsored, not by the universities, but by the Carnegie Corporation and the National Science Foundation. For ideas on testing we look to the College Entrance Examination Board and the Educational Testing Service; for overseas education we are turning to Education and World Affairs; and for educational television, to the Ford Foundation. To these organizations could be added all those agencies, public and private, that have funds and would like to encourage new developments in their own fields of interest; it is to these institutions that faculty flock in increasing number to negotiate their projects.

There is great value in these pipelines into institutions committed to supporting new ventures and new ideas, but the university must not allow itself to be factored out of the discourse. Any abdication of an active role in educational innovation would rob the university of an important claim to autonomy based on its contribution to change and innovation. Fortunately, the universities continue to play a substantial role in the programs and policies of these agencies themselves, either as trustees or as members of advisory committees.

But, in addition to this participation in the innovating agencies, university administrations will have to budget their own funds for educational experimentation to be conducted either by themselves or in concert with other universities. Nothing will better limber the universities' joints than the necessity for spending their own funds for educational ventures. In short, the university must keep its reputation as an initiating force. If a division of labor is generally accepted, and innovation is left to outside organizations, then initiative for change will have bypassed the university, and where initiative is not exercised, decisions will not be made. And where decisions are not made, the case for institutional autonomy is gravely weakened.

In addition to the maintenance of academic freedom and innovation, society is putting increased emphasis on planning for the future growth of higher education. Because of the importance and cost, higher education has become affected with the public interest. And as importance and cost increase, there is an irresistible pressure to force planning and decision making to go up the scale of available organizations: first states, then regions, and then the national government. At the same time, a larger and larger group must be involved in the planning process because the interest in decisions becomes more widespread.

As this widening circle of institutions and persons becomes involved in planning the future of higher education, the university is obviously forced to share its responsibilities for forward planning. This cannot and should not be avoided. But it is all the more critical that universities participate directly in these operations.

Yet, just as in the case of innovation, participation must be positive and constructive if it is to be effective. The defensive participation that is limited to viewing with alarm plans that affect one's own university will not give us a place at the planning table, nor will the equally limited role of participating only as applicant for funds. We must participate as institutions that have a sophisticated notion of the future needs of higher education at all levels. We must actually know what these needs are and what must be done to meet them, and we must be ready to explain that plans for our own institutions take this knowledge into account. And, finally, we must convince the interested public that, as universities, we are really both sensitive to and operate within the dictates of this larger public interest.

Conclusions

In conclusion, let me assert that the future of university autonomy turns directly on our capacity to persuade others that only through an appropriate measure of autonomy will academic freedom be protected; that the autonomous university can innovate and that the autonomous university can responsibly balance its own interests with those of larger public interests at all levels of society.

This will take some doing and the doing of it will fall largely on the shoulders of university administrators. But there are plenty of signs that today's administrators measure up to this large task. They are increasingly capable of exercising educational leadership. They have, for the most part, resolved ancient feuds with faculty that will make possible increasing internal cohesion. They are drawn into planning at all levels and frequently are the originators of farsighted views about the future directions of higher education. They are identified as the champions of academic freedom; it is their arm that must now be successfully twisted if a professor is to be silenced or dismissed. They are on the boards of state, regional, and national bodies, and more frequently than not are to be found as the executives in the same agencies. And, finally, they are involved in an almost continuous process of public education about the nature of the university and the needs of higher education.

In the end, the autonomy of universities will depend on the force and statesmanship of our university administrators. And, conversely, that statesmanship will have as its highest task the development of the appropriate and measured balancing of that autonomy with the idea of interdependence of universities when both the institutional interest and the general interest require. It is the great task of those who would lead our universities to manage this new order of university responsibility. Who can doubt but that we must and will succeed.

Myths and Realities
of Institutional Independence

LOGAN WILSON

ALTHOUGH PROFESSORS and others like to think of a Golden Age when the higher learning meandered without interference from administrators, trustees, or outside busybodies, W. H. Cowley has shown the mythical nature of this view. He has pointed out that college and university professors have seldom, if ever, managed their own affairs unchecked by any external constraints, and that one would be hard put to find a single example in the Middle Ages or later of a completely "free republic of scholars." That most venerable prototype, the University of Bologna, for instance, was originally run by the students themselves, who hired and fired the rector and the teaching staff until control gradually shifted to the civil government. Another frequently mentioned institution, the University of Paris, was really under the authority of the Church.

Contrary to popular thinking, moreover, the lay board of trustees for colleges and universities is not an American invention. It came to this country by way of Scotland and Ireland, whence it had been adopted from Holland and Switzerland. Cowley refers to the fact that laymen have been members of the governing bodies of most American institutions of higher learning since their beginnings, and makes similar observations about the long-established tradition of the academic presidency.

Countering the charge that American colleges and universities are "undemocratically organized and administered," he states:

"Why have institutions of higher education been established and by whom?" The answer seems clearly to be, first, that they have been organized to disseminate and to advance socially beneficial knowledge, skills, and attitudes; and second, that civil governments have created them for the good of the general community. They have not been founded for the sole or even the primary benefit of professors, students, trustees, or all of them taken together but, instead, for the benefit of society at large. Hence, in all countries civil government, the most inclusive agency of society, retains the right to set them in motion and, further, to require that their governing boards represent the public interest.[1]

[1] W. H. Cowley, "Some Myths about Professors, Presidents, and Trustees," *Teachers College Record*, November 1962, pp. 164–65.

This assertion seems to me to overlook the vested interests which have established many institutions and to overstress the functional importance of the mere legalities of charter issuance, but the essential concept is correct. As tax-exempt, nonprofit institutions, colleges and universities do exist to serve the common welfare. I agree further with Professor Cowley that the full control of a profession or occupation by those who practice it directly, be they teachers, lawyers, merchants, clergymen, or civil servants, is syndicalism rather than democracy.

Just as there are some academicians who might like syndicalism, there are others who would do away with all controls. You may recall Robert Hutchins' observation that professors really prefer anarchy to any form of government. Paul Goodman's book, *The Community of Scholars,* is an attack upon those administrative and other restraints which the author regards as being main impediments to the freedom of teaching and learning. His ideal institution would entirely eliminate ". . . the external control, administration, bureaucratic machinery, and other excrescences that have swamped our community of scholars."[2]

Despite complaints within the academic community about many forms of constraint, I believe that Cowley accurately summarizes the situation in most American colleges and universities, as follows:

Legal entities control professorial salaries, the physical circumstances under which faculty members work, and the statutes which regulate general institutional procedures; but they do not determine the "standards and procedures" of teaching and research. Nor, indeed, do administrators, who, in fact, almost universally blanch at the occasionally made suggestion that they should project themselves into such matters. Further, except for those in the lower ranks, academics decide as individuals what courses they will teach, the methods of instruction and examination they will employ, the time of the few office hours a week they will schedule, and the part of the day that their classes will meet. Such facts as these patently belie the criticism under discussion and, instead, sustain the generalization that professors have more individual freedom in deciding upon their procedures and in allocating their time and energies than perhaps any other variety of professional people.[3]

A widely distributed statement prepared by Editorial Projects for Education reminds lay readers that practitioners of the higher learning hold a position of power equaled by few other occupations in our society. They are granted a large measure of freedom to interpret, disseminate, and originate knowledge. Their custodianship is a critical one, and their influence on culture and society is indeed enormous. The environment in which they go about their daily tasks must be surrounded accordingly by many safeguards to insulate it

[2] New York: Random House, 1962. P. 168.
[3] Cowley, *op. cit.,* p. 168.

against improper outside pressures. Because they and the colleges and universities in which they work are committed to the pursuit and transmission of truth, academic freedom is thus a functional necessity rather than a luxury.

Proper and Improper Constraints

Insofar as the individual professor is concerned, the 1940 Statement of Principles of Academic Freedom and Tenure of the Association of American Colleges and the American Association of University Professors sets forth a widely accepted norm. Its pertinent parts read as follows:

(*a*) The teacher is entitled to full freedom in research and in the publication of the results, subject to the adequate performance of his other academic duties; but research for pecuniary return should be based upon an understanding with the the authorities of the institution.

(*b*) The teacher is entitled to freedom in the classroom in discussing his subject, but he should be careful not to introduce into his teaching controversial matter which has no relation to his subject. Limitations of academic freedom because of religious or other aims of the institution should be clearly stated in writing at the time of the appointment.

(*c*) The college or university teacher is a citizen, a member of a learned profession, and an officer of an educational institution. When he speaks or writes as a citizen, he should be free from institutional censorship or discipline, but his special position in the community imposes special obligations. As a man of learning and an educational officer, he should remember that the public may judge his profession and his institution by his utterances. Hence he should at all times be accurate, should exercise appropriate restraint, should show respect for the opinions of others, and should make every effort to indicate that he is not an institutional spokesman.

Insofar as the individual institution is concerned, there is unfortunately no generally accepted counterpart of the statement just quoted, even though it is recognized in most circles that a college or university must also be reasonably free and independent if it is to flourish as a disinterested center of teaching and research. One evidence of this recognition is that trustees are seldom elected by the people at large and when chosen usually serve for extended or indefinite periods. Direct democracy likewise is rarely the mechanism used for choosing presidents, deans, and other educational leaders, or for removing them from office. Professors, in turn, do not serve at the pleasure of their students, even though classroom reactions to teaching may be an important component in the judgment of their worth to an institution.

Institutions of higher learning, in short, must have leeway to rise above and go beyond immediately felt needs in their pursuit of knowledge as an end in itself. Without such freedom, their impressive accomplishments in the arts, humanities, and sciences would soon be matters of past history.

However all this may be, the contemporary college or university has a closer similarity to the community at large than it does to the cloister. To survive and be significant, it must be responsive to the world around it. In terms of its own character, it may respond selectively to the claims pressed forward, but it cannot be entirely aloof. Although academics may disdain the marketplace, their ethos cannot ignore the concerns of the outside world.

Because of the intricately involved relations between the typical American college or university and its wider environment and the swift tempo of change, it is perhaps easily understandable why there is no normative statement about institutional autonomy which corresponds to the 1940 Statement of the A.A.C. and the A.A.U.P. The American Council on Education's Commission on Administrative Affairs is making a comprehensive study of the whole question of institutional autonomy, and here I wish to give some preliminary views set forth for this commission by Charles H. Watts:

Institutions of higher education can best serve the society in the dual role of servant and critic. While they should be sensitive to changes in the popular will, they must also maintain their freedom from immediate pressures to change. Throughout their history, our colleges and universities have become increasingly autonomous. Now, however, it is generally recognized that an appropriate balance must be struck between the autonomy with which they govern themselves and the responsibility they have to the society in which they exist. This concept, along with the new belief that higher learning constitutes a primary national resource, makes it mandatory that we seek clear definitions of the kind and degree of autonomy our institutions need for effective operation and the kind and extent of accountability they owe to society.

As American society becomes larger and more complex and as higher education becomes more necessary to its well-being, the sources of pressure for change move from the groups which established or directed our colleges and universities (trustees, church groups) to agencies of the public (state and Federal governments, business and industry). In the sense that pressures from such agencies reflect genuine social needs, they are legitimate; but when they threaten the role of the institution as a critic of society, they are not legitimate. In responding to legitimate pressures, the institution must have the power to judge which among them it may properly meet. But where the pressures are not legitimate, the problem is more serious. For if the right to criticize is lost, the pursuit of truth is impossible.

Commenting on a solution of the problem, Watts goes on to observe that if our society were homogeneous, and if all of its segments had the same needs, there would be less variety in the types of colleges and universities we have. Any effort to define standards of autonomy and accountability must take into account that such variety exists and that this may be an important and necessary strength in our system of higher education. But this variety is likely to lessen in the future. And while a decrease in the variety of types of colleges and universities will make it easier to decide what degree of autonomy is necessary, it will also make it more difficult to maintain autonomy as systems of institutions develop and coordination among institutions increases. Moreover, the context in which these developments occur will be in flux too. We shall have to start with the premise that the relationships of any institution with other institutions and with society will be substantially changed fifteen years from now.

Since we do not know precisely what the new relationships will be, it will not be sufficient to set down abstract principles of autonomy and accountability. Such principles must be developed, of course, but alone they will not be very useful. In attempting to define our concepts of institutional autonomy, we must also carry out "field investigations" of specific infringements of autonomy. These two approaches—the inductive and deductive—should be coordinated so that as difficulties are solved at particular institutions, the solutions will contribute to the development of a set of abstract principles which will provide guidelines for a long time into the future.

It is apparent that at present we have no universally accepted norms of institutional autonomy, and hence lack precise guidelines to differentiate between proper and improper constraints. In extreme cases, of course, it is easy enough to recognize that an individual or group is improperly impinging upon the independence of a college or university. Likewise, when an institution's charter is sufficiently specific, the courts may decide whether its intended purposes are being subverted. Even so, some type situations may illustrate the difficulties inherent in deciding what is proper and what improper.

Let me illustrate. Is it proper for a state legislature to decree that all state-supported institutions must require a year of American history for the bachelor's degree? Should a professional association be allowed to determine an entire program of course offerings suitable for accreditation? How much voice should alumni have in the athletic policies of a college or university? Is it legitimate for local industry to exert strong influence on a liberal arts college to develop programs in engineering and business administration? Does the community have a right to hold an institution responsible for the off-campus behavior of its students? Is it improper for a political body or an affluent group of constituents to express displeasure toward a particular institution by reducing its appropriations or withholding customary support?

Variations of Constraint

Without attempting to answer these questions here, I shall now turn to a consideration of the variations of external constraint to be found among different kinds of institutions. The universe we are talking about includes 2,100 institutions. The state having the most institutions is New York, with 187, and the least is Nevada, with one. Although no precise count is available, it is estimated that there are upwards of 30,000 trustees for these 2,100 institutions. The average number of trustees for public institutions is ten, and for private institutions it is 24.

The U.S. Office of Education classifies institutions in 11 categories, according to types of programs, ranging from "terminal-occupational (below the bachelor's degree)" to "liberal arts and general with three or more professional schools."

Within this varied universe of higher education, it is to be expected that there should be notable differences in the kind and amount of external constraint. The A.A.C.–A.A.U.P. 1940 Statement, for example, makes allowance for special limitations on the autonomy of institutions having religious or other distinctive aims. An illustration of such a limitation in a Roman Catholic institution may be noted in this statement to its faculty: "While ———— College is operated under Catholic auspices, there are no regulations which require all members of the faculty to be members of the Catholic faith. A faculty member is expected to maintain a standard of life and conduct consistent with the philosophy and objectives of the college. Accordingly, the integrity of the college requires that all faculty members shall maintain a sympathetic attitude toward Catholic beliefs and practices. . . ." The actual control exercised by churches over affiliated colleges and universities, however, runs the gamut from domination of appointive powers and of curricular as well as extracurricular programs to a very loose liaison which may reflect itself only in devotional exercises and in the divinity school. As church-affiliated institutions grow in size and strength, their denominational ties tend to loosen and may eventually disappear entirely, as is demonstrated by the histories of a number of well-known institutions of higher learning.

Although publicly supported institutions are by definition more susceptible to political interference than are independent or privately supported colleges and universities, this form of external constraint is associated with a number of other circumstances. As a result of cultural, social, and economic differences among states and regions, rather than any marked variations in forms of government, political interference is more common in the South than in the North and in the Rocky Mountain region than in the East. In states such as California and Indiana where there are strong public institutions, outside interference is less prevalent than in those states which have never had the climate of opinion required for vigor and freedom in public higher education.

Of course, all colleges and universities are affected by some forms of constraint. These vary in time and space, and the burning issue of one era—for example, evolution—may be displaced by a quite different form of controversy in another—say, integration. As is generally known, the campus quite often becomes an arena where public controversy is focalized. (It is interesting to note that four recent A.A.U.P. cases from Southern institutions all involve politics and integration.)

In my judgment, privately supported institutions are just as likely to become targets of external onslaught as their public counterparts. Adversaries of private institutions often choose different weapons and less open modes of attack, however, and I would add that a weak, inadequately supported private college or university is probably the most vulnerable of all institutions to impingements upon its autonomy.

Consistently strong leadership, firm sense of purpose, adequate material support, constituency appreciation of the values of higher education—these are some of the desiderata which enable a college or university to resist the intrusion of improper external constraints. Weakness in one or more of these respects may cause an institution to be very susceptible to interference from the outside.

The Influence of Different Constituencies

Like the debutante's father who is fearful that young men may make passes at his daughter but is even more fearful that none will want to, every institution desires the interest and attention of its constituents but does not want their interference. Achieving and maintaining such a delicate equilibrium is not, to be sure, an easy task. The various constituencies—parents and alumni, taxpayers and benefactors, legislators and businessmen, John Birchers and Americans for Democratic Action, athletic partisans and esthetic devotees—all have their special interests and favored pressure points. Their influences, as Clark Kerr has mentioned in *The Uses of the University*, are both formal and informal. The conspicuousness of these and other groups varies widely from one institution to another and from one kind of external environment to another. Even the local community in which an institution is situated may range anywhere along a continuum from positive assistance to real hindrance. No campus exists in either complete harmony or discord with its wider environment.

Although colleges and universities like to uphold the fiction that they have complete jurisdiction over the curriculum, the interposition of outside forces is evident here too. Scholarly societies and professional associations intrude on local faculty authority by insisting upon certain levels and kinds of course offerings for the certification of graduates. Accrediting associations set minimum standards regarding such matters as admissions, frequency of class meetings, library holdings, and what not. The American Bar Association takes a hand in the internal policies of law schools, as does the American Medical Association in the affairs of medical schools. Of late, there seems to be a growing tendency, moreover, for the courts to hear cases in which individuals or groups question the authority of the institution in matters of student discipline, professorial grading practices, and other situations long regarded as strictly internal concerns.

In short, aside from those obvious instances of blatant interference with institutional autonomy, there is also a gray area ranging from accepted constraints to those of a marginal and questionable nature. The erosion of autonomy thus can come from friendly as well as hostile sources and can be unintended as well as calculated.

Growing Involvements

As Clark Kerr has stated, institutions abroad are more "inward-looking and self-contained," are less intertwined with their surrounding societies than those in this country. He says,

When "the borders of the campus are the boundaries of our state," the lines dividing what is internal from what is external become quite blurred; taking the campus to the state brings the state to the campus. In the so-called "private" universities, alumni, donors, foundations, the federal agencies, the professional and business communities bulk large among the semi-external influences; and in the so-called "public" universities, the agricultural, trade union, and public school communities are likely to be added to the list, and also a more searching press. The multiversity has many "publics" with many interests; and by the very nature of the multiversity many of these interests are quite legitimate; others are quite frivolous.[4]

Another leading critic of American higher education, Jacques Barzun, contends that it is just as important for a college or university to consider what it should not do as what it should do. His view is that a university should not allow itself to be diverted or

[4] Kerr, *The Uses of the University* (Cambridge, Mass.: Harvard University Press, 1963), p. 27.

distracted from its traditional purpose (the removal of ignorance) by outside demands. He protests the bombardment of outside demands since the last war, with mounting requests upon faculty and staff "to drop what they are doing and to go some place which is not related to their task. . . ." to help world peace or social welfare or local culture, "by providing the means, the place and the talent for some worthy cause—an exchange program, a clinic, a survey, a world conference on fingernail biting." In Barzun's opinion, yielding to these claims, regardless of their seeming urgency, will fragment and ultimately destroy an institution.[5]

With higher education's increasing importance to society, it seems to me that the diminution of institutional autonomy is more likely to come from yielding to these miscellaneous importunings than from being overwhelmed by the crude force of open interference. If a college or university permits itself to become a kind of supermarket trying to please all possible customers or a mere service station catering to every passerby, it can hardly expect to maintain even the fiction of autonomy.

In our pluralistic society there is unquestionably a need for many kinds of institutions of higher education, and for a wide range of purposes in any large and complex institution. The complexities we confront, however, increase rather than decrease the urgency of making rational decisions about who should undertake to do what in our vast collective endeavor.

As I have said elsewhere, we live in a highly interdependent era when we can no longer afford to operate with anachronistic ideas of institutional autonomy. Educational leaders can put their time to better use by being realistic about the unavoidable involvements of their institutions than by rhetorical defenses of fading ivory tower images. In my judgment, we must stop talking and acting as if our separated colleges and universities were islands or enclaves and face up to the inevitabilities of more coordination.

One of the facts of modern life we must accept, it seems to me, is that both private and public institutions of higher education are becoming more politicized. I do not use this term in an unsavory sense, but merely to denote undeniable claims of the larger society and the growing involvement of all levels of government with higher education. This being so, professional educators no less than politicians and bureaucrats should play important decision-making roles in a changing set of relations.

In 1957 the Fund for the Advancement of Education underwrote an inquiry which resulted in the pamphlet *The Efficiency of Freedom*, and the book *The Campus and the State*. It was hoped that this inquiry would lead to improved relationships under which the

[5] See Barzun, "What Is a University?" *College and University Journal*, Fall 1962.

essential freedom of each institution would be fully protected while the legitimate fiscal, management, and program interests of state government would be equally safeguarded. The study pointed out that excessive bureaucratic controls and all-embracing supervision are sure recipes for mediocrity in higher education. It also stressed that institutions themselves could do more in the future than they have in the past to enhance their reputations for efficiency and sound management.

Expanding relations between higher education and the Federal Government have likewise been a subject of inquiry during recent years. We are rather belatedly recognizing some of the implications of this growing involvement too. As Babbidge and Rosenzweig have expressed it, the heart of the problem here is often that of indirection rather than direction, and lack of control rather than control.[6] *The Educational Record* (April 1963) reports the results of a Carnegie Foundation–sponsored inquiry into the impact of Federal programs on twenty-six different campuses, as viewed by the institutions themselves. In general, these self-studies report many more good than bad effects of participation. They point to enlarged and improved research programs, faculty benefits, graduate student assistance, plant and equipment gains. They view with deep concern, however, the imbalance created in favor of science departments, the diversion of institutional funds for matching purposes, the neglect of teaching, and the inroads upon an institution's traditional areas of decision making.

Problems arising from the mutual relations of higher education and government illustrate some of the concerns requiring our attention. Others could be mentioned with regard to business and industry and the many interest groups which have a stake in educational decisions and actions. Within and among institutions, and between them and virtually all sectors of the larger society, there is a pressing need for improved mechanisms of communication, deliberation, and action.

The Optimum Institutional Environment

However paradoxical it may seem, it is clear that as a college or university grows in influence and power it becomes enmeshed in an enlarged web of relationships. Inherent in this involvement is the potential of compromised integrity and independence, so that closer surveillance and tighter internal organization are required as countervailing elements to offset centrifugal forces from extramural sources.

[6] Homer D. Babbidge and Robert M. Rosenzweig, *The Federal Interest in Higher Education* (New York: McGraw-Hill Book Co., 1962), p. 162.

Although some of the literature on academic freedom leaves the impression that the ideal collegiate environment is one in which outside constraints are at a minimum, from the point of view of the general welfare this is not the case. Colleges and universities must maintain their identity to survive and their integrity to be worthy of survival, of course, but they also have other important purposes.

At present, unfortunately, there is comparatively little systematic knowledge of theoretical significance about the complex interrelations of colleges and universities and their environments. We know that community junior colleges tend to be more closely related to social forces at work in their immediate locales than are institutions with more dispersed constituencies. A well-endowed and long-established private university is likely to be in a better position to resist encroachments than is an impoverished college with a vacillating past and an uncertain future. A cosmopolitan environment is undoubtedly more conducive to institutional autonomy than a provincial one. Diversified financial support is commonly considered preferable to reliance on a single source of funds. Members of the academic profession attach considerable importance to tenure rules as protections against outside interference. One of the traditional functions of boards of trustees is to act as buffers between institutions and their environments.

We are aware of all these things as well as other factors having to do with this whole area of common concern. Our real difficulty is that we lack the objective knowledge of causal relations needed to make well-informed decisions. Faculty persons are in the main oriented toward the problems of disciplines and programs rather than structural and functional problems of the institutions employing them. Administrative officers, in turn, are likely to be concerned either with quite specialized aspects of college and university operation or with the *ad hoc* promotional problems of keeping the institution moving—and often without regard to where it may be headed.

As a consequence, not enough attention is being paid to needed research in college and university organization and administration. The managerial revolution which has long been under way in business, industry, and government has been slow to get started in the groves of academe. I would urge that it is high time for us to allocate more time and energy to the structural and functional problems of educational institutions and to the development of a more efficient and effective system of higher education better suited to its own ends and the needs of society.

Form and Function

in American Higher Education

LOGAN WILSON

NOBODY HAS EVER fully described, much less thoroughly analyzed, that complex entity called "the American system of higher education." Many of our arrangements have resulted more from historic accident than from conscious design, and most of our 2,100 or so colleges and universities have been left relatively alone to develop in their separate ways. As a consequence, our countryside is dotted with a large number and great variety of institutions, ranging from inferior establishments to some of the world's most distinguished colleges and universities.

Since uninformed persons may have the mistaken notion that our lay trustees control everything, it must be explained to them that governing boards seldom really govern. In most situations they function through their executive officer, the president. He, in turn, delegates much of his authority to other administrative officers. The faculty also is involved in the decision-making process, and in some institutions even the students share in academic governance.

Contrary to what those neatly arrayed organization charts might lead us to believe, lines of real authority and responsibility are often difficult to trace. This sometimes confused state of affairs is often rationalized as academic freedom, however, and because many members of the academic community place a high premium on being able to pursue their own interests with as little restraint as possible, very few complaints are heard.

Outside observers are aware, of course, that we pride ourselves on the broad diffusion of power within our institutions and upon dispersed rather than centralized support and control from without. Beginning on the departmental level in colleges and universities, we have made a watchword of "independence." Proceeding upward to the national level, where the authority of the U.S. Office of Education is markedly less powerful than that of any foreign ministry of education, the spirit of *laissez faire* abounds.

Within recent years, to be sure, we have acknowledged the growing interdependence of departments, divisions, schools, colleges, and universities, and their relations to society at large. This is witnessed in many places by the creation of interdisciplinary fields, bureaus,

29

institutes, and other structural devices intended to bridge the gaps resulting from increased differentiation and specialization. Between campuses, we have of necessity begun to develop state-wide planning, state and regional coordinating agencies, consortia, and other voluntary groupings, and are attempting to think more systematically about the mounting Federal involvements in higher education. We have long recognized an intricate network of relations among individual scholars and scientists, administrative officers and others, as well as among institutions and the various interest groups within them. Today the unifying influences of state, regional, and national agencies and associations are not to be minimized.

Even so, I think the time is now at hand in educational ranks when we must admit that many of our structural arrangements are very loose-jointed and perhaps ill-adapted to rapidly changing circumstances. A colleague of mine has noted that, hypothetically, by 1980 we shall need to double the size of all existing institutions and establish 1,000 new ones with average enrollments of 2,500 simply to accommodate sheer numbers. Not only must vastly more students be taught, but also they must be taught more and in less time. Research and public service demands will press ever more heavily upon us.

In light of these enlarged and more complicated functions, what structural changes should we now have under consideration? How should we proceed on local, state, regional, and national levels? Will the initiative come from educators, or will changes be thrust upon us? In his history, *The American College and University*, Frederick Rudolph has said, "Resistance to fundamental reform was ingrained in the American collegiate and university tradition, as over three hundred years of history demonstrated . . . except on rare occasions, the historic policy of the American college and university [was]: drift, reluctant accommodation, belated recognition that while no one was looking, change had in fact taken place." [1]

I would note that resistance to organization and to change is no longer a tenable position for us and our institutions. Too much insistence on outmoded forms of sovereignty can lead only to chaos. In our technological age, the knowledge industry has become one of our most important industries, and higher education is in a pivotal rather than a peripheral position in the swift pace of events. We have no option, therefore, but to adapt ourselves and our organizations to changing circumstances.

Problems of Individual Institutions

To begin on the local level, every college and university must continuously examine its own reasons for being, assess its current strengths and weaknesses, and envisage what it hopes to be and can

[1] New York: Alfred A. Knopf, 1962, p. 491.

expect to become in the decades ahead. Too often in the past we have assumed that anything done in the name of higher education necessarily must be worthwhile. In part, because our institutions do have high purposes and do yield many intangible benefits to society, we have disliked using anything resembling the balance sheets of business enterprise to appraise our efforts.

Many of our institutions are trying to do too many different things. In manifesting what someone has called the "university syndrome," they spread their material and human resources thinly and as a result do nothing really well. Even in single purpose, liberal arts colleges, where the emphasis is almost entirely on teaching, there are often no applied criteria for judging teaching performance. Almost everywhere, the curriculum, or what is taught, is more the product of historic accretion than of contemporary design. New courses are added helter-skelter, and virtually nothing is discarded. The rigidity of departmental structures is such that new fields like biophysics, genetics, and linguistics cannot be readily fitted into the traditional scheme. The growth of semiautonomous institutes, centers, and laboratories poses still other structural problems. (I know of one university which had 80 such institutes at last count, and another which had 25 in the international area alone.)

Despite years of debate and inquiry within academic circles, there is still no consensus about such basic matters as the effects of class size on different kinds of learning, the valid uses of television and programed instruction, or what constitutes a balance between teaching and research. The academic sense of dignity of some would be offended by the thought of anything akin to unit costing or to the economic input-output analysis used to gauge productivity in other types of carefully reasoned endeavor.

I do not mean to imply, of course, that there has been no experimentation with the relations between form and function in the higher learning. We have found out much about the learning process, and there can be no question that most of our colleges and universities are better environments for teaching, research, and public service than they once were. Still, I would contend that higher education as a whole has lagged in the development and application of systematic knowledge about its own processes.

Although bureaus or offices of institutional research are already in being on a number of campuses, organized inquiry of this kind is still generally the exception rather than the rule. It is indeed ironic that academicians, who have become indispensable to the advancement of the larger technology, should have done comparatively little to develop a technology of education. The economists, for example, have developed extensive bodies of knowledge in such fields as agricultural economics and labor economics, but until quite recently they have paid very little attention to the economics of education. Or, to generalize about our whole profession, it is interesting, in view of the broad range of intellectual inquiry to be found in colleges and universities, that we do not know more conceptually about the activities common to our immediate enterprise.

Our lack of expertise about structure and function in higher education in our own country is often revealed when members of the American academic community are called upon to advise about educational matters in developing nations. Perspectives may be demanded which we have never thought about very much. Relations between means and ends which have merely been taken for granted must be assessed, and priorities evaluated. The time dimension must be taken into account. Careful consideration has to be given to alternative arrangements, with an eye to their efficiency and effectiveness. Where material and human resources are severely limited, any investment in education must be weighed alongside other investments.

Although we Americans already have three centuries of experience behind us in the evolution of higher education and have more resources than does any other nation for its further development, it is my judgment that we too must proceed less haphazardly in the future than we have in the past. Our resources for education are not unlimited, and we must use them to the best possible advantage. A logical place to start implementing this resolve, it seems to me, is within our colleges and universities.

State and Regional Problems

Turning now from problems of form and function on the local level, let us look at similar concerns on state and regional levels. American educators who have noted the Robbins Report on higher education in Great Britain have doubtless been impressed by the kindred nature of some of our problems. This report mentions that it would be a misnomer to speak of a system of higher education in England today if by system one means a consciously coordinated organization. There, as here, institutions have grown up separately, and what system there is has come into being as the result of a series of particular initiatives, concerned with particular needs, and providing no way of dealing conveniently with all of the problems of higher education as a whole. Despite the existence of a University Grants Committee and increasing reliance upon financing from the central government, surprisingly little planning and coordination have resulted. The report goes on to point out important changes now occurring, and to face up to the urgency of still more changes.

Although we are further along than the British in certain respects, virtually all of our states and regions now confront problems which cannot be solved by leaving institutions completely to their own devices. As the Robbins study states, it is difficult to defend the continuing absence of coordinating principles and of a general conception of objectives. This does not mean, to be sure, that all activities must be planned and controlled from one place, but it does suggest more attention to interdependence and less insistence upon independence. As William Fels has put it, this means that unlimited freedom of action must give way to the right to choose within a structure that limits but sustains choice.

One evidence of political limitations on institutional autonomy is an increase in the number of boards having responsibility for the supervision of more than one institution. Although nobody has as yet assembled complete and reliable information about such coordinating agencies, one source lists nine states as having single boards responsible for governing all public higher education. Twelve other states are reported as having boards with more limited authority over institutions which, in turn, have their individual boards.

Most of these "master" or "advisory" boards exclude professional educators from membership and are comprised of politically appointed laymen with a legislative mandate to establish and maintain coordination. Their most common function pertains to budgetary concerns, and the next most common is some form of program planning. Studies of future needs in higher education, standards, admissions, degree-granting qualifications, forms of accreditation, uniform reporting practices, and related matters are also typical concerns. In addition, many of these boards define institutional objectives, and establish the role and scope of institutions under their jurdisdiction.

Insofar as I am aware, no other state has gone as far as California in developing a fully integrated master plan. Its legislatively authorized Coordinating Council for Higher Education has prepared and begun implementing a plan for the "development, expansion, and integration of the facilities, curriculum, and standards of higher education, in junior colleges, state colleges, the University of California, and other institutions of the state, to meet the needs of the state during the next ten years and thereafter."

Even though educational leaders have played active roles in the California Council, and have been used in advisory capacities everywhere, it is pertinent to note that the initiative behind mandatory coordination in most states comes from outside rather than inside academic circles. In view of the entrenched tradition of institutional sovereignty, this is understandable, but the unfortunate aspect of it is that resistance to change often places educators in the role of passive observers rather than active participants in shaping the larger destinies of their institutions.

Moreover, it seems to me that we ought to be making systematic studies of these various schemes, assessing their uses and abuses, and displaying more initiative ourselves in trying to improve the efficiency and effectiveness of our common endeavor through joint enterprise. To the best of my knowledge, in only a small handful of states have the presidents of both private and public institutions voluntarily come together to form coordinating councils which make decisions and take actions of real import.

The fact that institutions can function jointly for some common purposes without being under outside mandate to do so is demonstrated by the existence of six regional accrediting associations. Further instances of the ability of autonomous institutions to work in harness without any compulsion to coordinate their activities are to be seen in the numerous consortium arrangements created in recent decades. Virtually every region and state now has groupings of this kind. They may involve the pairing of a small college and a large university, a newly established institution with an old one, a number of highly developed universities with a sharing plan for very expensive facilities, and what not. They range from simple, bilateral arrangements for the free exchange of student credits to elaborate, multilateral arrangements for joint faculty appointments, coordination of adult education and extension programs, pooling of library resources, cooperative use of radio and television facilities, and other mechanisms. The most comprehensive and formally organized interinstitutional as well as interstate forms of joint planning and activity are exemplified in the three regional compacts, but the sanction behind the Southern Regional Education Board, the Western Interstate Commission for Higher Education, and the New England Board of Higher Education is legislative rather than institutional.

It is no news to say that these trends are not always welcomed in academic circles. Some hold that most of the politically motivated schemes aim primarily at the reduction of expenditures rather than the promotion of expansion and improvement in higher education. Others may approve the ends in view but deplore the bureaucratic proliferations which seem to accompany these structural changes. Still others in educational ranks go along willingly only with *voluntary* coordination and planning which stem from the institutions themselves. Those who are dubious about the effectiveness of voluntary arrangements, however, argue that they tend merely to preserve the *status quo* of individual institutions and often ignore the larger public interest.

Meantime, the movements toward more cooperation and coordination proceed without benefit of very much careful analysis of the forms and processes entailed. Some advocates of particular institutions or particular kinds of institutions continue to display a reluctance to look realistically at what the division of labor ought to be within a given state or region for dealing with teaching, research, and public functions. Conversely, indiscriminate zeal for cooperation and coordination can lead into hastily considered arrangements which do violence to the integrity of institutions.

With the tremendous costs immediately ahead in the rapid expansion and improvement of higher education, we can no longer afford blunders in the locations of institutions, wasteful duplications of programs, unplanned and piecemeal local responses to wider needs, and the general lack of unity which have characterized too many of our collective endeavors in the past. To plan wisely and act decisively, however, we must be guided by judgments based on objective knowledge of the relations between form and function in higher education.

The National Scene

Although decentralization of support and control has long been a dominant motif in American higher education, the growing interdependence of our whole society has produced countervailing influences. These influences are centripetal in nature. Their operation takes place on all levels but comes into focus on the national level. Even the most provincial institutions are necessarily involved in them, and together they form an intricate communications network extending all across the nation. With nerve centers mainly in Washington and New York, numerous educational agencies and organizations, mostly voluntary in their membership, help to give coherence to the American system of higher education.

To begin with, there are dozens of national organizations of individual teachers, scholars, and scientists, ranging from the Ceramics Educational Council with about 125 members to the American Chemical Society with almost 100,000. Even more comprehensive alignments of persons in allied disciplines are to be noted in such organizations as the American Association for the Advancement of Science and the American Council of Learned Societies. Administrative and staff officers also have their national associations. Another basis of national organization is exemplified by segmental parts of institutions and of specialized types of institutions. Representatives of law schools, extension divisions, junior colleges, Protestant colleges, Catholic colleges, urban universities, unaccredited colleges, proprietary schools, and what not are banded together. In the field of student personnel work alone, there are at least thirty different associations, and there are more than fifty organizations of whole institutions and segmental parts of them.

In addition, there are several "umbrella" associations, such as the American Council on Education, which include not only institutions but also other associations.

At the national level there are other membership organizations and agencies which perform specialized services. Some examples are the Institute of International Education, the National Merit Scholarship Corporation, the Educational Records Bureau, the College Entrance Examination Board, and the Educational Testing Service. Many special purpose agencies have been established to handle common problems and cope with issues which cannot be dealt with unilaterally by the nation's 2,100 or so colleges and universities.

The large philanthropic foundations also need to be taken into account as influences on the development of higher education, for as Henry Heald, of the Ford Foundation, has recently noted,

> By their nature, the large foundations have a national view, and should be equipped to see education whole and in its relation to the rest of society. . . . Foundations have facilitated inter-institutional cooperation, drawn together schools and universities for work on curriculum and other matters of common concern, and helped related university resources to a range of needs from urban problems to international affairs.

Finally, at the national level there is the Federal Government itself, with dozens of its agencies involved in higher education. Every college in the country is now affected by Federal programs, and many leading universities receive the bulk of their research funds from these sources. Until now a relatively minor factor in American education, the U.S. Office of Education has a projected budget for 1966 of $1.866 billion. In addition the President's budget provides for $1.515 billion for new legislative proposals.

From these and other circumstances it is clear that important decisions are no longer being made exclusively at local and state levels, but increasingly are being made at the national level. Even at the national level, unfortunately, many associations and agencies are acting unilaterally. Vested interests are sometimes pushed without too much regard for the common good, and the agencies representing divergent points of view are so numerous that communication among them is in itself a problem. When the Congress addresses itself to nationwide concerns in higher education, it sometimes hears a babel rather than a chorus of voices speaking from the academic sector.

The need for more cooperation and coordination is thus as obvious on the national level as on each of the other levels. At every juncture we must cope more effectively with issues that involve inflexibility, autonomy, resources, priorities, planning, and the public interest. Local demands must be balanced against wider needs, and short-range pressures against long-range objectives.

The necessity for more and better education no longer has to be argued, nor does the urgency for making a greater investment in it. To move ahead expeditiously, however, we must change some of our ways of thinking about education in general and about higher education in particular. On every campus, more of our best academic minds ought to concern themselves with basic questions of form and function in higher education. Moreover, at the highest policy level, our system of education, hardly less than our postal system, merits Cabinet recognition.

In conclusion, I want to acknowledge that I have no answers to many of the questions raised. I might add that neither does anybody else at the present. Fortunately for all of us, we live in a democratic and not an authoritarian society; we are already developing the means of arriving at collective solutions to common problems. With the proper determination, I am sure that we can maintain and strengthen the American system of higher education to meet our nation's changing needs.

2

Institutional Modifications

New Patterns of
Internal Organization

JOSEPH AXELROD

THE OBSERVER of higher education must overcome several obstacles if he is to succeed in identifying the new patterns on American campuses. Though much that is new is taking place, everything that is new is not destined to be a new *pattern*. How is he to judge which are the emerging patterns and which are not? How many cases of year-round operation, for example, does he need in order to declare with confidence that this will become one of the future patterns in American colleges? (Even as he poses the question, he wonders whether the matter *is* quantitative.) Moreover, how can he be sure that a given innovation on one campus—an independent study program, or the requirement of a comprehensive examination for the bachelor's degree—is identical with innovations carrying the same label on other campuses?

Part of the difficulty arises out of reports both in the professional literature and in the popular press which attempt to create or preserve a particular institutional "image." Such reports often begin as distortions of the truth. Usually they remain so; but occasionally the publicized image serves as a pressure to establish itself in reality. Such phenomena complicate the task of identifying a new pattern, but the conscientious student of higher education must recognize that he cannot remain blind to them.

After other obstacles, one still remains. How shall he interpret the word "new," since it is *new* patterns he proposes to identify? "New" for how long? Since the end of World War II? Since the mid-fifties? Or since the turn of the decade, perhaps?

We shall arbitrarily say: Since the first Sputnik, for with it, a new era in American higher education began. It was about the beginning of this era that the first National Defense Education Act was passed, that the educational profession realized the temporary relationship of the forties and fifties between Government and higher education had become permanent, that the Federal grant university, as Kerr calls it, had come to stay.

There were also other signs of the new era. There was unrest in the undergraduate schools; the old-fashioned liberal arts college seemed unable to find its place in a rapidly changing world. "The liberal arts tradition is dead or dying"—Jacques Barzun's words were quoted everywhere, and few educators disagreed. [28] Literally scores of new colleges came into existence in the late fifties and early sixties, many of which devised plans that openly rejected the organizational patterns dominant in the mid-fifties.

More broadly, the beginning of the new era was marked by the rise of state master plans for higher education. The California master plan was drawn up in 1959 and enacted into law in 1960. [15, 4, 22] Concurrently, state boards responsible for teacher certification began to modify requirements, explicitly rejecting the philosophy that had dominated teacher education in the thirties and forties. At this time, too, the teachers college, as an institution, is alleged to have died. [66]

The general education movement, too, came to its end, and the term itself has almost fallen into disuse. Colleges have adopted a more neutral phrase, like "basic studies," to describe their broad-area programs. The Association for General and Liberal Studies—a new organization of college and university faculty who had been active in the general education movement—avoided the term when, in 1961, it selected its name. [3]

The general education reform in lower-division curricula and the molting of normal school into teachers college into multipurpose institution can both be seen as movements that emerged sometime around 1920, reached maturity in the forties, and approached old age in the fifties.

Only after these preliminary questions—What is a pattern? and, What is new?—have been answered can the student of higher education approach the problem of identifying the emerging organizational patterns.

Old Patterns, New Recognitions, and Plans for Reorganization

A selection of a handful of the published works that most accurately reflect the state of higher education in the late fifties—the last years of the old era—would, I believe, include: for the junior colleges, Medsker's study [52]; for the four-year colleges, the collection of essays edited by Sanford [60]; for graduate education, the works of Berelson and Carmichael [12, 18]; and for the professional schools, a study by McGrath. [48]

What does the picture reflected in these studies reveal about American higher education in the late fifties? It reveals a general failure. The junior college, forfeiting its identity, had done less than was minimally required to meet its major objectives. Four-year colleges, judged by any reasonable standard of accomplishment, were failing. Graduate programs were a mish-mash of sense and non-sense which provided for doctoral candidates, in addition to the experiences particular to each, the common experience of humiliation. And the professional schools admitted that their programs were falsely based, attempting, as they did, to contain an accelerating knowledge impossible of containment.

This was the verdict of the late fifties. By the mid-sixties, the situation has changed on every front. The years 1959–64 are the beginning years of a period of reorganization in higher education.

THE JUNIOR COLLEGE

The American Association of Junior Colleges was about forty years old when the junior college came under the scrutiny of Medsker and his staff. The judgment which the study reached concerning achievement of general education goals—"In the majority of two-year colleges, relatively little had been done to meet the objectives of general education"—is echoed in its judgments of other major functions. [*52*, pp. 23–27] A basic cause for the failure was the mounting pressure to offer courses exactly parallel to those in four-year institutions. "When this happens," Medsker declared, "the junior college forfeits its identity." [*52*, p. 53]

Loss of identity led to even greater loss of prestige. The other segments of higher education regarded the junior college as existing primarily to give inferior students *some* college training. A University of California chancellor, speaking at the end of the old era, expressed this thought exactly. He thanked the California junior colleges for their role "in building a great University of California"; because the junior college had performed the chore of providing lower-division education to the less talented student, "the University has been allowed to continue its pursuit of distinction," he stated. [*55*, p. 7]

This was the attitude dominant in the fifties. In the sixties it is dominant no longer. The state master plans have come into existence, and the junior college is destined to play an extraordinarily significant role in the future development of the nation. Like the university and the four-year college, the junior college is considered in the new age to have its own excellence which it, also, must pursue.

Growth in junior colleges during the first half-decade of the new era has been phenomenal. In New York State, for example, between 1953 and 1960, community colleges were established at the rate of about one a year. But this was too slow, reported Kenneth Doran, and in 1960 the Heald Committee report and the State University master plan called for more. From 1960 to 1964, ten were established. [*21*, p. 16] In early 1964, the Educational Policies Commission declared that junior college education must become universal in

America and that the content of studies must change—must now be "aimed at *intellectual* growth." [*25*, p. iii, italics added]

Experimentation in junior colleges with new organizational patterns has thus far, however, been limited. B. Lamar Johnson, who recently made a ninety-college survey focusing on the new patterns, concludes that many institutions have given "increasing attention to improving the processes and organization of teaching." As for concrete change, however, Johnson reports that "only a few faltering steps have been taken." [*38*, p. 14] Still, his report describes many innovations in physical facilities—push-button lecture halls, autolearning laboratories, new television production and reception areas, facilities for live long-distance interviews—and some curricular experimentation: programed learning, team teaching, independent study, and work-study programs. Only rare instances were found "of any attempts to break the lockstep of the traditional calendar." [*38*, p. 14] In late summer 1964, however, the Los Angeles Board of Education authorized a study to explore the possibility of year-round operation for the seven junior college campuses in Los Angeles, and similar steps are being taken elsewhere.

Though late in starting, the swell in developments in the public junior colleges has begun. The private junior colleges have traditionally participated in experimentation. The four-building Learning Center at Stephens College, for example, has resulted from new conceptions of both physical facilities and the organization of student out-of-class time. [*62*]

THE FOUR-YEAR COLLEGE

The pattern in recent junior college history—a general failure in the late fifties, followed by plans for revising the form and content of the educational experience—has reached a considerably more advanced stage on four-year campuses.

When Sanford's *The American College* appeared, it attracted the attention of college administrators and faculty throughout the nation. They were struck by the collection's new approach to higher education and were stunned by the picture it portrayed: "American colleges are failing rather badly. They fail to achieve their own stated purposes; and they fail by other reasonable standards of accomplishment." [*60*, p. 2]

Just as the junior college, by 1959, had lost its identity, seeking to shape an amorphous product, hoping every variety of four-year school would find it acceptable, so the undergraduate college by 1959 had lost its identity, supplying its students with a huge cafeteria of specialized courses designed in some vague way to meet the demands of the graduate schools. That the demands were often contradictory and sometimes more imagined than real only made matters worse.

But about the time *The American College* appeared, a myriad of new colleges came into existence. The sound of saw and hammer, argument and compromise, was heard everywhere—from Hempstead on Long Island, to Detroit to San Diego and Santa Fe; from Oakland in Michigan to Santa Cruz to Tampa and Sarasota. The new colleges all began by rejecting old patterns, even the best of the *old* patterns. Three gave themselves the name "New College," for their intention was—and is—to be born new and to remain perpetually new.

In April 1964, a conference on the experimental college, sponsored by Florida State University, took place at Wakulla Springs. Ten campuses were represented: Antioch, University of California (Cowell College on the Santa Cruz campus), Florida Presbyterian, University of Michigan (Dearborn campus), Michigan State, New College at Sarasota, Pacific (Raymond College), Parsons, Stephens, and Wayne State (Monteith College).

The colloquium concluded with an analysis of the over-all patterns in the ten institutions: Five are experimental entities within larger institutions. Nine base their curriculum in the liberal arts and general education. All have selective admission policies, include independent study both as a means of learning and as a goal of education, plan programs that are flexible in both content and rate of learning, specifically include evaluation officers to appraise the effectiveness of the program (and in some cases the achievement of individual students), give the library a central and unusually important role in the educative process, and set special criteria for the selection of faculty. There was much discussion about the elimination of grades and credits. There was a general recognition that the experimental college is and must be in a state of constant flux and change.[1] [*37*, pp. 3–7]

The curricula in all these colleges express dissatisfaction with traditional ways of organizing undergraduate instruction. The source of their inspiration is, rather, the rich tradition of nonconformity in American higher education, a tradition that produced such great experiments as the Meiklejohn college of the early thirties, the Hutchins college of the middle forties under Faust's deanship, and the Harold Taylor college of the late forties under Raushenbush's deanship. These three no longer exist as experimental colleges, but their influence has been incalculable.

The Small College to be established in 1969 on the campus of the California State College at Palos Verdes is illustrative of the new

---

[1] As early as 1958, Hatch began to collect data about ten experimental colleges of the late fifties: Austin, Bard, Goddard, Hofstra, New College (Amherst, Mount Holyoke, Smith, and University of Massachusetts), the Michigan State campus at Oakland, University of South Florida, Wayne State's Monteith, and Wesleyan University. Hatch's report states seventeen aspects of experimental colleges. Many of these anticipate the listing which emerged from the Wakulla Springs conference. [*31*] The experimental programs at Bard, Goddard, Monteith, New College (Massachusetts group), and Wesleyan were also described by Baskin. [*10*]

movement. The parent institution will not open until 1965, but already Small College is part of the plan. It will enroll 500 students and offer a specially designed three-year (twelve-quarter) B.A. program requiring year-round attendance. The student body will include the full range of abilities and backgrounds present in the total campus, which is being master-planned for 16,000 students. Small College will not set any blanket requirements for the degree (other than the minimal requirements of the State Education Code) because it plans to tailor-make each student's program. Instructional means will include independent study, programed instruction, and credit by examination. In addition, it will provide observation-internship experiences for graduate students in the regular college who plan to become college teachers. As at New College at Hofstra and Cowell College at Santa Cruz, it is anticipated that the operation of this separate experimental college will cost no more per student than the traditional program. [9, 13, 14, 36, 49]

While some of the new answers are being sought in the small, experimental college, other patterns are being created at larger institutions newly in operation or about to come into existence—at Boca Raton, Florida; Irvine, California; Oakland, Michigan; Stony Brook, New York; San Diego, California; Tampa, Florida; and at scores of other sites. These larger institutions also reject the organizational patterns dominant in the fifties.

A 1963 workshop at Boca Raton hammered out the philosophic framework for the new Florida Atlantic University. Participants recommended that the new institution "give major attention to the elimination of the lock-step, time-serving characteristics of conventional programs." They suggested the new university "organize student learning experience around substantial blocks of time" and "give more than usual attention to interdisciplinary study." Above all, it must seek "to avoid over-specialization which limits the breadth of intellectual understanding and reduces effectiveness in coping with the urgent problems of our generation." The recommended plan, moreover, emphasized the development of independent study programs and comprehensive examinations by means of which students are to demonstrate they have attained the goals set for the degree. [27]

The new patterns are stimulating curricular reform on hundreds of older campuses, from the University of Santa Clara to Southwest Missouri State College to the University of Toledo; from Coe and Beloit and Antioch to Southern Methodist and the City University of New York; from Montana State University to Pennsylvania State to the California State College at Hayward.

On some campuses, the reform is piecemeal; but on others, a complete overhauling is in process. The new curriculum at Beloit College, for example, will revolutionize every aspect of the instructional program. It is based on twenty-nine principles, among them the following: Course credit will replace hour credit. The interrelatedness of knowledge will become a basic mode of organizing the curriculum. Student achievement will not be measured merely by the passing of courses; area examinations and a comprehensive examination in the major will be required. Instead of admitting and subsequently graduating "peas in a pod," the college will accept a variety of students and help each to develop his maximum potential. Students will spend a smaller proportion of their time in class than formerly. During "vacation" terms, students will be involved in activities relevant to their education. High school and college will be looked upon as an eight-year unit rather than as two independent four-year units. Students will share a common academic experience both at the beginning and near the termination of their undergraduate careers. The degree program covers eleven "terms," each fifteen weeks in length: three underclassman terms, five middleclassman terms (two on campus, one on a field project done either in this country or abroad, two "vacation" terms), and three upperclassman terms. The content of the five middleclassman terms is to be tailored individually for each student. [*11, 33*]

Thus are the American campuses, old and new both, in ferment. This is the reply of the sixties to the standardized curriculum which the fifties inherited and proliferated. In the late fifties the liberal arts were said to be dead; in the mid-sixties, they are vigorously alive.

What has happened is simply that the liberal arts needed the time to redefine themselves for the new era. McKeon stated the point precisely: "The true function of the liberal arts . . . is to liberate men. They have performed this function in the past by adapting themselves to the problems men have faced, and they have become obsolete and ineffective from time to time by elaborating old methods without consideration of new facts or problems. New liberal arts must be devised for the problems of the modern world." [*50*]

In the new liberal arts college, both *form* and *content* must change. The external forms have already undergone palpable change. One takes no risk in predicting that the fifty-minute hour, the three-hour course, the two-semester year, and the four-year degree will have become old-fashioned before the end of the decade. But deep-seated change cannot occur unless the content of the curriculum as well as its external form is modified.

The content of each of the disciplines is itself undergoing rapid change. By the mid-sixties, even the traditional colleges are recognizing that a discipline is not a collection of subject-matter information, but a set of tools and methods by which a changing subject matter can be explored. Some recent changes in curricular *content* are so common they need only brief mention. Humanistic and societal studies now focus beyond the arts, letters, and social institutions of Western man. Structural linguistics revolutionizes the teaching of English and foreign languages. Basic studies science courses emphasize the tools and methods of science rather than current but changing factual information. Behavioral science emerges as an integrating framework for the several social sciences. The new biology is a new world. There is a new relationship between knowing and doing in fine arts courses.

On the whole, however, change in form alone—*old* content poured into new molds—has been a trap for many colleges during the first half-decade of the new era. Language staffs discover that the language laboratory is a troublesome space-eater because the courses have remained unchanged. A good proportion of the 250 colleges and universities offering credit courses on television to 250,-000 students discover that their telecourses must be something more than a TV camera focused on a man in a classroom. The new forms demand a new organization of content—indeed a *different* content. The independent study program results in more harm than good if the same mediocre readings on the same insignificant topics continue to be required.

But curriculum planners have another dimension in mind when they seek to change the content of a learning experience. This is the relationship which the student establishes between himself and the subject matter of the course—his "involvement." The profession, unfortunately, is still in the first stages of knowing how to explore this crucial aspect of the teaching-learning process. Pioneer work was done by five University of Chicago faculty members in 1949. [8] This early study helped focus attention on the different roles the effective instructor plays during a class hour; as he varies his role, the student's involvement is variously affected. This study also suggested that it is not the *fact* of overt student participation that matters, but the *nature* of his participation, and especially of his non-overt participation. This variable was identified as more significant in effective learning than other variables such as class size, which had attracted more attention. Much research has since been done, but, as McKeachie pointed out recently, no major breakthrough has yet occurred. [60, chap. 8]

An even more difficult problem must be solved by the new liberal arts college of the sixties: how to chain the powerful noncurricular forces. These appear to constitute even more effective educational means, along many lines, than the curriculum itself. "To design a college with only courses in mind," one observer writes, "is to overlook the most influential forces available for teaching." [39] These noncurricular forces have been studied in recent years, but as yet no mechanisms have been discovered for controlling and channeling them. [46, 54, 61, 63; 60, chaps. 13–15]

THE GRADUATE SCHOOL

At the close of the fifties, the over-all attitude toward the graduate school was one of ambivalence—severely critical and highly approving. In the academic world, much dissatisfaction was expressed, except by the graduate faculties themselves. The graduate school was, for the most part, looked upon good-naturedly as an antiquated system that slowly and patiently met every new condition with another patchwork reform. The graduate schools have the highest status in and out of the academic world, and those responsible for their programs are among the nation's best minds.

Researchers who studied the system in the late fifties found serious shortcomings. A 1958 article on graduate education summarized the recommendations of the Truman Commission of 1946: "The Commission pleaded for a larger conception of scholarship which would include 'interpretive ability as well as research ability, skill in synthesis as well as in analysis, and achievement in teaching as well as in investigation.' " Nevertheless, the article continued, "there is little present evidence that the recommendations of the Truman Commission have had practical effect, although there is continuing ferment over the issues raised." [45, p. 601]

Those who scrutinized the graduate schools a few years later were still impatient. "For more than fifty years," charged Carmichael in 1962, "the organization, methods, and policies of graduate schools have remained essentially unchanged; the policies and practices adopted in the nineteenth century are, in the main, still in force." [18, p. 159]

But change could not be held back. By the mid-sixties, many of the lines which had separated fields of knowledge had broken down. In area studies programs, space science, biology, behavioral science, and linguistics, traditional discipline boundaries are largely ignored in the most fruitful research being done. New degree programs are demanding combinations of skills and tools formerly fragmented by departmental walls; for example, advanced linguistic study now requires mastery of tools which have been developed jointly by humanist philologists, anthropologists, and mathematicians. [7, pp. 24–34] This cross-departmental communication is the wellspring for the great changes destined to reshape the graduate schools of the coming years.

The graduate schools of the mid-sixties take more seriously than those of the mid-fifties their responsibility in the preparation of college teachers. Leaders in higher education in the fifties became deeply concerned about the imminent, critical shortage of college teachers. The 1954 meeting of the Committee of Fifteen [29] was followed, in 1958, by another national conference, sponsored by the American Council on Education, where everyone admitted the situation was grave. [5] In 1959, the master plan survey team in California estimated their state alone would need an average of more than *three thousand* new faculty per year during the next fifteen years. [15, p. 121] But that same year, all forty graduate departments at Columbia University did not yield even a score over *three hundred* Ph.D.'s. [58, p. 179]

The 1958 Council conference joined other national groups in criticizing the graduate schools for having been slow to reorganize, but opinion differed about whether the change needed was a series of minor adjustments or a complete overhauling. Out of this Council conference came a number of specific recommendations that would lead to greater breadth in the doctoral program, to reduction in time spent in the program, to an emphasis on significance rather than novelty in the dissertation, and to a redignified master's program. [5, 26]

During the years following, important changes in graduate studies were made, but too slowly and too few to satisfy many of the critics. Rosenhaupt summarized the developments in the early sixties: "While new growth is stirring everywhere, powerful factors restrain it." [58, p. 179] And Orlans reported disquieting facts: In some universities, it took some graduate students several months to arrange an appointment with their thesis adviser. [53, p. 52] In the dozen universities receiving the largest sums of money from the Federal Government, a *fifth* of the faculty sample could greet few or no advanced graduate students by name. [53, p. 49] A survey of Woodrow Wilson fellows in the early sixties disclosed that those who attended the four graduate schools judged best in the country by a group of liberal arts chairmen (Berkeley, Columbia, Harvard, and Yale) were less satisfied with the size of classes and with faculty guidance than were the fellows attending other institutions. [53, p. 52]

One cause for the slowness of change appears to be ignorance about higher education. First of all is "ignorance of simple facts about graduate education" by the graduate faculties themselves [58, p. 179]; second is ignorance about the graduate school—and the university in general—as a social institution. Thomas W. Hamilton wryly remarks: "Perhaps some day we shall know as much about our colleges and universities as we now know about corporations, political parties, and teen-age gangs." [51, p. vii] Another cause for slowness rests in the delicately balanced system by which universities are able to support doctoral candidates and simultaneously instruct lower-division students at relatively low cost. The unsupervised teaching assistant, notorious in the forties and fifties, is now becoming somewhat less common, as a result of efforts made by some of the graduate schools and national discipline associations. Among graduate schools, Harvard has led the way in reforming this vicious pattern. [*64*] Among discipline associations, the Modern Language Association of America is one which has urged the graduate faculties in the foreign language field "to stop assuming that good teachers simply happen." [*47*, p. 7]

At the master's level, two developments have attracted wide attention. The first is the series of high-level master's programs, developed on about eighty campuses, designed for prospective teachers. Thirty of these programs carry the specific title "Master of Arts in Teaching." According to U.S. Commissioner of Education Francis Keppel, these programs "encourage high standards of scholarly achievement, professional competence, and long-term career commitment." [*40*, p. 253]

Second, special *three-year* master's programs are being conducted on some forty campuses. This attempt to break the old pattern, in which a single-year master's program disconnectedly follows two years of upper-division work, is worth looking at more closely. Typical of the movement is the three-year master's program at the University of Arizona. University officials hope that students who complete it "will have received a more thorough and demanding education and will have enjoyed experiences not available to most students in this age of mass and patterned education." Like other such programs, it is an integrally planned course of study covering three years of work. It retains students only so long as they maintain the program's high standards. The senior year includes an honors project and an apprenticeship; the graduate year includes training in independent research and experience in a supervised graduate assistantship. [*2*]

THE PROFESSIONAL SCHOOL

The history of the professional school during the late fifties and early sixties is as complex as that of the graduate school. In the late fifties, according to McGrath and Henderson, professional school curricula were moving away from a professional orientation toward a liberal arts framework. [*48*; *35*, p. 142] A distinction between "pure" and "applied" knowledge originally provided the basis for the uniqueness of their curricula; but since World War II, this distinction has been found to be no longer functional or philosophically defensible.

As the years moved toward the mid-sixties, the professional school's programs—we refer here to those that are still a vital part, psychologically and physically, of today's campus—tend to become indistinguishable from programs in the main body of the university. [*48*, pp. 50–59] It seems likely that the professional schools will carry on their separate existence for a time, but the pressures of economy and efficiency may bring about their demise eventually.

Many of the institutions now coming into being are not planning to have separate professional schools or even separately designated professional curricula. For example, the California State College at Palos Verdes is departing from the older state college pattern by planning neither a school or division of education nor one of business; this principle will apply to both its undergraduate and graduate programs. [14]

It thus appears that the professional school and the ivory tower will collapse together. This is a repetition, with variations, of the 1919–59 history of the teachers college.

The New Patterns: The Reply to Standardization

The intellectual in America has always been closely related to higher education. By the end of the fifties, the intellectual had finally arrived. He was highly respected in the workaday world. He was better paid than ever before. He was influential in government and industry.

Still, he was troubled. Although he was influential, he felt impotent. The campus intellectual of the fifties railed against loyalty oaths; in the end he signed them. He did not like the news that nineteen of the ninety-three fraternities and thirty-six of the fifty-five sororities on the University of California campuses refused to sign the nondiscrimination pledge,[2] but he did not allow it to interfere with his work. He was happy, at least, to hear the platforms on his campuses ring with the slogans of anticonformism. The watchword was "pluralism of values," and it was everywhere said that no single view could ever dogmatically be declared "the American view." But the nation as a whole craved an identity—craved one so badly, it was willing to pay any price.

The price was standardization. Could the colleges and universities of the fifties resist the onslaught? Could they keep their students, their faculty, their curricula—and, what is more important, the administrative relations among these—free from standardization? They could not. The platforms of the campuses of the late fifties continued to ring with the slogans of anticonformism, but the studies of college and university students—many of them unpublished—reveal the crushing fact: the primary effect of college and university experiences on students was simply that they had become more like one another.[3]

---

[2] This requirement was set by the Regents in 1959, with a fall 1964 deadline. [59] By January 1965, all but two fraternities and ten sororities had complied.

[3] Aside from the pioneer work of Newcomb and Jacobs, over half of the chapters (sixteen out of twenty-nine) in The American College bear on this question, as well as a substantial portion of the titles listed in the bibliography of the Center for the Study of Higher Education at Berkeley. [16] My thanks to Paul Heist for his help in interpreting for me some center data on this point.

A student entering college in the fifties who did not wish to be molded to a norm faced a wretched alternative: "Submit, or seek your education (without portfolio) elsewhere." Some of the most creative minds of the generation were expelled from the academic garden. Gamesmen, plodders, nonentities remained. They were turned out "capable" and "sharp" by the campus assembly line. "He's going to go places" was a phrase of approval, and it signified the student would take the path of involvement without commitment.

These students grew up to become the young faculty of the late fifties and early sixties—"a generation of gamesmen," Riesman called them, "bright but unconvinced men, who are erudite but poor specimens of mankind." [*30*, p. 20]

Higher education's achievement in standardizing the students of the fifties is commemorated in a folksong that became a hit in 1964. It begins with a description of the houses that, made of "ticky-tacky," look like a series of little boxes. The second stanza runs: "And the people in the houses/ All go to the university/ And they all get put in boxes, little boxes, all the same—/ And there's doctors and there's lawyers and business executives/ And they're made out of ticky-tacky/ And they all look just the same." [*57*]

But when the song reached its greatest popularity, the words were less true than when they were first sung. In the mid-sixties, students are becoming destandardized on many campuses. There is immense activity under the names of "honors programs" and "independent study programs." [*10, 19, 32, 44*] Moreover, the 1919–59 pattern that built a wall between the high school and the college is broken. The trickle of high school students taking courses on college campuses in advance placement programs in the early sixties will likely become a stream later in the decade. [*56*]

Admissions offices are concerned about the "creative" youngster who is not allowed in because he does not meet standards. The standards have not yet been changed, but students who are allowed in are not as quickly evicted as in the pre-1959 period. Administrators hope that the dropout rate among the more creative students, so great in former years, will decrease. Indeed, it is anticipated that the number of dropouts—which, in the forties and fifties, the process of standardization had brought to almost *half* of those who entered college [*60*, p. 631]—will decrease markedly as students become destandardized.

The first and most significant trend on American campuses during the current decade is thus the deconforming of students. The second is the deconforming of curricula.

The content of college and university curricula—especially during the crucial initial months when student attitudes toward the higher learning are being formed—has undergone rapid alteration during the last half-decade. In 1963, for example, a Harvard faculty committee declared its three-year-old freshman seminar successful, and the education editor of the *New York Times* saw a sign of the "beginning of an entirely different kind of general education—less uniform, less 'balanced,' less superficial, more tolerant of individual detours." [34]

At the close of the fifties, a university president, looking at curriculum change, said it "entails all the physical and psychological difficulties of moving a cemetery." [65] The major difficulty appeared to reside in a curious historical circumstance: the curriculum was grounded in the concept of number. Everything was by count: class hours, grade points, credits and courses, semesters and quarters and trimesters. So many credits for so many hours for so many weeks for so many years would earn a degree. Even some of the newest plans—the 3-3 of Dartmouth or the 4-1-4 of Gustavus Adolphus—suffer from dependence on counting. [20]

Leaders in higher education knew, as they faced the opening of this decade, that once the curriculum was freed from the yoke of number, they could manage the other curricular problems. But they understood the total problem well enough to know that this freedom could not come until the instruments measuring a college student's knowledge, in the fullest sense of the word, were perfected.

These two developments—dequantifying the curriculum and perfecting knowledge-assessing scales—are now moving toward one another, ready to join into a single movement. The pioneer work in joining these two was done at Chicago in the forties and at Michigan State, Shimer, and various other campuses in the East and Midwest in the fifties. Now it is the colleges and universities in Florida, Michigan, and New York that are leading the way.[4]

The response in the sixties to the standardization of the fifties affects faculty also. The large movement to destandardize is providing the motive force in bridging the gulf between teaching and research. By 1959, this gulf had become immense. By the mid-sixties, the ends of the teacher-scholar and the ends of the research-scholar, long due for re-examination, are beginning to be redefined, and the fields common to both are being rediscovered.

Recent exploration of the ends of higher education points to three major goals for colleges and universities, all revolving around knowledge: its daily production, its continuous reinterpretation and transformation, and its daily diffusion. The central concern of the true

[4] As new campuses are being planned in these states, the organizational pattern calls for an officer in charge of coordinating measurement of student achievement and campuswide efforts to evaluate the effectiveness of the educational program. Such officers are not new on American campuses. A 1959 volume on testing carries descriptions of seven programs of the fifties, several of which had such officers. [1] But on the whole, the system of grading on the basis of vague and often contradictory criteria dominated the fifties. [6] It is, therefore, significant that the pattern of the fifties is being broken in these three states and elsewhere. [42]

scholar is seen to lie, first and foremost, with reinterpreting the body of knowledge, assimilating the new into the old, reassessing and transforming the shape of the whole. Only after he achieves this central objective—and is habitually performing it—is he considered ready to move to his own particular function. The research-scholar moves to the augmentation of knowledge, the teacher-scholar to the transmission of knowledge. Let the former neglect the center and attend only to augmentation, he becomes a researchist. Let the latter neglect the center and attend only to transmission, he becomes a classroom manager. Worse still, having no intellectual life in common, each must then mistrust and belittle the other.

In 1959, there were probably fewer research-scholars on American campuses than researchists, and probably fewer teacher-scholars than classroom managers. It may take several decades to correct the imbalance in institutional ends, but the sixties have seen the beginning. Universities famous for publish or perish are beginning to look for teacher-scholars for their faculties. New criteria for promotion will have to be worked out; but the problem will be surmounted. Dean E. McHenry, chancellor at the new Santa Cruz campus of the University of California, admits that "recruiting a qualified teaching staff, because of the emphasis on instruction rather than research, might be a problem." But he has announced that he has worked out a plan which "calls for a new system of staff evaluation and promotion." [17] The president of that multiversity dares to predict what lies beyond: "The last twenty-five years have been the age of the specialist," Kerr declares, "but I have a hunch— a very strong one—that the next twenty-five years will see a rebirth of the generalist. It's inherent in the very nature of things. It *must* happen." [43]

The age of overspecialization, of rivalry and misunderstanding between researcher and teacher is beginning to end. In the late fifties, educational leaders like Meredith Wilson and Peter Elder knew that was going to happen. This snatch of dialogue which took place in 1958 shows how they anticipated the current trend:

WILSON: What is "research"? Veblen, in his *Higher Learning in America*, makes the comment that the real business of a university is not teaching but study. Now, what kind of study is appropriately research? Mr. Elder, I would like to find out where you separate these.

ELDER: I am not sure I can help you. I personally generally avoid the word "research" and use the word "study." I merely mean some people's individual study is "published" before a group of undergraduates in oral communication. Other people's study is published that way and also another way in order to help people living thousands of miles away and a number of years from the present time. I therefore haven't made any distinction between research and study and really do not wish to. [5, p. 18]

In 1963, Kerr listed a number of institutional changes which he believes are coming, in spite of much faculty hesitation and "even some resistance": the revamping of curricula and calendars; the renovation of undergraduate teaching; the revolutionizing of some fields of study (for example, biology); the mechanization of some aspects of instruction. But two changes, he believes, will be readily accepted: "One will be directed toward overcoming the fractionalization of the intellectual world, and the other will call for procedures devised to make administration more personal, including faculty administration." [41, p. 101]

We have just seen, briefly, the paths by which fractionalization in the intellectual world is being combated. But destandardization of faculty-administration relationships will come less easily. The progressive formalization of these relations in the fifties became too well-paved a road to be quickly replaced. During the last decade, faculties were increasingly caught up in the formal procedures of rights and privileges, tenure and free speech, loyalty oaths and due process. "Faculty government has become more cumbersome," Kerr declared, "more the avocation of active minorities; and there are real questions whether it can work effectively on a large scale, whether it can agree on more than preservation of the status quo." [41, p. 43]

There are notable exceptions, but a great deal of the interchange between faculty and administration (including the superadministration, that is, systemwide heads and governing boards of institutions and systems) is formal or threatening or bitter. Reasonable dialogue between the parties is the exception. The observer notes that both sides invoke truth, justice, democracy, and America. And in invoking these clichés, they choke off dialogue. But if dialogue is not kept alive and flourishing between faculty and administration, how can higher education's total contribution to society be kept flourishing?

To recognize this principle, however, only intensifies the dilemma. No one seems to be sure how the principle is to be implemented, how dialogue is to be kept alive. During the fifties, relations between faculty and administrators underwent cycles of tension and relaxation as procedures were established to safeguard faculty rights, ensure justice, guarantee academic freedom. [24] No one can possibly wish these undone. But it cannot be denied that the growth of these procedures played a major role in the progressive impersonalization of faculty-administration relations. Is it possible, during the years immediately ahead, that the power of these procedures can be harnessed and made to contribute toward the humanization of these relations? Perhaps we can take a lesson from the giant computers— themselves symbols of standardization—that are actually learning how to differentiate and individualize rather than standardize. J. A. Easley, for example, told participants at a 1964 conference how

PLATO, a new computer system, meets the needs of its users not *en masse* but individually. [*23*] Perhaps the answer lies not in combating bigness but in channeling its power.

The solution currently being offered, however, takes a different line of reasoning. If progressive impersonalization in faculty-administration relations comes from ever-increasing bigness, then humanization should occur if the structure, even as it grows larger, is made to appear smaller. This is the solution of decentralization. Decentralization is taking place on several older campuses [5] and on some new ones. At the University of California, Santa Cruz, for example, twenty or so small, liberal arts colleges will be established (about four in each half-decade) and a "campus core" will provide the home for the graduate school, the library, and certain facilities requiring elaborate paraphernalia. Cowell College, the first of the undergraduate colleges at Santa Cruz, will open next year with about six hundred students and thirty-five faculty fellows.

The concept of "modular" growth, according to Chancellor McHenry, although "new in an American state institution, is really medieval in conception." [*49*] Thus, possibly, a medieval concept of university organization holds the key for the solution to today's grave dilemma in faculty-administration relations.

These, then, constitute the four-dimensional response to standardization which we see emerging in the first half-decade of the new era: individualizing the student; freeing programs of study from the yoke of number; rediscovering the central and common goals of researcher and teacher; and humanizing faculty-administration relations.

But there is a larger context, and I should like to close by stating my conception of it.

The leading minds in America know that education, and higher education in particular, is the most powerful instrument our society possesses for effecting social change. Both in the era ending about 1959 and in the present era, educators have sought to discover how that instrument can best be shaped toward that end.

The search for this answer during the era just ended was exciting, haphazard, energetic, disorganized, and eventful. And, as we have seen, the verdict of the profession was that it was not successful. There appear to be four causes for its failure. Three were internal: insufficient information about education, particularly higher education, as a functioning institution in our society; a general misconception of the processes by which knowledge is transmitted; and an

---

[5] For example, at the University of the Pacific. The Claremont group, incidentally, is not a case in point, since the Claremont colleges have not *moved* from centralization to decentralization. Nevertheless it should be said that recent developments in academic decentralization could not have taken the shape they have, without the benefit of the experience of Pomona and her sister institutions.

emphasis on the constant production of new knowledge at the expense of the continuous reinterpretation of the whole body of knowledge. One cause was external: a society at war.

The search for the answer during the years following 1959 promises to be exciting, systematic, energetic, organized, and eventful. Let us hope that historians of American higher education, judging this search with the eyes of, say, 1999, will declare it was successful.

REFERENCES

Note.—This is a list of the literature cited in the paper; it is not intended to be a selective bibliography.

1. AMERICAN COUNCIL ON EDUCATION. Committee on Measurement and Evaluation. *College Testing: A Guide to Practices and Programs.* Washington: The Council, 1959.

2. ARIZONA, UNIVERSITY OF. *The University of Arizona's Special Master's Program.* Prepared by T. W. Parker. Mimeographed. 1963.

3. ASSOCIATION FOR GENERAL AND LIBERAL STUDIES. *Common Goals of Liberal and General Education.* Proceedings of the First Annual Meeting of the Association for General and Liberal Studies, Oct. 25–27, 1962. East Lansing, Mich.: 1963.

4. AXELROD, JOSEPH. "Coordinating Higher Education in California," *University College Quarterly,* May 1964.

5. ———— (ed.). *Graduate Study for Future College Teachers.* Report of the Conference on College Teacher Preparation Programs Sponsored by the Committee on College Teaching of the American Council on Education in Washington, D.C., April 30 and May 1, 1958. Washington: American Council on Education, 1959.

6. ————. "What Do College Grades Mean? A Survey of Practices at Four Institutions," *College and University Teaching,* Herman A. Estrin and Delmer Goode. Dubuque, Iowa: William C. Brown Co., 1964.

7. AXELROD, JOSEPH, and BIGELOW, DONALD. *Resources for Language and Area Studies.* Washington: American Council on Education, 1962.

8. AXELROD, JOSEPH; BLOOM, BENJAMIN S.; GINSBURG, BENSON; O'MEARA, WILLIAM; and WILLIAMS, JAY C., JR. *Teaching by Discussion in the College Program.* Chicago: College of the University of Chicago, 1949.

9. BASKIN, SAMUEL (ed.). "Higher Education: Some Newer Developments." MS in press. New York: McGraw-Hill Book Co. (See especially chap. 2, "The New Colleges," by Lewis Mayhew.)

10. ————. *Quest for Quality: Some Models and Means.* U.S. Office of Education, New Dimensions in Higher Education, No. 7. Washington: Government Printing Office, 1960.

11. BELOIT COLLEGE. *The Beloit Plan.* Prepared by Sumner Hayward. Mimeographed. Beloit, Mich.: The College, 1964.

12. BERELSON, BERNARD. *Graduate Education in the United States.* New York: McGraw-Hill Book Co., 1960.

13. CAIN, LEO F. "The Small College at the California State College at Palos Verdes." Address given at the National Conference on New Directions for Instruction in the Junior College, Los Angeles, California, July 16, 1964.

14. CALIFORNIA STATE COLLEGE AT PALOS VERDES. *The Academic Plan for the California State College at Palos Verdes.* Palos Verdes: The College, 1964. (Presented to the Chancellor and the Trustees of the California State Colleges, Feb. 26–27, 1964.)

15. [CALIFORNIA, STATE OF.] *A Master Plan for Higher Education in California, 1960–1975.* Sacramento: California State Department of Education, 1960. (Prepared by A. G. Coons, A. D. Browne, H. A. Campion, G. S. Dumke, T. C. Holy, D. E. McHenry, H. T. Tyler, and R. J. Wert.)

16. CALIFORNIA, UNIVERSITY OF. Center for the Study of Higher Education. *Bibliography of Publications.* Mimeographed. Berkeley: The Center, 1946. (The list contains 130 items written by center staff or based on research conducted at the Center.)

17. CALIFORNIA, UNIVERSITY OF. Santa Cruz Campus. University of California press release, dated November 1962.

18. CARMICHAEL, OLIVER C. *Graduate Education: A Critique and a Program.* New York: Harper & Bros., 1961.

19. COLE, CHARLES C., JR., and LEWIS, LANORA G. *Flexibility in the Undergraduate Curriculum.* U.S. Office of Education, New Dimensions in Higher Education, No. 10. Washington: Government Printing Office, 1962.

20. "Colleges *Can* Operate All Year," *Saturday Review,* Dec. 15, 1962. (A series of four articles by Edward H. Litchfield, University of Pittsburgh; Weimer Hicks, Kalamazoo College; Marjorie Freed, Antioch College; and Joseph E. McCabe, Coe College.)

21. DORAN, KENNETH T. "New York's Two-Year Colleges," *University College Quarterly,* May 1964.

22. DUMKE, G. S. "Higher Education in California," *California Historical Society Quarterly,* June 1963.

23. EASLEY, J. A., JR. "PLATO: A Computer-Controlled Teaching System." Paper presented at the Nineteenth National Conference on Higher Education sponsored by the Association for Higher Education, Chicago, April 21, 1964.

24. ECKERT, RUTH E. "The Share of the Teaching Faculty in University Policy-Making," *American Association of University Professors Bulletin,* Winter 1959.

25. EDUCATIONAL POLICIES COMMISSION. *Universal Opportunity for Education Beyond the High School.* Washington: National Education Association, 1964.

26. ELDER, J. P. "Revising the Master's Degree for the Prospective College Teacher," *Journal of Higher Education,* March 1959.

27. FLORIDA ATLANTIC UNIVERSITY. *A Proposed Statement of Beliefs for Florida Atlantic University.* Mimeographed. Boca Raton: The University, 1963. (Prepared by Samuel Baskin and revised to include comments from workshop participants, Sept. 23, 1963.)

28. "The Future of Liberal Education," *Saturday Review,* April 18, 1964.

29. *The Graduate School Today and Tomorrow.* Written by F. W. Strothmann on behalf of the Committee of Fifteen. New York: Fund for the Advancement of Education, 1955.

30. HABEIN, MARGARET L. (ed.). *Spotlight on the College Student: A Discussion by the Problems and Policies Committee of the American Council on Education.* Washington: The Council, 1959.

31. HATCH, WINSLOW R. *The Experimental College.* U.S. Office of Education, New Dimensions in Higher Education, No. 3. Washington: Government Printing Office, 1960.

32. HATCH, WINSLOW R., and BENNET, ANN. *Independent Study.* U.S. Office of Education, New Dimensions in Higher Education, No. 1. Washington: Government Printing Office, 1960.

33. HAYWARD, SUMNER. "Five Experimental Programs in Undergraduate Liberal Arts." Paper presented at the Nineteenth Annual Conference on Higher Education sponsored by the Association for Higher Education, Chicago, April 20, 1964. (The five colleges described are Raymond, Oakland University, Kalamazoo, Earlham, and Beloit.)

34. HECHINGER, FRED M. "A Move to Free College Freshmen," *New York Times* (Western Edition), March 13, 1963.

35. HENDERSON, ALGO D. *Policies and Practices in Higher Education.* New York: Harper & Bros., 1960.

36. HOFSTRA UNIVERSITY. *A Proposal for a 3-Year Autonomous Undergraduate Degree-Granting New College at Hofstra University.* Prepared by the staff at New College and the Bureau of Institutional Research at Hofstra University. Hempstead, L.I., N.Y.: The University, 1964.

37. JOHNSON, B. LAMAR. "Behold You Have Created a New Thing: A Conference Summary and Critique." Address delivered at the Colloquium on the Experimental College, sponsored by Florida State University, Wakulla Springs, Florida, April 8, 1964.

38. ———. "Islands of Innovation," *Junior College Journal,* February 1964. (The full report of this survey appeared in March: *Islands of Innovation: A Report of an Exploratory Survey of the Utilization of Junior College Faculty Services.* Los Angeles: University of California, 1964.)

39. KEETON, MORRIS. "The Climate of Learning in College," *College and University Bulletin,* Nov. 15, 1962.

40. KEPPEL, FRANCIS. "Master of Arts in Teaching," *American Education Today,* ed. Paul Woodring and John Scanlon. New York: McGraw-Hill Book Co., 1963.

41. KERR, CLARK. *The Uses of the University.* Cambridge, Mass.: Harvard University Press, 1963.

42. KURLAND, NORMAN D. "New York College Proficiency Examination Program," *Current Issues in Higher Education,* 1963, ed. G. Kerry Smith. Washington: Association for Higher Education, 1963.

43. LEONARD, GEORGE B. "California: What It Means," *Look,* Sept. 25, 1962.

44. LEWIS, LANORA G., in cooperation with BRYAN, J NED, and POPPENDIECK, ROBERT. *Talent and Tomorrow's Teachers: The Honors Approach.* U.S. Office of Education, New Dimensions in Higher Education, No. 11. Washington: Government Printing Office, 1963. (A statement based upon the transcript of proceedings of an April 1962 Conference of the Inter-University Conference on the Superior Student.)

45. LITTLE, J. KENNETH. "Graduate Education," *Encyclopedia of Educational Research.* New York: Macmillan Co., 1960.

46. LUNSFORD, TERRY F. (ed.). *The Study of Campus Cultures.* Papers Presented at the Fourth Annual Institute on College Self-Study, University of California, Berkeley, July 24–27, 1962. Berkeley: University of California, 1963. (By R. W. Tyler, H. S. Becker, B. R. Snyder, B. R. Clark, C. R. Pace, T. Newcomb, M. A. Trow, J. Floud, J. King, and R. H. Sullivan.)

47. MACALLISTER, ARCHIBALD T. (ed.). "The Preparation of College Teachers of Modern Foreign Languages," *Publications of the Modern Language Association of America,* May 1964.

48. MCGRATH, EARL J. *Liberal Education in the Professions.* New York: Teachers College, Columbia University, 1959.

49. MCHENRY, DEAN E. "The University of California at Santa Cruz." Address given at the National Conference on New Directions for Instruction in the Junior College, Los Angeles, California, July 16, 1964.

50. MCKEON, RICHARD P. "The Future of the Liberal Arts." Paper presented at the Nineteenth National Conference on Higher Education sponsored by the Association for Higher Education, Chicago, April 20, 1964.

51. MAYHEW, LEWIS B. *The Smaller Liberal Arts College.* Washington: Center for Applied Research in Education, 1962.

52. MEDSKER, LELAND L. *The Junior College: Progress and Prospect.* New York: McGraw-Hill Book Co., 1960.

53. ORLANS, HAROLD. *The Effects of Federal Programs on Higher Education: A Study of 36 Universities and Colleges.* Washington: Brookings Institution, 1962.

54. PACE, C. ROBERT. "Images of American Colleges and Universities," *Higher Education: Its Multiple Facets,* A Report of the Eighth Far Western Conference of Fulbright Scholars. Los Angeles: University of California, 1963.

55. PETERSON, B. H. "The Role of the Junior College in California," *California Education,* October 1963.

56. RADCLIFFE, SHIRLEY A., and HATCH, WINSLOW R. *Advanced Standing.* U.S. Office of Education, New Dimensions in Higher Education, No. 8. Washington: Government Printing Office, 1961.

57. REYNOLDS, MALVINA. "Little Boxes." Discs issued by Columbia, #4-42940, and by Victor, #47,8301.

58. ROSENHAUPT, HANS. "Graduate Education," *American Education Today,* ed. Paul Woodring and John Scanlon. New York: McGraw-Hill Book Co., 1963.

59. *San Francisco Chronicle,* May 29, 1964.

60. SANFORD, NEVITT (ed.). *The American College.* New York: John Wiley & Sons, 1962.

61. SELVIN, HANNAN C. "The Impact of Higher Education on Student Attitudes," *Unity and Diversity in Higher Education.* A Report of the Seventh Far Western Conference of Fulbright Scholars. Berkeley: University of California, 1962.

62. SMITH, SEYMOUR M. "New Logs and Old Learning," *Improving the Efficiency and Quality of Learning,* ed. A. E. Traxler. A Report of the Twenty-sixth Educational Conference Sponsored by the Educational Records Bureau and the American Council on Education. Washington: American Council on Education, 1961.

63. STERN, GEORGE G. "Student Values and Their Relationship to the College Environment," *Research on College Students,* ed. Hall T. Sprague. Boulder, Colo.: Western Interstate Commission for Higher Education, 1960.

64. *Teaching Fellowships in Harvard College: A Survey by the Committee on Teaching as a Career.* Cambridge, Mass.: Harvard University, 1960.

65. WILSON, LOGAN. "A President's Perspective," *Faculty-Administration Relationships,* ed. Frank C. Abbott. Washington: American Council on Education, 1958.

66. WOODRING, PAUL. "The Short, Happy Life of the Teachers College," *American Education Today,* ed. Paul Woodring and John Scanlon. New York: McGraw-Hill Book Co., 1963.

Changes within the Liberal Arts Colleges

MARY WOODS BENNETT

THE LIBERAL arts colleges share with a variety of other educational institutions the dubious distinction of participating in the well-advertised crisis in American higher education. Although their contribution to the solution of the problem of numbers seems destined to be relatively small, they are under pressure to accommodate their fair proportion of the burgeoning horde of college-bound youth. Along with larger and more complex institutions, they view with alarm the likelihood of a severe shortage of teacher talent in the near future, and, with a few fortunate exceptions, they are concerned about their ability to pay competitive salaries to desirable recruits in a sellers' market. They are acutely aware of continually rising costs of higher education and of the real possibility of pricing themselves out of the market in an effort to make tuition cover a reasonable share of such costs. Far more than is true of colleges and universities maintained at public expense, or of the great universities which enjoy generous private support, the independent colleges are, as a group, plagued by questions about their own viability.

While Beardsley Ruml and Jacques Barzun may seem to constitute an unlikely team, they have effectively, if unwittingly, cooperated in delivering a one-two punch which has had a shocklike impact on the responsible officers of most liberal arts colleges—on trustees, faculty members, and administrators. Whether they have delivered a knockout blow, forced the victim to defensive tactics, or stimulated an effective counterattack remains to be seen. In any event, few faculty members are so deeply buried in their disciplinary ivory towers, few college presidents so distracted by the multitudinous demands of their jobs, few trustees so irresponsible, as to be wholly deaf to the warning that measures to ensure the very survival of the institutions they serve may be their paramount concern for the foreseeable future. Doubtless, we owe much to the two dissimilar colleagues who have hammered the lesson home.

Capacity for Change

It is not our task here either to defend or to challenge the thesis that the liberal arts college is obsolete. Nor are we to concern ourselves specifically with the "pursuit of excellence"—whether in curricular organization, in student performance, or in instructional method—important as it may be to keep before ourselves the goal of quality in these matters while we wrestle with problems of quantity and cost in higher education. Rather our assignment is to consider the means, the organizational devices, by which institutions take stock, make policy, develop, and carry out procedures for the attainment of their corporate purposes and for dealing with the pressures of the times. For the liberal arts college, especially the independent college, the organizational capacity to effect drastic changes may well be the key to survival when such changes are required to keep an institution both educationally stimulating and financially solvent.

When compared with other types of educational institutions of collegiate or university level, the liberal arts college is relatively small in size, simple in structure, unitary in function. More than its sister institutions, it can, or could, support the appellation: "community of scholars." Yet it is not immune to the divisive influences which have created some of the acute organizational problems of the multiversity. Its scholar-teachers, especially the younger ones, may well place concern for their discipline, and for their status in it, above concern for the general problems of the college in which they teach. Traditional departmental organization, with departmental loyalties strengthened by ever-increasing emphasis on specialization, may negate the opportunity for, and practice of, a unitary approach to policy and decision making by the faculty as a whole. The problems of numbers faced by higher education on a national scale may well result in modifications of a college's organization and methods of work even though the absolute size of its own student body, faculty, and campus changes relatively little. In a word, we cannot get by with a slide rule for institutional problem solving when our sister institutions, with which we must do business, are using computers. The "machinery" gets more elaborate, the personnel required to tend it grows, and so may distance—psychological and sometimes physical—between the faculty and president, while many solutions of the sort which once emerged from faculty meetings now pour out of the IBM machine.

Levels of Power

Typically, the liberal arts college is governed by a board of trustees which has ultimate responsibility for its destiny. Typically, such a board vests administrative authority in a president whose charge includes all aspects of the college's operations. Typically, the faculty is involved, through formal delegation of responsibility or by custom, in various aspects of administration, especially those relating to curriculum, instruction, and the academic careers of students. Within each category—the board, the presidency, the faculty—the extent of constitutional power and the manner in which it is exercised, varies widely, and among categories there are almost as many different patterns in the interplay of authority and accountability as there are colleges. Frequently there is a discrepancy between that which is legally permitted and that which is commonly practiced. Few boards and presidents are as autocratic as they could be according to the letter of the law. Many faculties exercise, through various advisory bodies and roles, more influence than is indicated by the official statement of their functions.

Presently there is much concern about administrative efficiency in colleges, the several strands of the argument indicating the principal types of current organization. In the absence of unequivocal answers from the realm of management as to optimal structure and procedure for getting the business of the college done, spokesmen for all interested parties, within the college and outside it, offer their opinions. Underlying the presentations of the various points of view are a universal concern for doing the job well, and a common conviction that new methods will have to be found or old ones adapted to meet changed conditions. But there is no agreement as to means. One group of arguments is advanced in favor of strong board and presidential authority on the grounds that institutional self-study can be more searching, bold steps more readily undertaken, necessary cuts in program or personnel more easily effected, by a relatively detached administrative group concerned with the institution as a whole. The traditional conservatism of faculties, their understandable self-interest where their own departments are concerned, the undesirability of distracting them from the essential tasks of teaching and scholarship, and the cumbersomeness of the usual faculty committee apparatus are all cited as arguments in favor of authority vested in the president and his aides. Another group advocates as strongly the primacy of the faculty in college governance, pointing out the degree to which essentially academic decisions ramify into all aspects of college operations, and stressing the desirability of democratic organization within the college. As the first set of arguments may suggest a bypassing of the faculty on matters of legitimate concern to them in the interests of firmness and efficiency of action, the second set tends to attribute to the faculty wisdom in all things. It is hardly surprising that a third group of spokesmen considers the merits of a faculty-administration council to give continuing attention to long-term over-all plans for the college, and of other means for securing the maximum benefit of faculty advice and participation in academic administration without involving faculty members in excessive busywork, administrative officers in frustrating delays, and the institution itself in confusion bred of simple failure to divide the labor adequately and keep the channels of communication open.

Administrative Needs

Today's college president is head of an exceedingly complex organization, all the complexities of which he must master for his own effectiveness and his board's understanding. He must find and retain a faculty which can keep the college "in the running" with curricula intelligently conceived and effectively taught, and he must have some administrative help in getting the job done. He must also have some specially equipped assistants who can cope with the consequences of the fact that even a little college is big business these days. He must encourage both administrative officers and faculty to give continuous attention to long-range planning. He and they will be most effective if each thoroughly understands the problems of the others as well as his own, and knows the limits of his own responsibility in the total enterprise.

A blueprint cannot be provided, but past experience is reassuring —with a few well-understood loci of final authority identified, a college may organize itself effectively in any one of a variety of ways. The traditions and present circumstances of the college, the character of the faculty, and the personality of the president will be as important in determining the course the organization will take, and its effectiveness, as will the bylaws of the board. The one course the college may not take if it is to survive is to leave to chance its own pattern of change, thus leaving the way clear for the development of intramural struggles for authority and prestige. In today's academic climate, an institution will change. Its only choice is whether it will change planfully or no.

Alterations in Institutional Attitudes and Behavior

DAVID RIESMAN

THE MAIN STORY of what has been happening to our pace-setter institutions of higher learning has recently been wittily and pene-tratingly stated in Clark Kerr's *The Uses of the University*. Some of the major themes can perhaps be summed up by saying that the academic guilds or disciplines have become the main intellectual and emotional homes of that minority of faculty members who set the modern style and, correspondingly, that the institutions where they happen to be teaching or the communities where they happen to be living have somewhat less call upon their interest and dedication.

Institutions at or very near the top of the academic profession can evoke institutional loyalties because their senior faculty do not view themselves as transients—though they may still be weaned away now and then—while at the same time, the undergraduates in such institutions are sufficiently rewarding to teach so as to com-pete with fair success with the graduate students and postdoctoral fellows for a place in the academic span of attention. And at the very bottom of the academic procession, college presidents can de-mand institutional loyalties because their faculty are captives, and the presidents can be despotic because they can tell some of their faculty that, if they don't like it there, they can go back and teach in the tenth or eleventh grade rather than in the thirteenth or fifteenth. In between these extremes, one does find institutions whose presidents—perhaps because they cannot help it—are more oriented to their local communities than to the academic guilds at large.

Nine years ago, when I was working on a study commissioned by the Fund for the Republic concerning academic freedom, I was curious about the different relative degrees of freedom possessed by the Big Ten state universities: why, for example, was the fac-ulty at Wisconsin, even in the noonday sun of Senator Joe McCarthy, more intrepid and less anxious than the faculty at Ohio State Uni-versity? Despite its national distinction, Ohio State then, and apparently now, is vulnerable to legislative and communal pressures in southern Ohio; and what is said by the Columbus *Dispatch* and by the state legislators in Columbus, weighs more heavily on that university than what is said by the sympathetic paper edited by

William Evjue in Madison—or by the Cowles Press in Minneapolis vis-à-vis the powerful University of Minnesota. I'm sure that many factors of political and cultural history and administrative courage and competence are involved here, among them being the "southern exposure" of Ohio State.

At such an institution, one may be grateful for the power and leverage of the academic disciplines which provide a faculty veto—in the worst case, simply by moving away—over institutional and communal provincialism. These latter qualities often predominate in some of the small, locally oriented liberal arts colleges, religious and secular. Sometimes these parade the virtues of smallness and declare that they "build character," perhaps as a substitute for building other equally valuable qualities; and they also suffer in the academic marketplace, because they have little to offer to the academic professionals who may want to live in a certain tension between local and institutional or denominational commitments and departmental and professional ones.

Teaching and Specialization

In this new world, the liberal arts themselves tend to become a specialty like any other. At a conference of honors program people at Columbia in May of 1964, a brilliant physicist at the University of Pennsylvania declared that no bright physicist was going to teach his subject as a service to nonscientists. Everybody would have to learn it as if he was being prepared to "do physics." Indeed, he would not know how to teach it in any other way. And recently sociologists at Smith College were saying that the products of the leading graduate schools are rarely prepared to teach sociology to undergraduates in a good liberal arts college, for the specialties they have learned to be concerned about can be taught only to graduate students or at best to advanced undergraduates who are going on in the field. Only in the humanities, and not always there, do the liberal arts remain nonvocational in this new sense, although one can find people who are teaching English literature, not so much for those who want to "do literature," but for those who are going to teach English literature to the next generation.

I am not, incidentally, suggesting that education as if one is going to become a specialist is necessarily not liberal. That depends on how it is done, how it is received by the student, and how he learns to put into context the various specialties to which he gains the courage to expose himself. Nor am I saying, as many have, and as is surely partly true, that research now has priority over teaching. Probably the great majority of college and university faculty members are still primarily teachers, whose last piece of research was their Ph.D. dissertation and who may complain of their heavy teaching loads while secretly welcoming this alibi for not meeting the other and now more prestigeful payroll of publication.

But what I think *has* declined is the role of the teacher-scholar in contrast with the role of the teacher-researcher. That is, there are plenty of teachers—for example, sisters teaching in one hundred and fifty small Catholic women's colleges—who have little hope or opportunity for research. (Among other movements, the Sister Formation Conference has helped create a greater research orientation among teaching sisters.) At most of the junior colleges, public and private, teaching loads are too heavy, and student-serving demands too great for research to be feasible, save for the most energetic. And, of course, in the large university there are numerous teaching assistants and ancillary personnel—for instance, those teaching language (not linguistics) courses—who are not really committed to research. There is a place for these people, even if they do not fit our standard image of academic man.

But in comparison with the teacher-researcher, there is less place and less prestige for the person who regards himself as a reflective and civilized student of his subject without feeling he must do extensive research in it. There never were many such people on the American academic scene, and the majority of professors, when I was an undergraduate, who claimed to be scholars were either ham actors, or pedants, or both. But the *scholar* is not an active colleague on a team or part of an academic production line so much as a man who reads and reflects and enjoys learning, and in the continuing debate on research versus teaching, this particular species tends to drop from view.

Allegiance to a Discipline

The attenuation of local ties should *not* be viewed as a loss of intellectual vitality, but rather as a change which has its many gains as well as losses. It means, as I have already implied, that faculty members who are visible to their guilds are relatively free from institutional and communal pressures not to publish their findings or to punish them for what they have written or said. No less important, the support of the academic discipline provides a countervailing power against the accepted pragmatism and drive for quick results of obvious and direct benefit to the society that were until recently characteristic of most Americans. The guilds could protect the longer view, the search for knowledge, as the phrase goes, "for its own sake," even to the point of a certain glorying in uselessness.

Of course, what is regarded as useful changes with ideology and with experience. Some Ivy League universities I know still worry that they are getting too many bright students who are going on to graduate school, and not enough who will go on to strike it rich in oil or real estate. But in the future it may matter more to their financial solvency to be able to get grants from the NSF and NIH than to possess alumni who have become entrepreneurs in the profit-making rather than the so-called nonprofit areas of our organizational life. Furthermore, Federal money based on quality of proposals acts as a countervailing pressure to the parochialism of a particular state legislature, the pieties of a particular community, or the timidities of a board of trustees which fails to act as a buffer against local vigilantes.

The Power of the "Guilds"

Furthermore, should one regard these developments purely as reflecting the trading instincts and desire for mobility of enterprising faculty members and department heads, this also would be a mistake. The power of the guilds cannot be understood simply as one might understand the power of the carpenters' union or even of the American Medical Association. It reflects the intramural developments within the active specialties which make it exciting today to work in biophysics, or macroeconomics, or in Far Eastern history, or many other fields. The morale of the subdividing disciplines is great because the new recruits have found frontiers within their own intellectual enterprise and therefore can take in each other's intellectual laundry without concern about whether freshmen students in survey courses care for it or not—in fact, the freshmen had better care for it if they want to be recommended to graduate school.

And the university presidents, if they are ambitious for their institutions, cannot help but work with the guilds and win their approval for what they are trying to do. It would be a rare university president who would turn down a chance to bring a nucleus, let us say, of psycholinguists, to his institution because this might unbalance the budget vis-à-vis some other field, for he would rightly hope that this coup would be the source of strengthening the institution in other areas if he could only get his faculty members, department heads, and deans to be sufficiently entrepreneurial.

Of course, when a faculty in a particular field grows beyond a certain size, the danger is that the members need to talk only to themselves for company. The curse of the small college for the alert ambitious guildsman is that he can't find anyone else to talk demography or microbiology with, and the virtue for the scholar is that he can find other people, even students, with whom to talk about many things. But if one is, let us say, at Berkeley, with seventy political scientists, he may not even have time to get outside his field. One could make a nice study of the lengthening amount of time spent at conventions as the guilds grow larger (and more affluent) and need to have time for more papers. If what I have described were the only tendency, then we could say that the traditional missions of higher education had been narrowed to the single mission of advancing the disciplines. We could envisage the day described in Derek Price's *Science Since Babylon,* when all the trees in the Canadian forests are being cut down, not for the Sunday *New York Times,* but for the *Physical Abstracts* and the tens of thousands of professional journals to which all but a handful of people then living will be contributing.

New Academic Missions

However, the traditional missions are still alive, though the addition of new missions has in many places altered their significance. Among these new missions is one which appeals to many of the best college students, especially at the most academically prestigeful institutions: namely, the mission to the less privileged in our own or in other societies. A student who may feel that the multiversity has become too big and impersonal, and who may not always be prepared to study a subject in the sequences and hierarchies organized by the subdepartments, may find that helping a slum Negro youngster learn English or sitting with an abandoned patient in a mental hospital provides a feeling of personal relation and responsibility lacking in the curriculum. The Peace Corps or civil rights activity may provide similar compensation. When some universities have become planetary in the sense of sending anthropologists and development experts to Pakistan or Tanzania, some of their students may be discovering the underprivileged right next door.

Of course, this is only a small minority of students, just as only a small minority resist the liberalizing impact of higher education by joining the Young Americans for Freedom and other student right-wing cadres. But the former group of compassionate students may be showing how the universities can tie themselves, as some are beginning to do, to local school systems or distant beleaguered colleges, such as the relation that Brown University has set up with Tougaloo or the University of Wisconsin with Texas Southern University, North Carolina College at Durham, and North Carolina Agricultural and Technical College.

One stimulus has come from the natural scientists and mathematicians, who thought teaching sufficiently important (along with the discovery that children themselves learn through discovery) to invade the previously snubbed or disregarded territory of the secondary schools, even the elementary schools. A few men have even begun to reverse the supposedly natural order of things, which is that if you are distinguished enough, you need neither learn anything about teaching nor teach anyone less advanced than a postdoctoral fellow. In the post-Sputnik excitement, some of these scientists and mathematicians came to be regarded as imperialists for their guilds, robbing the cradle for recruits. But a great many are more than that, sensitive to the humanistic qualities of their subjects and not wanting the young to be barred from such excitement by rote learning.

General versus Parochial Interests

It seems to me that these specific or guild-oriented missions may be replacing the kinds of relationships which universities such as Wisconsin and Minnesota have traditionally had with their state as sources of enlightenment and extension services in the broadest sense. In spite of all the talk about states' rights in education, it may be that a state is an insufficiently relevant boundary for a major institution which wants to draw its students, and certainly its graduate students and faculty, from a national and international orbit, and to decide on the relevant problems without asking on which side of the Delaware or the Mississippi they fall. Even the leading, once-regional institutions appear to me to be going national. Rice University doesn't want only to serve Texas and the Southwest; it wants to serve science and space and general culture wherever these are to be found. The University of North Carolina has not abandoned its state or regional concerns, but it has tended to merge them with its national ones. The problem then becomes one of which this group is very conscious, namely, to find new functional specializations not based on geography, or only in part based on geography, so that every institution doesn't try to do exactly the same thing and appeal to exactly the same constituencies.

It goes without saying that there are many exceptions to what I have said. All geological strata coexist in a large decentralized society such as ours. There are still many institutions which serve a particular sex, a particular ethnic group, a particular denomination (or all three at once), though there are fewer and fewer which serve only a single occupational calling. And I think that the future of the single-mission institutions is dark. Only a minority of women currently prefer the colleges set aside just for them; as we all know, a larger and larger proportion of the college-going population is going to coeducational public institutions. There is a danger that the public institutions will restrict their undergraduate and perhaps even their graduate enrollments largely to residents of the state, and thus short-change the whole society, which is looking for geographical as well as for other forms of mobility, and in which the most privileged youngsters, privileged by backing and talent, will still attend institutions which draw from the nation as a whole. A statewide mission, in other words, is usually a tax-based deprivation rather than an opportunity for growth. Of course there are still state problems and local problems, but the intellectual centers that can be expected to help in resolving them may not be located next door.

Research and Development in Higher Education

There is one mission which the university serves, but which, on the whole, has been insufficiently appreciated in higher education: the research and development function of higher education itself. The guilds are oriented to their substantive subject matters and hardly at all to the question of how these are taught, and certainly not to the institutions or institutes through which they are taught. (Individual academic entrepreneurs may write textbooks, and their publishers may compete for their renown; but both are small businessmen, not generally given to R&D on the learning process.) When a college or university could count on a constituency, it could take for granted—often erroneously, to be sure—that it understood its needs and that these did not require systematic investigation.

Today, however, the increasingly national orbits of higher education signify that institutions no longer can automatically assume that they know who their customers are or what they may require. Institutional, or in-house, research has its own dilemmas—for instance, concerning the publics to whom it is responsible (dilemmas etched by Professor Martin Trow of the Center for the Study of Higher Education at Berkeley[1]), but in any case, such research exists in only a few places, such as Minnesota, and in a few regional groupings, such as the Southern Regional Education Board or the New England Board of Higher Education.

One possible source for the incipient interest in institutional research arises in the realization among administrative leaders that the institutions they direct escape their understanding as they diversify and search actively for faculty members, for administrators and other personnel, for students, and for grants and brand-name recognition. Correspondingly, those faculty members who are wholly geared to their discipline have a difficult time grasping the complexity of their own institutions, although this seldom leads them to support institutional research, since they may continue to believe that they understand their environment. In any case, they are perhaps less willing to spend time outside the classroom counseling students, talking to College Nights at high schools, serving on admissions and other committees, and performing all the other tasks that, in a country formerly Puritan, once helped to subsidize

---

[1] "The Role of the Social Sciences in Planning for Higher Education," *Proceedings of the Symposium on Undergraduate Environment* (Brunswick, Maine: Bowdoin College, 1962), pp. 13–21.

the apparent idleness of scholarship. Since many faculty members have in some measure withdrawn their attention from what they may regard as the ancillary busywork of academia, more formal methods such as institutional research may be called upon in substitution.

The Problems of Size

In this process, the large university faces the danger of coming to resemble Big Steel, though hardly as inflexible or as periodically inattentive (for better or for worse) to non-egocentric definitions of the public interest. Big Steel suffers in part because it is big, its size a memento not to functional scale but to vanity, greed, and bad judgment. It is possible that there may come a time when research will suggest to the university that there may be a certain ceiling beyond which economies of scale are more than overbalanced by the long-run drawbacks of monstrosity. It is interesting in this connection that the Robbins Report in Great Britain is willing to consider enrollments up to 10,000 in an effort to reverse the characteristically British preference for "thinking small," even though it is still true that the new British universities plan to remain residential. Also relevant is the decision of the already mammoth campuses of the University of California not to grow any larger, and of two of the universities now being created, to attempt subdivision in interesting ways.

Still another model, which I regard as extremely valuable, or rather a set of models, is offered by the three great State Universities of Michigan, each of which has set up a satellite smaller college: Oakland University of Michigan State, Monteith College of Wayne State, and the new residential experimental college being planned at the University of Michigan. All these indicate that the big institutions need not necessarily simply grow larger by accretion. Such experiments are missions to higher education itself.

There is no single discipline which can be counted upon for that mission, and many can be counted upon to oppose it, whether as a distraction or a competitor for funds and administrative attention. But if the institutions are to keep up with the changes now occurring within them, I believe they can no longer play it by ear, but need the help that R&D already gives other, less backward, perhaps less competitive, industries.

Changes in the State College System

JOHN E. KING

THIRTY-FOUR YEARS ago, in the fall of 1930, there were 1,189,000 students enrolled in U.S. colleges and universities. At that time the phrase *state college system* might have caused one person in higher education to think of the land-grant colleges which have now evolved into land-grant universities; another might have thought of the 250 or so teachers colleges and normal schools which in that year enrolled 264,000 students and were supported by public funds. It is to the latter of these systems that I shall apply the term "state college system."

In the fall of 1964, the state college system consisted of approximately 200 publicly supported four-year institutions of higher education.[1] Most of these have been in existence since before World War I and have come through a pattern of development from normal school to teachers college and from teachers college to state college. The roles of more than half of the member colleges of this system have changed from "primarily teacher education" to "enlarged public college." Recently, more state colleges have been established in states like California, Minnesota, Texas, and New York. Others are in the process of being established.

Patterns of Evolution

Since there were 250 of these colleges in 1930—and several have been established since—and since more than 5 million students were enrolled in U.S. colleges and universities in the fall of 1964, it may be of interest to consider what has happened to the colleges not included in the 200 I have referred to as now constituting the state college system. The answer is: they have evolved. During this generation state colleges have not died or faded away; they have evolved. Normal schools have evolved into teachers colleges; teachers colleges have evolved into enlarged public colleges; enlarged public colleges have evolved into medium-scope universities; and some medium-scope universities have evolved into complex public universities. Nearly all of the 250 teachers colleges of 1930 can be followed along this channel of evolution.

[1] Listed in the February 1963 Analysis of AACTE membership as 80 "primarily teacher education" and 127 "enlarged public colleges."

There have been some alternate patterns. These include junior colleges evolving into four-year colleges, private colleges into publicly supported colleges, and, in some cases, state colleges into university branches or campuses. To use a biological definition, the 250 teachers colleges of 1930 have evolved by a "process of differentiation to a more highly organized condition." They have rolled out and unfolded, and they continue to do so.

Institutions in the state college system, whether or not they have come through the first and second evolutionary stages of normal school and teachers college, are generally regional colleges. The areas they serve may be primary, involving mainly students who live at home and commute to the college campus; they may be secondary, involving a sort of *nostrum mare* based on transportation facilities or economic and geographic linkage; or they may be tertiary, involving an entire state or extremely large geographic region cutting through two or more state boundaries. In many cases a combination is involved.

Regional Functions

Within its region the state college attempts to serve the higher education needs of the population. These needs fall quantitatively into three categories: (1) teacher education, (2) liberal arts and preprofessional education, and (3) technical, terminal, and business education. A fourth need often develops when the state college is located in a larger center of population and results in: (4) professional, graduate, and special curricula.

When the region served by the state college has been distinctive enough, and the leadership of the college courageous, tough, or shrewd enough, startling developments have resulted in some cases. The extent to which these regional higher education needs have been met by state colleges varies widely. Many factors have influenced what happens at such colleges. In addition to the leadership of the administration, faculty, alumni, and of local legislators and civic leaders, the following factors can be extremely important: the per-capita wealth of the state in which the college is located, the proximity of a particular college to other institutions of higher education, the political strength of the private colleges and state universities and/or land-grant universities in the state. The University of Southern Illinois is an example of what can take place when many of these factors are parlayed to meet the higher education needs of a distinctive region. Frankly, I have never seen more earth-moving equipment in one place than I saw on that campus a few years ago.

While the development of state colleges has been vital and strong for the last fifteen years, there are some states in which these colleges have seemed to slumber like blue-chip stocks and are now suddenly bursting into growth. New York State might be said to be an example of this—with twenty-three buildings going up at one time on its new campus, State University of New York at Albany. In other states, to show how sensitive these colleges are to the needs of their regions, there are individual colleges on the verge of being discontinued or radically changed in their missions by actions of legislatures or boards. Thus our state college system reflects with sensitivity the needs, hopes, and sometimes the struggles of the people of various states, regions, and communities.

Up and Out?

If the past is prologue, it seems likely that state colleges will continue to evolve as population increases and our college enrollments in the United States reach more than 8 million by 1974, as has been predicted. Along with the junior colleges and branch campuses of the state universities in certain strategic population centers like Kansas City and St. Louis, they will bear the brunt of the heavy increase in college enrollment during this ten-year period.

It is also likely that, since our population is both increasing and moving from rural to urban, the state college system will evolve itself out of existence by that time. In other words, by 1974 most state colleges will have become, or be on the road to becoming, medium-scope public universities and, in some cases, complex public universities.

If the state colleges do evolve even more rapidly during the next ten years and if they do share, along with the junior colleges, a major responsibility in meeting the higher education needs of what has been predicted to be a tidal wave of college students, there are problems to be faced.

Prospects and Problems

The most frequently mentioned problems immediately ahead are those of budgeting, staffing, and providing physical facilities. It is my belief that we will all be surprised at how willing the American taxpayer, state legislatures, and Congress will be to solve these problems in our time, at least insofar as they can be solved by tax funds. We have been helped so much by Castro, the Chinese Communists, and the strength of Russia that I believe we will see solutions to our financial problems that are, at present, difficult to envision. I am afraid that, as a college administrator, I have been guilty of excusing myself from facing certain realities in college administration for a long time because of lack of budget. In the future the public, the legislature, and the Congress will ask what we need in order to provide quality education for millions of young Americans, for adults who will have to be retrained, and for people who merely want to continue to learn. We are going to have to prepare rather carefully designed programs to accomplish these missions. We are going to be given pretty much everything we ask for, but it is not going to be quite the paradise we might have imagined it would be. There are going to be a number of embarrassing questions asked us about quality control, productivity of needed manpower, the kind of value patterns which our graduates will reflect in their lives as citizens, and so on. In fact, some of us may live to wish we were back in the good old days when we would have been glad to do all these things, but we just didn't have the budget.

These changing opportunities and challenges bear on autonomy and interdependence of institutions. It is my belief that in the future the administrator—or administrators and faculty members—of developing state colleges will depend very much on voluntary interdependence with a wide variety of state agencies, nonprofit corporations, government agencies, and other higher education institutions. It may be that at my college in Kansas we will be carrying on fairly symbiotic relationships with ten or twelve Federal agencies; a half-dozen state agencies which are already involved in our control; our Board of Regents; a voluntary higher education commission which relates us to all the private colleges, junior colleges, and other higher education institutions in our state; several accrediting agencies; and a multitude of other organizations and groups. I do not see any loss of autonomy in this emerging situation. It is complicated and it will probably lessen the extent to which a president of a state college can speak for his institution at the drop of a hat the way Robert Hutchins used to speak for the University of Chicago.

This emerging situation may have enormous benefits for the state colleges and their faculty members and for the students and public they serve. There is a possibility that within the coming ten-year period the state colleges may no longer be thought of as the "boondocks" by young Ph.D.'s produced on great comprehensive campuses. I am afraid that this kind of thinking has lasted twenty-five years; and it is unfortunate, because state colleges have been largely responsible for extending opportunities for higher education to the children of median- and low-income families; for providing teachers for our schools, and for making possible social mobility for a large segment of our population.

As we think of the future in terms of autonomy and interdependence, there are three hopes I will voice for the state college system and its members, no matter how far they evolve or how complicated they become:

1. That they will always serve to make possible universal opportunity for education beyond the high school. There is grave danger that some of our colleges, upon being swamped with students, will

attempt to become selective by means of high tuition or questionable entrance requirements.

2. That there will always be a commitment to the responsibility for teacher education on our campuses. This must continue to result in a total engagement of all possible resources in the pre-service and in-service preparation of teachers; and the academic and human climate on our campuses should be such that teaching as a profession compares favorably with other professions.

3. That as we grow in strength, support, and vitality, we will still try to work harmoniously and helpfully with the private colleges and junior colleges. Those institutions will need encouragement from us in our dealings with legislatures and Congress, and they need from us, now and in the future, understanding of their roles and importance.

This is especially true of the private colleges that are having difficulty defining their missions and obtaining support. Show me a state college administrator who believes we can successfully operate higher education in this country without private colleges, and I'll show you an administrator who could adjust quite well to higher education administration in a totalitarian country.

Changes in Junior Colleges and Technical Institutes

LELAND L. MEDSKER

THE NATIONWIDE growth of the junior college, and to a lesser extent of the technical institute, is now so well known that it needs no documentation. Less has been recorded, however, about the changes taking place within these institutions—changes which bear on their basic structure, the relationships among them, and their role within the complex of higher education.

In a sense, the junior college provides a good example of an evolving institution which, when it reaches adulthood, achieves the independence for which it has aspired during its adolescent years only to discover that the complexities of maturity are such that much of its new-found freedom is lost through the necessity of amalgamation with other institutions and agencies in order that it may meet the exigencies of the times.

The two-year college in America, for the most part, developed as a segment of the public school system. It was nurtured by that system, much as its early advocates thought it should be. Since in so many instances it was under the control of local school boards, its activities were not always well known nor was its staff free to operate as an independent unit. The last decade, however, has been a period of rapid maturing for the junior college. Increasing enrollments, community pressures for additional services, and other factors caused society to take a new look at this mid-level institution. The emerging concept of the "community college" meant not only that it undertook new responsibilities but that the general public became increasingly aware of its potential for service.

Partly as a result of these developments, and in accordance with other societal trends, certain developments both within and among junior colleges began to take place. Certainly the junior college is not unique in this respect since all types of educational institutions have been subject to change. However, the following six developments have made the public junior college a very different institution today from that of a short few years ago.

Changes in the Pattern of Local Control

One of the most pronounced changes pertains to the types of districts which maintain and control junior colleges. Until recently the dominant pattern of such control was for the junior college to be in a district which was also responsible for the elementary and secondary schools. Except in a few states, the trend now is for the junior college to be maintained by a separate district, with its own governing board. In California in 1960, for example, there were 56 districts maintaining junior colleges, of which only half were separate districts, the others being high school or unified school districts. Today, 56 of the 66 districts which maintain junior colleges in that state are autonomous. As a result of new legislation in a number of states, including Ohio, Missouri, Illinois, Pennsylvania, Oregon, and others, the trend is in the same direction.

The separate district ordinarily has several distinct characteristics. It is almost always larger than a local public school district, with the result that it has a larger service area as well as a broader tax base. In fact, many junior college districts are finding it necessary to establish two or more campuses in order to serve the area. Second, and of greater significance, the educational policies and the faculty personnel policies in this type of district are likely to be more liberal and to resemble those found in four-year institutions than is true of the junior college that is under the jurisdiction of a local school board. In short, the junior college in the separate district tends toward the collegial pattern.

Even in certain states where the junior college is administered under other school units, the trend is toward separate, distinctive campuses and a fair degree of autonomy in administration. Florida and Washington are good examples. All this says something about the climate of an institution, about its ability to act independently, about its opportunity to innovate, and about many other features which make it less like a secondary school.

Accelerated Pressure toward Multifunctions

Although much has always been said about the responsibility of the public two-year college to serve both the transfer and the nontransfer student, as well as to render a myriad of community services, recent developments bring the matter of the multipurpose institution at the junior college level into sharp focus. Increasing selectivity on the part of four-year institutions, which diverts a growing percentage of lower-division students to the junior college for their first two years' work, creates for this institution a heavy responsibility for the transfer function and the necessity for it to articulate its efforts with those of the four-year institutions to which its students transfer. At the same time, the current accent on vocational and technical education places the junior college in a position where it either must discharge this function adequately or turn the responsibility over to separate vocational or technical institutes. The technical institute, on the other hand, is frequently called upon to increase its academic offerings, not so much to enhance its vocational program as to make it possible for its students to transfer. Thus the dilemma of whether there can or should be a comprehensive institution is compounded. Needless to say, new funds for vocational training will accentuate this problem.

Certain other questions relating to autonomy arise in connection with the new emphasis on technical education. One of these grows out of the fact that administrative agencies at the state level often tend to become specific concerning the exact nature of vocational-technical programs and thus leave little to the imagination and educational philosophy of local colleges and technical institutes. Something of the same situation also exists when junior colleges depend too heavily upon local advisory committees for suggesting nature and content of vocational offerings. While the use of advisory committees is to be encouraged, a question arises whether the individual institution should exercise a degree of autonomy, at least by encouraging advisory committees to think in terms of broad educational needs rather than only in terms of needed vocational skills.

A move in the direction of interdependence is found in the practice of voluntary cooperation among junior colleges with respect to vocational offerings. Increasing costs in technical education and a belief that educational institutions should coordinate their efforts to reduce unnecessary duplication of offerings have resulted in efforts on the part of junior colleges in certain areas of the country to plan cooperatively with other nearby junior colleges for an appropriate distribution among them of training programs in highly specialized fields. Many people believe that this type of planning will increase. In any event, cultural pressures are great on both the junior colleges and technical institutes to perform a dual role. There is, then, the subtle fact that any imbalance in the discharge of the two functions leaves either institution in an unfavorable relation to the other and thus, in the final analysis, not completely autonomous.

Identification of the Junior College with Higher Education

The tendency of the junior college to be dissociated structurally from the public school system probably stems more from pragmatic reasons than from philosophical ones. There are, however, many indications that it is in transition in terms of its identification with other segments of education. Traditionally associated with secondary education, and often described as "the thirteenth and fourteenth grades," junior college education is now subject to a different perception. Despite its local control and its closeness to the community, recognition of the fact that its activities are post-high-school in nature and that normally it serves a high proportion of baccalaureate-bound students leads planning agencies, the lay public, and the profession to categorize it as higher education. Thus, as master plans for higher education are developed in the various states, the junior college is almost invariably considered one of the family of higher institutions.

This tendency has many corollaries. Of these, perhaps the most significant is that of faculty involvement in policy making. The issue of faculty authority as manifested by the growth and development of faculty senates and similar arrangements in junior colleges is one of the most discussed topics in many states, including California. Without doubt, a new era has arrived in which the junior college faculty will be much more involved in policy making than it has been in the past.

Accompanying this trend is the growing practice of using professional rank as a means of assigning, promoting, and dealing with the teaching staff. Today, approximately 24 percent of the public junior colleges in the country and 13 percent of the private institutions have adopted faculty rank as a basis for operation.

Changing Practices of Faculty Recruitment

Traditionally in public junior colleges a high percentage of teachers has been recruited from secondary schools. In fact, many high school teachers are still given the opportunity to move into the junior college. But there is an increasing tendency to recruit junior college teachers from among students who are completing graduate studies. In a few states a good number are also recruited from four-year colleges. Thus, the reference point of the beginning junior college teacher is changing from the traditional secondary approach to a feeling of closeness to the college and university setting. At the same time, the teacher certification requirements for junior college faculty in some states are either being eliminated or modified.

Increasing State Concern for Junior Colleges

An evident trend is the extent to which the various states are evincing interest in and concern about junior colleges. This may seem more an external than an internal development, but it has implications for the matter of autonomy and interdependence. One indication of the trend is the frequency with which planning agencies and legislative bodies give an important place to the junior college. Almost without exception, studies concerning the projected needs for higher education in the various states point to the important role of the two-year college in meeting these needs. Similarly, interim legislative commissions frequently deal with junior college problems and recommend legislation concerning this level of education. There is evidence that in most states the need for increases in state aid to local junior colleges is recognized. Interestingly enough, in this connection two different plans are developing. A few states, including Massachusetts and Minnesota, have recently established fully state-supported and -controlled junior college systems. Other states are either considering or moving in the direction of a separate state board for junior colleges, but still allowing considerable control at the local level.

Formation of Strong Professional Associations

A distinct trend among two-year colleges is their tendency to form strong professional groups at both the state (or regional) and national levels. In many states the associations maintain central offices, with paid professional assistance. The American Association of Junior Colleges maintains a large office and staff in Washington and serves its constituent members in various ways. One outcome of such organizations is that the individual institutions work together in a way that leads to joint and cooperative action on legislative and other matters.

Conclusion

While these various changes within junior colleges are by no means all-inclusive of developments taking place in most public two-year institutions throughout the nation, they are sufficient to pinpoint the basic question of whether this particular type of institution is headed in the direction of autonomy or interdependence. Without doubt certain of the forces at work lead to greater autonomy. Having come of age and severed its connection with the public schools, and having assumed a multiplicity of responsibilities as a mature entity, the junior college in many ways is more autonomous than it formerly was. But just as no man is an island, neither is any institution completely independent. There are forces which cause the junior college to look outward and to take on informal as well as formal relationships with other agencies. The various points of identification with higher education, for example, serve to throw it into a never-ending relationship with other higher institutions. The matter of interinstitutional change is the subject of other papers in this volume, but it should be noted that many of the characteristics and requirements of interinstitutional relationships stem from the changes that are occurring within individual institutions.

Perhaps the matter of autonomy versus interdependence should be viewed as a continuum, at least for such institutions as junior colleges. Given the independence that is generally accorded distinctive colleges, their surrender of certain individual rights and privileges may fall at a number of different places along the line and not necessarily at either end, depending upon the issue. The problem, then, would seem to be that of their using wisely the opportunities for preserving considerable autonomy and at the same time of embracing interdependence to the point that services are enhanced and uniformity is minimized.

3

The Emergence of State Systems

State Systems and Plans for Higher Education

LYMAN A. GLENNY

PRIOR TO 1945 the lack of system and rationality of organization in higher education stamped the development of colleges and universities in most states. The great wave of new institutions which swept from coast to coast during the eighteenth and nineteenth centuries left most of them, public and nonpublic, independent of all others. Each had its own lay board of trustees, each pursued goals, established programs, and sought students with little or no regard for what other institutions, distant or near, were doing. Although programs were quite similar, geographic distance contributed to their separateness, and denominational aspirations negated concern for coordinating activities.

Early in this century a nominal cooperation was sought through state associations or councils in which most institutions, public and nonpublic, held membership. But the one- or two-day annual meeting of these organizations interfered little with collegiate independence. With rare exception the associations lacked a professional staff to provide continuing leadership, and few ever attempted state-wide studies of any kind or adopted policies having an important impact on higher education. The meetings were structured more as forums to air plans and problems than to construct controlling policies. They did, and still do, ameliorate tensions among institutions on many matters. But, in such councils, each institution, represented in its sovereign capacity by its president, has felt no great compulsion to put the collective interests of education above its own self-interest.

In the 1920's the normal schools and teachers colleges in many states were deprived of individual boards and placed under a single governing board, frequently the state board of education. Several states also adopted a governing board for all state-supported institutions. These early developments, however, made little impact on the "happy anarchy" and the tremendous diversity dominating American higher education until after World War II.

Diversity continues to be cherished and encouraged by all, but today the unlimited freedom of a college or university to pursue a self-determined destiny is rapidly being curtailed among the public institutions and even has prospects of diminishing among the nonpublic

86

ones. At the state level the new watchwords are cooperation and coordination, with institutional independence only within certain new parameters. The classic condition of autonomy in higher education still prevails in only ten states. In all others, some rather formal structure, legal or voluntary, advises, persuades, or orders public, and occasionally nonpublic, institutions into a degree of co-ordination formerly thought to be impossible and undesirable.

The new coordination did not arise out of foresight by educators but from demands of legislators and governmental agencies for more efficient use of public monies. They wanted to eliminate wasteful duplication of programs resulting from competition among state institutions, to facilitate realistic and scientific budget requests, and to establish the rationale for developing new institutions and campuses. In attempting to protect the integrity of their own institutions, educators until recently generally have opposed increased coordination, particularly through new state commissions and boards with legal power. The need for coordination and greater central planning is now apparent to most leaders of higher education, especially in the public sphere.

Recognition of need has not been accompanied by agreement on the most effective means for achieving coordination. No two states have identical organizations for the coordination or governance of two or more institutions or systems of colleges. Nor is there a commonly accepted scheme of coordination. These conditions are not surprising since coordination is a relatively new concept in higher education. Unlike individual universities or colleges that attempt to emulate or duplicate existing prestige institutions, coordinating structures and functions have grown out of the direct felt necessities and experiences of the particular states. The recognized need for coordination has led to organizations and modes which, with rare exceptions, reflect directly the traditions, values, and practices of the people of the state. A widely emulated pattern or model co-ordinating system has yet to be established. Where borrowed patterns have been used, the resulting operations are so determined by state environmental factors and attitudes that different systems emerge.

Despite the singular characteristics of each state educational system, at least three distinct types of state-wide organization aimed directly at coordination can be detected. These are the voluntary organizations, such as those in Indiana, Colorado, Michigan, and Minnesota; the single board system for both coordination and governing of all state institutions, used in New York, Iowa, Florida, Oregon, Georgia, Mississippi, and thirteen other states;[1] and the coordinating board or council plan which is superimposed upon the

---

[1] Alaska, Nevada, Hawaii, and Wyoming have only one state institution.

existing pattern of institutions and governing boards, as now found in twenty-one states including California, Illinois, New York, Ohio, Virginia, Oklahoma, and Utah.

Voluntary Systems

Without exception the well-known voluntary structures have arisen only after the state legislature orders one or threatens to establish a single governing board or a coordinating agency with legal power. One of their main purposes is to ward off imminent threats of outside controls.

Membership on the voluntary coordinating council or committee always includes the presidents of the institutions in the system and/or executive officers of systems of teachers or state colleges. Indiana allows one or more additional staff persons, usually the budget and financial officers, from each institution. Minnesota also includes two members of the governing boards of institutions or group of institutions. Of the voluntary systems, the Indiana Conference, established in 1951, has the longest history and is thus considered the most successful. The Minnesota Liaison Committee was legislatively authorized and became operational in 1959,[2] the Colorado Association of State Institutions was formed in 1961,[3] and the Michigan Council of State College Presidents, a long-existing organization, began its coordinating efforts in 1961. Staff work for these systems is donated by the institutions, and in Colorado and Michigan full-time executive officers are employed to direct studies.

Since 1959, two other long-standing voluntary systems have given way to legislatively established agencies. The California Liaison Committee, which operated with moderate success for over a decade, was replaced by the California Coordinating Council for Higher Education in 1960.[4] The Ohio Inter-University Council, formed in 1950, may continue to operate, but in 1963 Ohio established the Board of Regents, a coordinating agency with more power than most now in existence.[5] These two former voluntary systems, along with that of Indiana, had often been cited as models by the critics of the more formal agencies described below.[6]

Until the last five years the voluntary organizations, with the exception of the now defunct California Liaison Committee, were almost exclusively concerned with budget preparation and dividing legislative appropriations. As legislatures have become interested

---

[2] *Report of Liaison Committee on Higher Education in Minnesota,* 1959–60.

[3] *Articles of Association of State Institutions of Higher Education in Colorado,* January 1961.

[4] State of California, *Education Code,* div. 16.5.

[5] State of Ohio, *Revised Code,* sec. 3333.01-3354.18.

[6] M. M. Chambers, *Voluntary Statewide Coordination in Public Higher Education* (Ann Arbor: University of Michigan, 1961).

in long-range planning and in program allocation among institutions, these agencies have also concerned themselves with additional responsibilities. The short-term record of accomplishment of voluntary councils seems undisputed.

On the other hand, the councils appear not to meet long-run expectations of the state government or the public. Both the California Liaison Committee and the Ohio Inter-University Council were replaced for their failure to deal adequately with the problems and issues confronting higher education in their states. The existing Colorado and Michigan voluntary agencies are also in danger of replacement. Early in 1964 the Colorado legislature prohibited the voluntary organization from continuing, and it is now operating under a temporary one-year authorization.[7] In Michigan, a "blue ribbon citizens committee" has under consideration a formal coordinating agency to provide more extensive coordination than by voluntary means or than by provisions of the new Michigan constitution.[8]

Single Board

The original coordinating mechanism was the single governing board for a group of like institutions or for all the state degree-granting or state-aided institutions (Florida, 1905; Iowa, 1906).

The members of the state-wide governing board are appointed by the governor of the state, usually for terms of six or seven years. Presidents of institutions do not sit on such boards but are usually in attendance at board meetings. Often they constitute an advisory council to the board on policy matters. The title of the chief officer may be secretary (Iowa), president (New York, New Hampshire), or chancellor (Oregon, Georgia). The number of central office staff members ranges from a handful to several score, and staff titles are those familiar in administrations of large universities.

Theoretically, a board with complete governing powers over all public institutions could achieve the maximum in coordination. But the adverse attitude of collegiate administrations toward these boards and the serious political problems encountered in approving the constitutional amendment usually required to establish a single board have prevented a major increase in their number. Only New York, Arizona, and New Hampshire of the states with more than two state institutions have adopted a single board system since Oregon and Georgia did so in 1931.

The Board of Trustees for the State University of New York was

---

[7] Letter of May 11, 1964, to the author from Harry S. Allen (staff director of the Colorado voluntary association).

[8] Discussed at meeting of Governor Romney's Citizens Committee on Higher Education, May 1, 1964, at which the author was present.

created in 1948 to coordinate the state-supported institutions.[9] It is a single governing board with full power over major operations of the many state campuses. It should be noted, however, that although this board controls the State University of New York, it is subject to the state-wide coordination plans and policies of the Board of Regents of the State of New York.[10] In 1961 the legislature gave the regents master planning controls over all of higher education in the state and thus strengthened their historic power as a coordinating board.[11]

As a result of a state survey in 1948, Arizona's three state institutions were placed under a single governing board.

In 1963, the two New Hampshire public teachers colleges were made state colleges and placed under the Board of Trustees of the university. The planning and development of public junior colleges continue under the State Board of Education and, as in New York, a coordinating board is authorized to coordinate over-all planning.[12]

The failure recently of the single board concept to gain acceptance among the states as the agency for state-wide coordination is attributed chiefly to the general aversion to rigid centralization and also to the preference for the coordinating board. As noted, the threat of establishing "one big board" has been the primary factor in the creation and maintenance of the voluntary systems.[13] The single board has been vigorously opposed by most educators, who see a leveling and averaging of all institutions under its control.

The negative attitude may have grown out of observation of, and experience with, the single board that governs a group of teachers colleges (now state colleges or universities) in many states (for example, Wisconsin, Pennsylvania, Minnesota, Texas, California, Tennessee, Oklahoma). In the past such boards have governed, often through the state department of education, as if all the colleges were almost identical, although recently an increasing amount of diversity seems permissible (for example, in Illinois). A study which analyzed operational differences between the single state-wide board and the coordinating board concluded that the single boards consciously avoided the much-feared uniformity attributed to them,

---

[9] *Laws of State of New York*, chap. 8, sec. 351.

[10] The Board of Regents of the State of New York, created in 1784, is often considered the oldest coordinating agency in the country. The state constitution gives power to the lay regents to approve and register new academic programs and charter institutions. However, the regents did not use such powers to "coordinate" in the sense used in this paper until the 1961 statute provided the board with master plan powers over all institutions in the state, public and nonpublic. Pennsylvania has a somewhat similar history of state-wide coordination.

[11] *Laws of State of New York*, chap. 388, sec. 1.

[12] *New Hampshire Laws of 1963*, chap. 303.

[13] See Howard L. Bevis, "Symposium: How the Dual System of Higher Education Functions in Ohio," *Annual Conference on Higher Education in Michigan* (Ann Arbor: University of Michigan, 1955).

and also concluded that they were no more effective in coordination and planning than were the first coordinating boards.[14]

Nevertheless, these adverse attitudes cause heads of colleges and universities facing legislative action to support a coordinating board as against the single governing board. However, no state with a single state-wide governing board has decentralized and changed to a coordinating board arrangement.

The Coordinating Board

The coordinating board (commission, council, committee), often referred to as the "super" or "higher" board, is rapidly gaining ascendancy over all other methods of coordination. While the single governing board arrangement has gained only three new adherents in over thirty years, no less than thirteen new coordinating agencies have been formed in the past four years and several existing agencies have been given coordinating powers. The total in existence is now twenty-one.

The popularity of these agencies can be attributed to the ease of establishment by state legislation, to their desirability in the eyes of the institutions when compared to a single governing board, and to the improvement in quality of professional staffs and the resulting improvements in practices of coordinating agencies. Existing institutions and governing boards continue to operate. The coordinating board attempts to provide order and planning either by regulating directly certain phases of operations such as programs and budgets, or by advising the governing boards, legislature, and governor of desirable courses of action, or by both means. The composition of the coordinating agencies ranges from all public members appointed by the governor to all members representative of institutions or governing boards.

Superficial similarities allow the casting of all these boards into a single classification, but differences in membership composition and in authorized power show two major subtypes with important variations. These differences in the composition and power of the central agencies cause considerable controversy among educators.

COMPOSITION

Oklahoma and New Mexico, the first coordinating agencies, were composed entirely of public members appointed by the governor. At least seven additional states followed this lead. The merits of this form of membership are considered to be impartiality toward each institution and protection of the broad public interest in con-

[14] Lyman A. Glenny, *Autonomy of Public Colleges: The Challenge of Coordination* (New York: McGraw-Hill Book Co., 1959), pp. 225 ff.

sidering total state needs. Legal restrictions usually prevent appointment to the board of members directly (or at times indirectly) associated with any institution in the coordinated system.

In 1960, Utah departed from this familiar form and, in addition to the six public members, allowed one representative each from the three governing boards. The Illinois board in 1962 was organized with two representatives from each of three governing boards, eight public-appointed members, and the state superintendent of schools. Both boards have a majority of public members, so that impartiality and the state-wide perspective remain as the operating assumptions. At the same time the boards maintain intimate contact, through institutional representatives, with the problems of governing boards and the institutions.

Wisconsin, in 1955, was the first state to ignore the principle of a majority of public members: the university and state college boards provide five members each, the governor appoints only four, and the state superintendent sits ex officio.

In 1960 the new fifteen-member California Coordinating Council was composed of representatives from the state university, the state colleges, the public junior colleges, the nonpublic institutions, and only three members appointed by the governor. (The California master plan proposal had not called for any public members.[15]) The legislators of New Hampshire (1963), Missouri (1963), and Maryland (1962) have established agencies without public members. All members are presidents of institutions and/or members of governing boards.

The reasons offered by college administrators in support of this type of membership rather than impartial lay members are almost identical to those presented in favor of "voluntary" systems of coordination: (a) the functions of coordination can be limited to those of immediate concern to the institutions by persons intimately familiar with their problems, functions, and programs; (b) coordinating policy is formulated best by those directly responsible for the welfare of the institutions, with a maximum of autonomy for the colleges and universities.

POWERS OF COORDINATING AGENCIES

The amount of legal power the board will have over the institutions will be determined primarily by the composition of the board, whether it is composed of a majority of public members or of a majority of members with a direct stake in collegiate institutions. Boards controlled by public members tend to have final authority

---

[15] California State Department of Education, *A Master Plan for Higher Education in California, 1960–1975* (Sacramento: California State Department of Education, 1960), p. 43.

over important educational policies; those controlled by collegiate members tend to have advisory powers only.

With the exception of Utah, the agencies with a majority of public members usually have final approval of all new degree programs of the public institutions and have budget responsibilities which may involve detailed analyses and budget consolidation. The newest of these agencies (New York, under its increased authority; Illinois; and Ohio) must also approve establishment of new campuses of state institutions, and develop and keep current a master plan for all higher education in the state. Some agencies have many additional final powers over such matters as tuition, admission standards, buildings, records, and dormitory rates. All agencies make recommendations to the governor, the legislature, and the governing boards.

With the exception of Wisconsin, those agencies with a majority of college representatives have power only to plan and to recommend. They have no final authority over institutions on any policy matter. The titles of agencies in South Carolina, Massachusetts, and Maryland indicate their advisory nature.

Legislatures delegate substantive powers to boards of public members, whereas boards of institutional members are delegated little, if any, power. Quite probably the institutional member boards do not want power. In Wisconsin powers have been delegated, but the committee has been reluctant to use them. Part of the tradition of autonomy is to avoid exercising any control over sister institutions—except through pre-emption of appropriations.

What kind of membership is desirable in a coordinating board? What powers, if any, should such an agency exercise? The opposing answers to these two questions create the major issues about coordination today.

Whatever the answers are, the public member agencies appear to have greater longevity and increased legislative support in comparison to boards of institutional members. The older coordinating agencies consisting entirely of public members (New York, Oklahoma, New Mexico, Texas) have never been in serious legislative jeopardy. In New York, New Mexico, and Texas, new legal powers have been granted, mostly over planning, programs, and new campuses. Recently, the Oklahoma State Regents have undertaken considerable planning activity, a rejuvenation which already has gained the board new respect from both the institutions and the legislature. The North Carolina board was given a legislative vote of confidence in 1963 when a move was made to change its membership by including institutional representatives. No agency of this type has been discontinued in any state.

On the other hand, those coordinating agencies with majority or total membership of college representatives appear to have a more uncertain and shorter existence. The Wisconsin Coordinating Committee was formed in 1955, at the same time as the Texas commission. The committee and the joint staff (one member from the University of Wisconsin and one from the state college system, plus subordinates) performed their functions for seven years, often with plaudits from the legislature, governor, and outside observers. However, in 1962 both the governor and legislature expressed concern about the superficiality of budget coordination. By the spring of 1964, newspapers reported "an open war" between the university and the colleges over expansion plans,[16] and a citizens committee, appointed as a result of a legislative joint resolution, was engaged in a thorough study of means for improving coordination. In June, the citizen group advocated a reorganization of the Coordinating Committee to provide a majority of public members and a staff independent of any institution.[17]

Maryland probably holds the record for a short-lived coordinating agency. Authorized in 1962 as a result of a state survey conducted by outside consultants,[18] the Advisory Council of institutional members lasted for just one year. Its failure has been attributed to "self-interests" of the institutions involved.[19] The 1964 legislature reconstructed the coordinating body as an all-public-member agency.

The Kentucky council, first formed in 1934, has fluctuated in legislative favor. In 1956 a full-time staff person was authorized, but when he left in 1958 the agency reverted to its former easy-going operation, without a staff. In 1962 the council was reorganized, some public members added, and funds again appropriated for a central staff. The 1963 biennial report of the agency indicates that it still has not assumed all the functions originally authorized in 1934.[20]

The new California Coordinating Council has been in operation since 1960. It is engaged in extensive studies, including adult and medical education, unit costs, and building utilization. However, the legislative analyst, the State Department of Finance (the governor's financial arm), and others in the official family have raised questions about its effectiveness in making recommendations on budgets and salaries and in fulfilling the provisions of the master plan. The coun-

16 *The Capital Times* of Madison, Wis., printed the headline: "Seek Control of Higher Education, State Colleges Hurl Challenge at U.W." See also *Milwaukee Journal*, March 1, 1964, and April 12, 1964.

17 Wisconsin Legislative Council, "Second Progress Report of the Subcommittee on Education to the Committee of 25," June 18, 1964 (Mimeographed; Madison: Wisconsin Legislative Council), p. 10.

18 *Public Higher Education in Maryland, 1961–1975*, Francis E. Rourke, Director, Report of the Commission for the Expansion of Public Higher Education in Maryland (Baltimore: 1962).

19 Southern Regional Education Board, *State Legislation Affecting Higher Education in the South, 1964*, First Report, March 25, 1964, p. 10.

20 *Report of the Council on Public Higher Education for the Biennium Ending June 30, 1963*, dated January 1964.

cil states in its annual report that it has been unable, through recommendations to the governing boards, to make progress in shifting students from the state colleges and universities to the junior colleges and in increasing the proportion of students in the upper divisions of the senior institutions. In lieu of relying on the governing boards, the council calls upon the State Department of Finance to work toward these major master plan goals by managing the priorities for new instructional facilities.[21] However, a member of the master plan survey team and a consultant to the council, who recently raised several policy issues in relation to the responsibilities and role of the council on master plan and budgetary functions, concludes that the council "can and will be of greater service" as it clarifies its role on the issues.[22]

The Missouri commission, the New Hampshire board, and the South Carolina advisory committee have yet to establish records for evaluation.

Institutionally dominated systems find themselves in an uneasy position. This can be attributed to the same factors that led to the demise of the voluntary structures in Ohio and California—failure to deal adequately and speedily with expansion and development issues.

The effectiveness of an agency composed of a majority of public members as compared to one composed of a majority of institutional members is revealed primarily by the execution of coordination policy. With the exception of Utah, the public-member agency normally has outright approval or disapproval of all new programs and campuses of the institutions.[23] It can review operating and capital budgets in sufficient detail to determine whether planned institutional expenditures conform to over-all plans. It may also have other powers over admission standards, tuition, fees, auxiliary enterprises, and allocation of appropriated funds, which enhance the coordinating effort considerably.

Agencies composed of institutional representation may have a mandate to develop and implement a master plan, but their very composition and limited powers appear to make effective fulfillment a remote possibility. Satisfaction with the *status quo*, self-interest of institutions, and domination by the largest and oldest universities seem to prevail. New programs of institutions usually are not reviewed at all, and budget recommendations are directed at the "gen-

[21] Coordinating Council for Higher Education, "Budget Report to the Legislature 1964" (Sacramento: February 1964). See pp. 42–46.

[22] T. C. Holy, "The Coordinating Council for Higher Education in California," *Journal of Higher Education*, June 1964, pp. 320 f.

[23] The Utah Coordinating Council is an exception to the generalizations. With advisory powers only, it has had effective program control through recommendations to the governing boards. The detailed, professional studies that support its program and budget recommendations may help to account for this success.

eral level of support" sought, as in California and Wisconsin. Recommendations to governing boards may be acted upon in whole or in part, or may be ignored entirely with no fear of legal sanctions by the coordinating agency. If ignored, the agency may persuade the legislature to take the desired action.

Coordinating attempts of these advisory agencies so far show results not unlike those of the voluntary systems which they resemble in practice.

Coordinated Planning

If master planning is desirable, is it better to have a coordinating board with power to develop and execute plans or to have state executive and legislative agencies perform these functions with advice from a coordinating agency without legal powers? In the long run, which arrangements can fulfill best the promises of a master plan, protect the public interest, and preserve essential institutional autonomy?

The answers to these questions become extremely important as one realizes the scope and probable impact of long-range planning. The chief feature which distinguishes the new concept of coordination from the old is master planning. In 1959, a report on the single board and coordinating agencies indicated that the weakest and most poorly performed function of all agencies was planning.[24] Today, planning is the chief function specified in virtually every law establishing a new agency. The Illinois, New York, and Ohio statutes require a "master plan," and the Missouri law a long-range "coordinated plan."

Master planning is relatively new in higher education, even newer than the coordinating agency which is now charged with its development and periodic revision. The characteristics which distinguish the master plan from most state surveys are the variety of subjects studied; the volume of data collected; the depth of analyses; the integration of programs, budgets, and building priorities to provide a unity of purpose; the full inclusion of the nonpublic institutions; and the means for step-by-step implementation of the plan, with simultaneous review and revision leading to fulfillment of major goals.

The wide publicity given to the adoption of the California master plan of 1959–60 provoked other states to emulate the idea, if not the exact features, of the plan. "Master plans" have been completed or are in process in Georgia, Utah, Illinois, Oklahoma, New York, Texas, Missouri, and several other states, and these follow state-wide studies of North Dakota, South Dakota, North Carolina, New

[24] Glenny, *op. cit.*, pp. 74, 265.

Jersey, Virginia, Maryland, Kansas, Nebraska, Montana, and other states made in the late fifties and early sixties. Some plans are no more than general surveys called master plans, but others are truly comprehensive in their scope. The nonpublic institutions, the orphans of most state surveys, are brought into active participation in master planning either under law, as in New York and Pennsylvania, or on a voluntary basis, as in California, Illinois, Oklahoma, and Kansas.[25]

In the past outside consultants have conducted state surveys in collaboration with in-state specialists, but the tendency now is to charge the coordinating board with full responsibility for master plan development and to use nationally recognized consultants sparingly. California and Utah used no outside consultants; Illinois retained one on junior colleges; New York and Oklahoma had several for short terms. Ohio is using a group of outside consultants to provide "the basis for a master plan" to be developed and formulated later by the new Ohio Board of Regents and its staff. Whether or not the coordinating agency or some other group develops the master plan is determined largely by the experience and professional competence of the staff permanently employed in the coordinating agency.

The major features of master plans are too numerous to list in great detail, but generally they will emphasize:

1. The development of colleges to serve commuter students, primarily two-year institutions, but also new four-year college and university campuses.

2. The placing of junior colleges clearly in the realm of higher education, giving them new status in the state organization and more state aid and supervision.

3. Means for providing programs for the undereducated and for improving the quality and number of technical and semitechnical programs.

4. The development of graduate, professional, research, and specialized undergraduate programs, and the organizational means for controlling their proliferation in the several public institutions in order to achieve maximum use of resources at minimum costs.

5. The use of admission standards and tuition rates to funnel students into desired types of institutions and programs.

6. A system for developing project priorities in capital construction among institutions and campuses (a feature that will be stimulated by the Higher Education Facilities Act of 1963).

[25] Statutes requiring master plans usually specify that nonpublic institutions "be considered in arriving at recommendations," but few studies other than in these states have actually collected as detailed data from them as from the public institutions. Some nonpublic institutions, unless required by law, may not wish to participate.

7. Increased utilization of physical plant by scheduling late after-noon and evening hours and year-round operations.

8. The need to increase the supply and competence of faculty members, make better use of those most competent, and increase their productivity and effectiveness through various new instructional techniques.

9. Greater cooperative effort among all institutions, public and nonpublic, and continued planning to keep the master plan fresh and up to date.

The highlights of the master plans of two large states, California and Illinois, indicate that comprehensive master plans contain certain common goals but important differences in means for achieving them.

Both the California and Illinois plans place increased reliance on junior colleges to meet the surge of new enrollments, attempt to divert students normally projected for entry into state senior institutions into the junior colleges, and provide extension of graduate and professional work only under controlled conditions. Both use admission standards, program control, greater state aid to junior colleges, and a coordinating agency as means for achieving the main planning goals.

In California, detailed features of the master plan, such as programs to be offered by the various types of institutions, are placed in the statutes of the state. In addition, the Coordinating Council recommends to the governing boards as well as to the governor and legislature desirable means for continuing implementation of master plan features. As previously stated, governing boards have not necessarily responded to recommendations, and the council must then turn to the state executive agencies and legislature for action.

In Illinois, the Board of Higher Education, within well-defined legal limits, has the power to approve individual programs at each institution and to review budgets in great detail. To implement the master plan, the board also proposes to use minimum admission standards, tuition and fees, construction priorities, and control over revenue bond projects. The underlying philosophy is to maintain desirable flexibility and adaptability in meeting rapidly changing needs without the necessity of turning to state executive agencies and the legislature. With the advice of the board, appropriations are determined by the legislature.

The extensive statistical studies supporting the California and Illinois master plans are typical of those conducted by the single boards and coordinating agencies having a professional full-time staff. They make or recommend major planning decisions only after a thorough fact-finding and review process. Most often an inventory is made of the programs and functions performed; the costs involved; the potential enrollments at various levels; the ability levels and other characteristics of students; the availability and quality of faculty and instructional and research facilities; the rates of college-going in various sections of the state; other data on finances, organization, and operations of the institutions to be coordinated; and projections of the state's ability to finance higher education. (The costs of computer time alone in a recent master plan study were estimated at $150,000.) Continuing reports permit subsequent revision and execution of the plan without the dislocating features of a one-time master plan effort.

The functions of budget and sometimes program review (formerly the preoccupation of single boards and voluntary and coordinating agencies) become the chief administrative means of control over a master plan (or survey). The recent practice of staffing these agencies with research-oriented persons, primarily from social sciences, has developed new perspectives in the coordination of budgets and programs.

BUDGETING OPERATIONS

In the past years, budget review was simple and unsophisticated, consisting of little more than adjusting, in conference with the college presidents, the total amounts to be requested from the state. Today, with experience and closer cooperation of institutions, formulae have been developed and refined. Some formulae have now become very complex, with separate subformulae for academic staff, library, nonacademic personnel, physical plant maintenance, and administration. In addition, a sliding scale of weights is often used for budgeting the various levels of instruction, from freshman to doctorate levels. By considering a greater number of factors, the coordinating agencies attempt to make the formulae more objective, and hope to reflect the variety of programs and functions of the several institutions. Experience has shown that formulae must be constantly re-evaluated to keep them timely and equitable and to reflect as accurately as possible the changing assumptions which serve as their basis. (The Texas commission and the Florida Board of Control have developed formulae which have attracted the attention of agencies in other states.)

Increasingly, unit cost studies are used as a basis for budget review and program development and allocation. These studies, too, are much refined over the old methods. Instead of dividing the total state appropriation by the total number of students to get a per-student cost, agencies of New Mexico, Utah, and Colorado, among others, gather data to show the detailed costs of courses offered and, to a lesser degree, costs of other phases of operations. The California Coordinating Council is now conducting a detailed cost study for its public institutions similar to that undertaken in 1952–54, but using the procedures substantially as developed for the California-Western Conference Unit Cost Study of 1954–57, sponsored by the Fund for the Advancement of Education.[26] Indiana already uses a modified form of these procedures; Illinois will start a unit cost study in the fall of 1964.

BUILDINGS

New and improved scientific techniques are also in use for developing building budgets for legislative consideration. Ten years ago few institutions had ever conducted a building utilization study.[27] Today, almost all public and many nonpublic institutions have made one or more such studies. Some coordinating agencies, notably New York and Illinois, plan to collect, every year or two, detailed data from all institutions, public and nonpublic, in the state. Wisconsin and Indiana already do this for their state-supported institutions. These studies provide information on the type and quality and the number of square feet of space used for a variety of purposes. They also show the size of classrooms appropriate to the size of classes taught, the effectiveness of scheduling procedures, and the number of students that can be accommodated in existing buildings according to various standards of utilization. As space studies have been improved, so have the coordinating procedures for establishing priorities of new buildings among the various campuses. The requirements of the Higher Education Facilities Act of 1963 on utilization of existing instructional and library facilities in determining project priorities will further stimulate the use of more refined studies and data. Also the act brings the nonpublic institutions into the state studies, as was already the case in California in 1953–54 and Illinois in 1962–63.

Fortunately, as recommendations and decisions on coordination become more objective and factually established, legislative action tends to follow coordinating agency recommendations rather than political expediency in approving building projects. The long-range construction plan also provides the legislature with a clear picture of what future state-wide financial needs will be for the capital expenditures of state higher education.

PROGRAMS

The rather dramatic changes in budgeting functions of the coordinating agencies are easily surpassed by changes in program func-

[26] "California and Western Conference Cost and Statistical Study, Reproductions of Original Forms and Instructions," Office of President, University of California, Berkeley, 1954.

[27] John Dale Russell and James I. Doi, *Manual for Studies of Space Utilization in Colleges and Universities* (Athens, Ohio: American Association of Collegiate Registrars and Admissions Officers, 1957), p. 10.

tions. Whereas programs were formerly considered only in conjunction with budget review, now they are given a prominent place in agency activity. The laws give some coordinating bodies the power to approve or disapprove new instructional programs, new departments and schools, branch campuses, and new research and public service programs. Data collected by coordinating agencies for purposes of program analysis cover such items as the number and types of different programs, the number and size of classes, total credit hours produced per class and program, credit hours produced per faculty member, and other factors which show scope, quantity, and productivity of the instructional enterprise.

Operating within the context of a long-range plan, the coordinating agency, with this information, has an opportunity to encourage development of quality in all the new programs necessitated by new students, technological breakthroughs, and graduate and professional specializations. Programs are assigned to those institutions which merit consideration on an honest appraisal of efficiency and quality of their operations and future potential. The agency prevents continuance or duplication of unneeded programs. With power over the planning and allocation of programs, the budgeting process becomes a meaningful method of enforcing the plan.

Major Trends in Coordination

The descriptions above of plans and planning and of the various systems for state coordination reveal that in the postwar years a marked about-face has occurred in most state systems of higher education from the near-anarchy of over a hundred years. Some major trends in the last few years are:

1. The number of state-wide voluntary coordinating agencies remains static, although their operations have broadened in scope. All of them now employ a small central professional staff.

2. The single board for governance and coordination is no longer widely adopted as a means for achieving coordination.

3. Coordinating (super) boards are rapidly becoming the principal scheme for coordination of state systems.

a) Some have advisory powers only. For the most part these are composed primarily of members representing institutions and governing boards.

b) Others have from a narrow to a wide range of powers over programs, budgets, admission standards, tuition, and other matters. These agencies are composed of all, or a majority of, public members not directly connected with any public college or university.

4. Representatives of nonpublic institutions are sometimes given membership on coordinating boards with advisory powers. Nonpub-

lic institutions are usually given consideration in formulating state master plans.

5. The chief function of most agencies has changed from budgeting to planning for orderly growth of higher education in the state.

a) Budget and program review have become primary means of implementing master plans rather than goals in themselves.

b) The scope of subjects studied and the volume of data collected and analyzed is increasing rapidly. Use of computers has accelerated this trend toward more scientific studies.

6. Staffs of coordinating agencies are larger in size, more professional, and better skilled in research techniques.

7. Many public institutions now exercise their autonomy within boundaries set by state plans in the form of law and/or coordinating agency policy.

8. The Federal Higher Education Facilities Act of 1963 appears to be lending impetus for power to be given to a coordinating body concerned with both public and nonpublic institutions in the states. The act will also stimulate better and more frequent state studies of building utilization.

These trends provide evidence that the states and their colleges are in the dynamic process of meeting the challenges offered by T. R. McConnell, chairman of the Center for the Study of Higher Education at Berkeley, in his recent book *A General Pattern for American Public Higher Education*. He stated:

> The great need in public higher education is for constructive, collaborative, and comprehensive planning, and for purposeful sharing, as well as purposeful division, of responsibilities. If colleges and universities are to meet future needs, they will have to engage in extensive experimentation and encourage fruitful innovation.[28]

A Selected Bibliography

In the preparation of the paper the author used approximately ninety master plans, surveys, and other documents from the various states. He also used correspondence with staff members of coordinating agencies of fourteen states and with several nationally recognized authorities on state planning and coordination. The sheer bulk of these materials makes undesirable their listing here. General references follow.

Brumbaugh, A. J. *State-Wide Planning and Coordination.* Atlanta, Ga.: Southern Regional Education Board, 1963. 50 pp.

Chambers, M. M. *Voluntary Statewide Coordination in Public Higher Education.* Ann Arbor: University of Michigan, 1961.

Glenny, Lyman A. *Autonomy of Public Colleges: The Challenge of Coordination.* New York: McGraw-Hill Book Co., 1959. 325 pp.

[28] New York: McGraw-Hill Book Co., 1962. P. 169. This book includes an excellent review of the sources of controversy among institutions that lead to a formal coordinating agency.

MCCONNELL, T. R. *A General Pattern for American Public Higher Education.* New York: McGraw-Hill Book Co., 1962. 198 pp.

MARTORANA, S. V., and HOLLIS, ERNEST V. *State Boards Responsible for Higher Education.* U.S. Office of Education, Circular No. 619. Washington: Government Printing Office, 1962. 254 pp.

MOOS, MALCOLM, and ROURKE, FRANCIS E. *The Campus and the State.* Baltimore, Md.: Johns Hopkins Press, 1959. 414 pp.

Public Higher Education in California

EDMUND G. BROWN

CALIFORNIA'S emerging system of higher education has been described many times—both in glowing and in critical terms. Our critics have said that our classes are too large. Indeed, in some instances they are. Others have warned that the larger campuses of the University of California are in danger of becoming educational factories. This danger would be very real if we did not continue to stress quality of education as well as quantity. Critics have also said that the faculties of our universities are permitted too much time for research while our state college faculties are permitted no time at all. These criticisms, and others, have been directed at us from a variety of sources. We know that we have not yet achieved perfection; we're aware that shortcomings exist and we are doing our best to correct them.

On the other hand, those who view our system as a whole and who weigh our goals against our progress often tend to minimize our problems. Dr. James Conant, for instance, has commented: "The pattern of higher education in California seems to me a highly promising one for the United States in the second half of the twentieth century. Clearly the California system provides relatively free higher education on an extremely flexible and broad basis. All this has been accomplished while the scholarly, scientific, and professional standards in the university have been maintained."

California has, in fact, developed a unique system of tuition-free education, from kindergarten through graduate school, for all qualified students. The system did not evolve overnight, nor was it the product of any single state administration. Rather, it is the result of the determination of the people to make a massive investment in an educational system which cuts through all barriers of race and socioeconomic background. California long ago rejected the notions that only a select few should be eligible for postsecondary education and that the quality of our colleges and universities would be diluted when they became available to all.

Public Concern and Population Growth

There is no need to recount the dramatic statistics of California's growth. Today the state has a population of over 18 million, and projections indicate that the figure will reach 40 million by the turn of the century. Much of our population growth can be attributed to immigration from other states. And we are fully aware that most of those who move here are deeply concerned with education. When a newcomer is asked why he settled here, chances are he will mention the excellence of the public schools, colleges, and universities. Tuition-free campuses, located so that college-age children can live at home and still get a first-rate education, create opportunities for a better family life and for the achievement of the highest degree of education of which young people are capable.

Because of this concern with education, California ranks first in the nation in the percentage of grade-school pupils who finish high school, and among the highest in the proportion of high school graduates who go on to college. Education has been a major factor in the development of technological industry in the state and it has raised the whole tone of California life.

These facts are well known. And, as a result, literally hundreds of inquiries come to us every year from trustees and administrators throughout the world asking how California, with its tremendous growth, has been able to provide quality higher education. A few years ago, for example, Great Britain's Robbins Committee came to the United States to investigate means of educating large numbers of students instead of an elite few. They visited the University of California, whose faculty includes more Nobel laureates than any other school in the world. They toured our state college system—the largest system of four-year colleges in the country and the second largest in the world—and they visited some of our seventy-four junior colleges.

In talking with that committee, or with others who study our system, we do not claim perfection. We have many problems, mostly related to growth, but we are determined to plan for the educational pressures of the future before we are engulfed by them. Within the next six years we must provide the desks and teachers for 1 million more students in the grades from kindergarten through junior college alone. And by 1970 we shall have to double the capacity of the University of California and triple the capacity of our state college system.

Financing Higher Education

The people of California have given evidence that they can and will meet this challenge. Between 1959, when I took office, and 1964 the state invested a total of $8.5 billion for all educational purposes. In the November 1964 elections voters approved still another $380 million bond issue, of which more than 70 percent was earmarked for the construction of new public higher educational facilities. In 1964 the state spent $2,500 to keep each student in the University of California for one year; it cost $1,100 a year for each student in a state college; and local and state governments spent a total of $625 for each student in junior college. Californians recognize this as the best investment the state can make in the future and testified to this faith by committing themselves to additional expenditures for higher education.

These figures are cited here to provide an idea of the unprecedented growth and the financial problems the state was facing in 1959 when a group of educators set out to draw up a Master Plan for Higher Education. They knew that California's population would increase by 85 percent by 1980. And they knew that it was the state's policy that every California child who has the ability also has the right to attend a public institution, without charge. They knew, too, that the phenomenal rise in enrollment was creating the strongest need for organizational change in public school education since the late nineteenth century, when lower schools were in the process of moving from semiautonomous local units into a system coordinated by an over-all state board of education. They knew that higher education in California had to be coordinated and that a plan was needed to span the years from 1960 to 1975.

The Master Plan

The master planners considered the idea of a single board with jurisdiction over all aspects of the system of higher education. But such a board, they thought, would minimize competition between the various campuses and the idea was rejected. The alternative—a single board for every campus of every institution—would increase competition, but it would decrease coordination. That idea, too, was rejected. What was finally decided upon was the unique California Master Plan for Higher Education which gives the over-all system both coordination and competition. Under this plan, one governing board is responsible for the University of California and its nine campuses; the State Board of Education, which formerly governed both the state colleges and the junior colleges along with the secondary and elementary schools, was given only partial responsibility for the junior colleges—local boards for each district now share this responsibility; and in addition, a separate board of trustees was established for the state colleges.

Beyond all this there was a need to minimize duplication and waste created by competition among the three segments of higher education. To accomplish this the planners created the Coordinating Council for Higher Education. The plan gives those directly concerned with higher education twelve of the fifteen seats on the coordinating council, and first crack at solving their own problems.

We do not claim that our growing pains have subsided, or that our plan has created an educational Utopia. But we have achieved a sizable measure of progress. For example, nine new campuses have been established for the University of California and the state colleges; seven additional sites are being studied and will be authorized as soon as practicable. The junior college system has expanded to seventy-four colleges and the state has given the local districts new financial support.

Cooperation within the System

The three segments of higher education, after negotiations with the Coordinating Council, have agreed that three of every four high school graduates going on to public higher education will start in the junior colleges. The master plan specifies that only the top 12.5 percent of the high school graduates may attend the University of California as freshmen and only the top one third may attend state colleges as freshmen. But all members of the graduating class may attend the junior college in their district. If they prove themselves in junior college to be superior students, they may transfer as juniors to a state college or to the university. Or, if they are less academically inclined, they may take vocational training in a junior college instead.

The three segments have also agreed that the state colleges will take a greater percentage of the undergraduate load and that the university will increase its emphasis on graduate work. Medical training is an example. The University of California's two existing medical schools (at San Francisco and Los Angeles) now graduate 172 physicians each year. But even modest projections show that an additional 350 physicians will be needed each year by 1971. We have, therefore, begun plans for a new medical school at San Diego which will admit a class of 100 by 1967. In addition preliminary plans are being made to establish a medical school at the university's Davis campus, and a third school may be authorized in the future.

The study of law provides another example. Our projections show that the need for lawyers in California will double by 1980. The university's law schools at Berkeley and Los Angeles must be expanded as rapidly as possible to capacities of 1,000 students each. A new law school at Davis will admit its first class in 1966; and a second in southern California must be established before 1975.

Increasing Demands

These same pressures exist throughout higher education and, accordingly, our Coordinating Council has launched the most comprehensive cost and statistical analysis yet attempted anywhere. Plans are being made to meet unprecedented needs in the fields of dental education, nursing, college libraries, continuing education, junior college organization, facilities use, and the supply and demand of faculty. Even with all the plans that have been and are being made, however, we are still not meeting the demands made on the system. In the fall of 1964, for instance, the California state colleges had to turn away 7,500 students, simply because there was no room for them. Some students at two southern California colleges were actually sitting on the floor in classrooms. And the University of California registered 3,000 more students than they had expected.

This development naturally raised problems for the university's budget. But every year brings financial problems, and we are working hard to make sure that we do not become the best educated bankrupt state in the nation. The master plan includes economy measures. Year-round operations are already scheduled and will be a reality in a few years, allowing an increase of from 15 to 25 percent in enrollments in existing facilities. In addition, we are continuing to raise tuition for out-of-state students so that California will not be financing the education of students from areas that are not themselves investing in public higher education.

California's educational program, I believe, demonstrates that we have taken the initiative in solving our problems and have not hung back waiting for national action. But although we are making a major investment in education, we are strong supporters of Federal aid to education. Currently the state receives millions of dollars each year in Federal aid for higher education, in addition to millions of dollars in research grants. The National Defense Education Act has been helpful to California and Californians rejoice in congressional efforts to broaden this act. We do not fear Federal aid because we know that it does not mean Federal control. Even under an expanded Federal aid program, California would remain independent.

Conclusion

In closing, I should like to turn to another area—the freedom of thought which we have in our educational system and which we intend to maintain. Some college presidents may not take it kindly when we succeed in luring distinguished faculty members to the new campus of the University of California at San Diego, or to the cluster of colleges to be established at Santa Cruz, or to San Francisco State College. But we shall continue to compete with other institutions throughout the nation for the finest minds and the greatest teachers in every field of higher education. We shall not compete only on the basis of salaries, or on the fact that our institutions are located in beautiful landscapes and a delightful climate, but on the most important factor of all—freedom of thought.

Great schools have survived without large sums of money, and even without a high degree of public interest and enthusiasm. But they cannot survive dictation from outside their own ranks concerning what the teacher can teach and what he cannot, or what the student may hear and what he may not, or what fields of inquiry are open and what are closed. Education today is being challenged by those who would clamp the lid on intellectual inquiry, but we in California are determined to counter such efforts with all the force we can muster.

By the same token, we shall press our belief that the mind of the student is not a bottle into which pre-mixed ideas should be poured. It is a muscle, to be strengthened by exercise and matured by vigorous use. A major duty of higher education is to challenge intellectual dependency, encourage controversy, and keep the world of ideas stimulating. This spirit is far more important than huge sums of money or campuses equipped with the latest models of test tubes.

Californians have determined to provide the bricks and the buildings, and the dollars, but they will go even further in centering their effort around the single aim of quality. The ability to educate vast numbers of students while maintaining high quality and freedom of thought is a distinguishing characteristic of California's system of higher education. The goal is to give our state's college and university students the finest education available anywhere in the world. To do this, in the words of President Clark Kerr, we will work not to make ideas safe for students, but to make students safe for ideas.

The New York State System

JAMES E. ALLEN, JR.

THE REPORT of a 1960 study of higher education in New York State described the state's machinery for the control and operation of higher education as "one of the most complex in the whole country." As one in a position to know, I consider this easily one of the major understatements of our times!

Yet underlying this complex and often confusing legal administrative structure, there are certain fundamentally sound principles and patterns of organization which, if not always clearly perceived, are nevertheless a source of great strength in New York State as we strive to meet today's vast needs and tremendous problems in higher education. The following is a brief over-all picture of this structure, the interrelationships involved in it, and the steps being taken to equip it better for meeting the needs of the future.

Regents of the University of the State of New York

The history of the legal structure for governing higher education in New York State goes back to 1784, five years before the founding of the Republic. In that year the state legislature created a corporation entitled "The Regents of the University of the State of New York" which was empowered to found schools and colleges.

Today the University of the State of New York (not to be confused with State University of New York) consists of all the colleges and universities, both public and private—approximately two hundred in number—which have been incorporated by the state Board of Regents or are subject to visitation by the regents. Under the law this unique university includes, in addition to institutions of higher education, all secondary schools and such other institutions, schools, museums, libraries, organizations, and agencies for education "now or hereafter incorporated by the state." Thus, the University of the State of New York comprises the entire educational system in New York State, from the kindergarten to the graduate school, public and private.

The governing head of the University of the State of New York is the state Board of Regents, a body of fourteen laymen, elected by the legislature, each for a fourteen-year term. The executive officer of the regents and the professional head of the university is the state commissioner of education who also holds the title of "President of the University of the State of New York." He is appointed by the regents and serves at their pleasure. The State Education Department is the executive agency for the regents and the commissioner.

The regents are vested with the responsibility of determining the "educational policies" of the state, consistent with the constitution and statutes, and are authorized to establish rules carrying into effect the laws and policies of the state relating to education. They are directed by law "to encourage and promote education, to visit and inspect its several institutions and departments, to distribute to or expand or administer for them such property and funds as the state may appropriate therefor or as the University may own or hold in trust or otherwise, and to perform such other duties as may be entrusted to it."

The regents and the commissioner of education are authorized to inspect and require reports from any institutions in the university. The regents may suspend or revoke the charter or any of the rights and privileges of any institution which fails to make any required reports or violates any law or any rule of the regents.

In addition to their broad coordinating and supervisory roles for all of education in the state, the regents have certain specific responsibilities for higher education. These include the responsibility for the promulgation and revision, at least every four years, of a "Regents Plan" for the expansion and development of higher education in the state.

The Regents Plan must "include the plan and recommendations proposed by the State University trustees and the plan and recommendations proposed by the Board of Higher Education of the City of New York and may include plans with respect to other matters not comprehended within the plan of state and city universities, including but not limited to, improving institutional management and resources, instruction and guidance programs, financial assistance to students and extension of educational opportunities through library resources and television."

In the development of their state-wide plan, the regents must give "due recognition to the plans and contributions of the private institutions." In other words, the regents are charged with the review and coordination of higher education planning and development in the state to the end that all needs are met in such a way as to make maximum and efficient use of all facilities and resources, private as well as public.

The four major segments of higher education over which the regents preside are: (1) State University of New York; (2) City

University of New York; (3) the community colleges; and (4) the private colleges.

State University of New York

In 1948, the State University of New York was created "within the higher education system of the state as established under the Board of Regents." At its outset, the State University was comprised of a nucleus of 28 postsecondary institutions already in existence: ten teachers colleges, six agricultural and technical institutes, five institutes of applied arts and sciences, the State University Maritime College, the College of Forestry, and the five contract colleges at Cornell and Alfred Universities. Today, State University comprises 58 units: three university centers, two medical centers, a Graduate School of Public Affairs, 24 state colleges (including the former teachers colleges and the two-year agricultural and technical institutes), and 28 locally sponsored two-year community colleges.

The State University is governed by a Board of Trustees appointed by the governor. The trustees are responsible for "the planning, supervision and administration of facilities, and provision for higher education supported in whole or in part with state monies" under the State University law. Each university center and college of State University is locally administered by a council consisting of nine members appointed by the governor. Each council exercises certain powers with respect to its institution, subject to the "general management, supervision, control and approval of and in accordance with, rules established by the State University trustees."

City University of New York

The second major segment of higher education in New York State is the City University of New York. The City University consists of four senior colleges: the City College, Hunter College, Brooklyn College, and Queens College, offering four-year, graduate, professional, and two-year programs; and six two-year community colleges sponsored and administered by City University under the program of the State University.

The City University is governed by the Board of Higher Education of the City of New York, whose members are appointed by the mayor. (The president of the board of education for the public school system is an ex officio member.) Like State University, City University has certain legal relationships with the Board of Regents of the University of the State of New York, as do all the private institutions in the state. Thus, the degrees, and the programs and curricula leading to degrees, must be approved by the Board of Regents. The Board of Higher Education has legal relationships also with the State University. Under this relationship the curricula and budgets of the community colleges sponsored by the Board of Higher Education must be approved by State University. The naming of a president of a community college sponsored by the Board of Higher Education must also be approved by State University. State funds for City University are channeled to the City of New York via the State University.

Public Community Colleges

In New York State public community colleges are locally sponsored and administered but financed jointly by local and state funds. In the fall of 1964 there were 28 of these colleges in operation—six in New York City and 22 distributed throughout the rest of the state.

Local sponsorship is required by law in order for a community college to be established. Although such sponsorship can be by a county, municipality, or school district, all but two New York community colleges are in fact sponsored by counties. The local sponsor provides one-third of the finances for current operating purposes of community colleges, the student and the state each also providing a third. The local sponsor and the state divide evenly the costs incurred for capital development of these institutions.

The administrative responsibility for public community colleges rests with local boards of trustees. The membership of these bodies again reflects the joint local and state interest in community colleges. Of the nine trustees on each local board, four are appointed by the governor and five by the local sponsoring agency, and all are persons residing in the area of the local sponsoring jurisdiction.

The public community colleges are supervised by the State University. The trustees of the State University must approve establishment of all new community colleges, in accordance with the State University's master plan as approved by the regents and the governor. As in the case of all institutions of higher education, the curricula offered by community colleges leading to a degree are subject to approval by the regents.

Private Colleges

In addition to a rapidly expanding system of public institutions, New York State is richly endowed in the number, diversity, and quality of its privately controlled institutions. Currently there are 141 privately controlled colleges and universities operating as a part of the University of the State of New York. They include 109 four-year colleges and institutions, among them such renowned universities as Cornell, Columbia, Rochester, Fordham, and New York University, and such well-known liberal arts colleges as Colgate,

Hamilton, and Vassar. All these and many others that could be named, as well as the 32 privately controlled two-year colleges, are subject to the superintendence and visitation of the state Board of Regents.

The range in diversity displayed by the privately controlled colleges taxes easy description and represents, I believe, a basic strength of higher education in the state. Some are single-purpose colleges to train secretaries, business leaders, clergy, or scientists. The services of these institutions are needed and appreciated. So are those of the general-purpose institutions, be they universities or four-year or two-year colleges. Every degree program they offer is registered by the State Education Department on the approval of the regents and contributes to New York's total strength in higher education.

Other Features of the Statutory System

Other features of the statutory system of higher education in New York State include: the State Dormitory Authority, the Regents Scholarship Program, the Scholar Incentive Program, the Higher Education Assistance Corporation, and the State University Construction Fund.

DORMITORY AUTHORITY

The State Dormitory Authority, created by the legislature in 1944, is a "public benefit corporation" within the University of the State of New York empowered to construct, equip, and maintain student housing facilities, academic buildings, libraries, laboratories, classrooms, or any other structures "essential, necessary or useful for instruction in the higher education program" on the campuses of any public or private institutions located in the state which are "authorized to confer degrees by law or by the Board of Regents." In addition to such facilities, the Authority may also provide housing accommodations for the use of married students, faculty, staff, and their families at private institutions.

REGENTS SCHOLARSHIP PROGRAM

The Regents College Scholarship Program was first established by the legislature in 1913. Nine different types of scholarships and fellowships are specified by statute, covering both undergraduate and graduate study. All are awarded on the basis of competitive examinations. Stipends range from $250 to $750 depending on the recipient's financial need. In 1964, 70,000 people held regents scholarships and teaching fellowships amounting to $24.3 million.

SCHOLAR INCENTIVE PROGRAM

In 1961, the legislature created a new "Scholar Incentive Program" for all New York State students attending an institution of higher education in the state full time and maintaining satisfactory academic records. Stipends range from $100 to $300 a year for undergraduate students and from $200 to $800 a year for graduate students. The awards are payable directly to the students for use in meeting tuition charges at the New York State institution of the student's choice. Approximately 134,000 students annually participate in this program. The dollar amount of Scholarship Incentive Program awards made to students for 1964–65 was $26.2 million.

HIGHER EDUCATION ASSISTANCE CORPORATION LOAN PROGRAM

Another feature of New York State's Student's Financial Aid Program is a state-wide, bank-guaranteed loan program. This program is governed by the Higher Education Assistance Corporation created by the legislature in 1957 as a nonprofit corporation. Its purpose is to improve the higher education opportunities of state residents who attend college within the state or elsewhere, by lending or guaranteeing the loan of funds through banks to assist them in meeting their expenses for higher education.

The maximum loan which any student may receive or have guaranteed for any school year is $1,500, with a total maximum of $7,500. Under the program, the qualified student borrows from a bank on a promissory note. The corporation pays all interest while the student is in college and any interest above 3 percent thereafter. The colleges play a key role in certifying the student and his need. The corporation receives state funds as a reserve in order to guarantee the loans made by banking institutions. This reserve is 10 percent of whatever is outstanding. Since 1958 (and as of July 31, 1964), the corporation had made 127,281 loans worth more than $95,538,000—and its business is expanding rapidly.

STATE UNIVERSITY CONSTRUCTION FUND

State University in recent years has had to embark on a vast program of capital construction to keep up with rapidly increasing enrollments, both current and projected for the future. To help the university handle the financing and management of the construction of needed new facilities, the legislature in 1962 created a new agency, the State University Construction Fund. Bonds issued by the Housing Finance Agency of the state (for construction of facilities other than dormitories and related facilities, which are handled through the Dormitory Authority) are amortized by university income which the Construction Fund draws upon to repay the Housing Agency.

Concluding Comments

In conclusion, the New York State statutory system for higher education has the framework within which a strong system of colleges and universities has developed and flourished. No state can boast of a finer group of institutions of higher learning than can be found in New York. This historic system has made it possible to take the steps necessary to meet the challenge of higher education in our time. State-wide plans have been developed and are being kept up to date. With the strong support of the governor and the legislature, major steps to expand opportunities and improve quality are under way.

The system is sound in principle and uniquely suited to the great diversity of needs and resources which exist in the Empire State. Among its strongest points are: (1) It lodges in one agency, the Board of Regents, the authority to plan, coordinate, supervise, and evaluate all of higher education, public and private—including also the elementary and secondary schools, the libraries and museums—thus enabling the state to use its resources in meeting its educational needs in the most efficient and economical manner possible. (2) It provides maximum protection against interference by political groups or by agencies in or out of government which have special interests.

There are, of course, some weaknesses in the New York pattern. It is a complex system, involving many procedural controls and complicated interagency relationships. It often moves too slowly and with an unnecessarily heavy hand. There is need for greater decentralization of administrative functions, particularly in the State University. Also, the system places an extremely heavy burden on the regents and the State Education Department.

Happily, most of those concerned with the welfare of education in the state are aware of these weaknesses, and efforts are constantly being made to identify and eliminate them. The regents, for example, recognize their role primarily as one of planning and policy making. They delegate administrative matters to their staff and leave the operation of higher education to the appropriate institutional authorities.

But despite any weaknesses that exist, the system has stood the test of time and it offers advantages for meeting the tremendous educational task ahead which few states can match. The greatest weakness in the New York system may well be the failure of the state to make the most of the potential inherent in its legal structure. It is my hope that in the days to come, as plans evolve and innovations unfold, this weakness, too, will be overcome, enabling the state to reach new heights of achievement in higher education.

The North Carolina State System

JOHN T. CALDWELL

IN 1931 NORTH CAROLINA "consolidated and merged" three separate institutions into a single three-campus university designated "The University of North Carolina." This legislation brought together the three separate boards of trustees into one governing board, but preserved the identity of the separate campuses in name. The Act of Consolidation did not deal at all with the other nine state-supported senior colleges or with the more than forty independent and church-related institutions. It was, nevertheless, a step which recognized the values of coordination and unification.

In 1955 the North Carolina Board of Higher Education was created by statute to "plan and promote the development of a sound, vigorous, progressive, and coordinated system of higher education in the State of North Carolina." The nine senior colleges as well as the consolidated university retained their own governing boards, but all of them came under the authority of the new board. It is essentially a planning and coordinating authority, but its statutory powers have permitted it at times to make other judgments and decisions of a governing nature which have challenged decisions made by the individual boards.

The original Community College Act of 1957 gave the Board of Higher Education jurisdiction over institutions created under its provisions. And the Higher Education Act of 1963 did four things to the existing "system": (1) It confirmed the consolidated university in its unique "university" role, conferred upon it exclusive authority for awarding the doctorate, and made provision for adding campuses beyond the three in existence. (2) It raised three junior colleges to senior college status. (3) It provided for the creation of "comprehensive" community colleges under the jurisdiction of the State Board of Education (*not* the state Board of *Higher* Education) and for transfer of the earlier public community colleges to the same jurisdiction. (4) It made the state Board of Higher Education the licensing authority for institutions of higher education.

Since passage of the 1963 act, the Board of Higher Education has instituted the practice of inviting all the heads of public colleges plus five representatives of the private institutions to attend each of its meetings.

Another administrative development vitally affecting the operation of higher education culminated in 1957 in the creation of a Department of Administration in the state government. This department is charged with preparation of the state budget and budgetary control, preparation of all capital improvement plans and control over their execution, and control of purchasing and contracts. No institution is exempt from full control. Separately constituted is the State Personnel Board which administers the state's classified personnel system from which only college and university teaching personnel and certain administrators are exempt.

The state's General Assembly makes separate appropriations to each college, to the university trustees and its Consolidated Offices, to each of the three campuses of the university, and to special university units such as the Division of Health Affairs, the Agricultural Experiment Station, the Agricultural Extension Service, and a few others under university control. Each separate appropriation is heavily line-itemized.

That is the structure of higher education in North Carolina. Within this structure all the usual problems of coordination and governance are represented, but very few solutions have been found which could be applied elsewhere.

Conflicts of Authorities

A common observation in the state is that the machinery for the administration of higher education is excessive in quantity and complexity. Is it? In what respects? One way to answer these questions is to suggest that if certain elements were eliminated, the criticism would disappear. First, further reduction in the detail of appropriation acts for both operational budget and capital improvements and further reduction of detailed administrative control from state financial officers and staff would be welcomed. Second, the university has not enjoyed being questioned and blocked by the state Board of Higher Education in a few instances on matters of judgment in which the university has exercised historical, statutory, and obvious professional competence. This kind of friction is inevitable where coordinating bodies are superimposed over governing boards.

It is doubtful that any *coordinating* authority can be effectively exercised without some encroachment on an institutional board's *governing* authority. The unhappiness which occurs when two overlapping levels of responsibility each assert the organizational axiom that authority must be commensurate with responsibility may be unavoidable. Only an abundance of good judgment, good sense and experience, and clear channels of communication can resolve the definition of boundaries; statutes cannot. One alternative to the present arrangement in North Carolina would be to remove the university from the jurisdiction of the Board of Higher Education. This would have apparent advantages to the university, of course, but disadvantages would accrue to the over-all coordinative function intended to be performed in the state's interest by the Board of Higher Education. With the university and the community colleges both removed, the coordinative role of the state board would be unrealistically limited. No doubt additional mechanisms would then have to be invented to achieve planning and coordination among the university Board of Trustees, the Board of Higher Education controlling senior colleges, and the Board of Education controlling community colleges!

Need for Professional Personnel

Professionals in higher education are confronted with troublesome dilemmas, one of which is encountered in the growing staffing requirements in coordination, control, and financing. For example, on the one hand they insist that state and Federal programs and controls affecting higher education should be staffed with people "who understand higher education," meaning people who have been "pros" themselves and who should be recruited from the ranks. Yet scholars for the classrooms and laboratories of the nation are scarce, as are able institutional administrators. Presidents do not wish to lose either personnel or their time to expanding staffs of state control agencies.

State-wide planning and coordination are requisite, however, and must be performed well, or else whatever resources of money and personnel are committed to the task will be wasted for taxpayer and institutions alike. Institutions must cooperate in their own interest to make good personnel available on both full- and part-time assignments. Coordinating boards must make certain to staff themselves with sound people.

Since the quality of higher education is demonstrated in the classroom and laboratory or not at all, the whole purpose of organization and administration at every level must be to develop and support that quality. If the intelligent allocation of resources is the objective of planning and coordination and governance, then its ultimate purpose is to sustain quality in the classroom and laboratory. These truisms suggest a set of rules with respect to the organization of state-supported higher education:

1. Responsibility for all decisions, educational or financial, that bear directly on learning and research should rest to the maximum practical degree with the institution, meaning its faculty, administration, and local governing board (if a board is provided).

2. Staff should be added at any higher level over the institution

only to provide information and judgments of a broader character than lie within the capability of a single institution, but not to substitute judgment on a matter within the constituted competence of the institutional level.

At every level the professional staff should be clearly adequate to assemble information for planning, administrative, and governing purposes; to make proper analyses and judgments; to provide helpful information to the institutions in the system; and to keep all parties adequately informed and involved in the exercise of coordinating and/or governing authority. (The North Carolina Board of Higher Education has since its founding had too small a staff to perform its functions. It has only recently been expanded to a more adequate level.)

The *total* machinery should be properly articulated and balanced so as to realize maximum results in each of the parts. In North Carolina, state legislative and administrative control in excessive detail thwart the possibilities of over-all planning and coordination (by Board of Higher Education and university trustees) and has the effect of blunting institutional initiative and efficiency.

Several "layers" of administrators, as in North Carolina's system, suggest the need always to define roles to realize maximum possibilities in the division of labor. For example, in the consolidated university the president takes major responsibility for handling relations with the university board, the Board of Higher Education, and the General Assembly, leaving the several chancellors relatively more free to develop institutional programs and other relationships. The rule is to cast the officers at each higher level so far as is possible in a role which does not burden the institutional executive, but relieves the latter, supplements his role, and assists him in the accomplishment of authorized institutional objectives.

In summary, every institution wants autonomy even while it submits logically to pyramiding authority for the sake of "coordination." North Carolina's system of higher education is no exception. It has all the formal machinery needed—and more!

Higher Education in New Mexico

HAROLD L. ENARSON

WE DEAL WITH difficult, even exasperating, issues in our search for the delicate balance between the autonomy and independence of the college or university on the one hand and the insistent requirements of coordination on the other. Only in the Great Books are such issues settled to anyone's satisfaction. As for me, I have concluded that in his grasp of the nature of incompatibles, James Thurber has the edge on Plato and other Great Coordinators. Thurber's "war of the sexes" reminds us that there are irreconcilables in life. There *are* problems which, because they cannot be solved, must—even as an unruly spouse or a wart on the nose—be lived with.

Statutory coordinators and college and university presidents, like the husbands and wives in Thurber's cartoons, operate from different premises even as they live (to a degree) in the same premises. The college or university president wants to do what he wants to do. This is commendable (to a degree) and is called "autonomy," or "independence," or even "integrity"—all virtues which lead our "captains of erudition" to stand six feet six inches high in defense of these precious values. The state-wide coordinator also wants to do what he wants to do, which is to put all state institutions in a single corral for purposes of feeding, branding, and general management. This, too, is commendable (to a degree) and is called "coordination," "avoidance of wasteful duplication," and "planning for balanced growth"—virtues which lead our coordinators to stand six feet six inches high in defense of *their* values.

When strong men (and strong institutional competitors) collide with one another and with state coordinators, something has to give. Obviously we cannot all have our way. No college or university stands totally apart from its neighbors; the day of the self-sufficient, truly autonomous college or university is ended (if, indeed, it ever existed). It is essential that the institutions of a state work in concert with one another, that *system* be substituted for isolation, insularity, and imperialism. Lowell's famed vision of America, "aglow with universities and colleges like a field with campfires of an army on the march," is incomplete unless there are vital connections—in communication, supply, and coordination—between the campfires. But by the same token, our institutions of higher learning must be allowed to *enterprise*. Otherwise there will be nothing really worth coordinating.

New Mexico is one of approximately forty states with some sort of state-wide machinery for coordination. Although New Mexico is small in size (only one million persons), it is generously sprinkled with publicly supported institutions of higher learning—seven in all. Our decade of experience with the Board of Educational Finance, a special kind of "statutory state system of higher education," may illuminate some of the issues in the struggles over coordination. Therefore, I should like to describe the situation which led New Mexico to set up the Board of Educational Finance, outline briefly the development of this agency, and comment on its strengths and weaknesses. In concluding I should like to comment on the limitations of this particular model of a statutory system.

Background

The Constitution of New Mexico directs that the management and control of our institutions be vested in separate boards of regents for each institution. Our regents take their management responsibilities seriously, as well they might. For in the small towns and cities of New Mexico, our institutions are "smokeless industries," cherished for their payrolls as well as their learning. Thus institutional image and aspiration have been joined with community image and aspiration. Since, in the culture of the frontier, growth *per se* is equated with progress, each of the institutional presidents used to enter the legislative halls prepared to battle for his share. Though the New Mexico legislature is noted for its tolerance of noisy dissension, by all accounts the fight got out of hand. Each institution had its friendly legislators, its troops awaiting the call to action, its own arsenal of statistics to prove its case. Not surprisingly, statistics could seldom be reconciled, institutional and personal jealousies were magnified, and the legislature became increasingly exasperated with the whole show. Neither the process of jungle warfare nor its fruits were satisfactory to the legislators *or* to the colleges and universities. Thoughtful legislators concluded that there was a public interest in higher education and that it was more than the sum of the interests of the separate instiutions. And so, by act of the legislature, the Board of Educational Finance was launched in 1951, with the active support of some, though not all, of New Mexico's educational leaders.

Functions of the Board

In essence, the legislature decided to move the battle of the budget outside its halls and into a new specialized budget agency reporting to it. The charge to the new agency was briskly to the point:

There is hereby created a board of educational finance whose function shall be to deal with the problems of finance of those educational institutions designated by Sections 11 and 12 of article XII of the Constitution of the State of New Mexico. The board shall be concerned with the adequate financing of said institutions and with the *equitable distribution* of available funds among them. The board shall receive, adjust, and approve the budgets, submitted by the several institutions prior to the submission of said budgets to the budget officers of the state and shall exercise such other powers as may hereafter be granted it by law. [Italics supplied.]

The board has nine members, appointed to staggered terms of six years, and not more than five may at the time of their appointment be members of one political party. The board is required to appoint a "full-time executive secretary who shall be an experienced educator of demonstrated competence in the fields of institutional management and finance." And in a final flourish the legislature included a unique provision, namely, that:

the necessary expenditures of the Board, under a budget subject to and approved by the Board of Finance, shall be prorated annually among the educational institutions in proportion to the size of their total budget.

The Board of Educational Finance is now in its thirteenth year of operation. It has survived changes within the board and the staff, shifts in political control in the governor's office and the legislature, occasional outbursts by outraged institutional presidents and sniping by other agencies of state government. In the last three sessions of the legislature, the Board of Educational Finance's budget recommendations have been accepted by the governor and the legislature, which is a good measure of the confidence enjoyed by this agency. Moreover, the board generally enjoys the respect, grudging at times, of the educational community. In short, most of the players prefer the present ground rules. No one seriously proposes a return to the old free-for-alls, which had about as much dignity and equity as a tag wrestling match.

Merits of the Board

What has been the special merit of the Board of Educational Finance? Simply this: It has provided a quiet forum where educational matters can be brought under intensive, professional staff review followed by dispassionate analysis and discussion by a lay board that takes its job seriously. To an impressive degree, analysis by professional staff has been substituted for public squabbles. Over the years the Board of Educational Finance's studies—thorough, searching, and of high professional calibre—have helped "educate" the institutions themselves in the economics of institutional management. The staff of the board has done this through a continuous program of staff analyses which have built skillfully upon the internal management reviews of the various institutions. However, it has not been the quality of its research which has done the most to build the prestige of the Board of Educational Finance. Rather, it is the conviction that through the Board of Educational Finance we have achieved a greater measure of equity in the distribution of the educational dollar and a greater measure of efficiency in the expenditure of that dollar. In the contest for funds, the board's insistent question: "What's best for New Mexico?" has put the spotlight on the choices faced by the institutions and by the state. The result has been more thoughtful, dispassionate decisions in the allocation of the higher education dollar.

New Duties

Several additional duties have been thrust upon the Board of Educational Finance, extending both its powers of review and of allocation. Thus new graduate programs must be approved by the Board of Educational Finance (and by the State Board of Finance) before they can be started; expenditures for purchase of real property or construction of buildings or other major structures must also be approved in advance by both boards.

The Board of Educational Finance also approves out-of-state travel and defines "residence" for use by the institutions in determining out-of-state residence tuition. The responsibility for allocation of the proceeds from state educational institutions bond issues has been placed on the board, also with the concurrence of the State Board of Finance. And as recently as 1963 and 1964 the legislature charged the agency with state-level responsibility for approval of new branch colleges and junior colleges and for distribution of funds appropriated by Congress for the colleges and universities of the state.

This accretion of powers has not taken place without a parallel growth of concern on the part of the institutions. The board's oft-repeated disclaimer that it has no direct operating power over the institutions has not been entirely persuasive. The board *can* overrule the judgment of the faculty, the president, and the regents on the need for new graduate programs. The board *can* "discount" for purposes of capital outlay planning the anticipated funds which might be realized by land sales or other transactions which have historically been the exclusive concern of a local board of regents. Insofar as the board alters the capital outlay priorities set by the regents of an institution, it is open to the charge that it substitutes its educational judgment for that of the regents who are legally responsible for the management of the enterprise and presumably closer to the problem. And, in policing the initiation and development of new branch colleges, the Board of Educational Finance clearly is engaged in defining the market and, to that extent, the role of the institution in the educational economy and policy of the state.

Sources of Tension

It is little wonder that some regents have expressed serious concern about the expanding power of the board and wondered out loud "What are regents for?" However, such criticisms fall wide of the mark. The existence of a state-wide public interest requires the voice and arm of a state agency to protect that interest. Moreover, to date the Board of Educational Finance has, for the most part, ridden with a light rein. It has scrupulously avoided detailed intervention in the affairs of the institutions. It does not police individual salaries, regulate the development of new courses, or dictate the internal distribution of the institutional budget. In applying the most sensitive of its powers—the approval or disapproval of new graduate programs—the board has required proof of demonstrated need. To date, head-on collisions have been avoided. This will not always be possible, and vigorous protest can be expected whenever the board rejects proposed graduate programs that enjoy the strong support of faculty, institutional officers, regents, and (in some instances) community interests.

A reviewing agency will inescapably make some unpopular decisions; and the institutions will have "saddle sores." (The board can only hope for an "equality of dissatisfaction" on the part of the competitors.) Such conflict is built into the system. One can only hope that the tension will be creative, that occasionally consensus will emerge from conflict, and that in all cases the referee's decision will be accepted in good grace by the losers.

Surely no one has made a persuasive case for turning the clock back. There is little evidence, in New Mexico and elsewhere, that back-room bargaining under the aegis of a "voluntary coordinating agency" will promote a public interest that transcends the interests of competing institutions.

Some Pitfalls Ahead

There are some real concerns with possible directions the Board of Educational Finance might take. These concerns are less often voiced, but far more serious.

First, "success with the legislature," in the sense that the legislature accepts the Board of Educational Finance's budget recommendations without modification, may be less impressive than it appears. There is always a possibility that future boards will second-guess the legislature rather than press for deserved levels of support for higher education in New Mexico. In some states that I have studied, educational budget agencies survive and find favor because they provide a respectable professional veneer for decisions that are basically strategic and political. To put it bluntly, they tell the legislature what it wants to hear. This has not happened in New Mexico; but it could happen.

Second, the impressive outpouring of financial and other reports, and the wealth of "comparative statistics" should not obscure the fact that few statistics can be truly comparable. Our seven institutions are remarkably *unalike*—in purpose, in size, in emphasis, even in aspiration. The constant reiteration of comparisons infers the desirability of conformity. It is fashionable to lament the disease of proliferation, but as Dr. Herman B Wells reminds us, "next to proliferation, uniformity is the greatest enemy of distinction—uniformity of treatment of departments, of individuals, and of subject matter. They are not all of equal quality and to try to treat them all precisely alike is a great mistake." [1] I am sure that Dr. Wells would agree that the impulse toward uniformity of treatment of whole institutions is folly of an even higher order.

The Board of Educational Finance's fact-gathering machinery is impressive—a tribute to the diligence and the talent of its architect, Dr. John Dale Russell, who served with distinction as the first chancellor of the board. But it does not follow that the annual budget recommendations flow inexorably from the analysis of the evidence. In last analysis, the board's recommendations reflect values and convictions. No protective cloak of professionalism should obscure the highly subjective nature of the board's budget recommendations. In short, neither the legislature nor the public at large need be mesmerized by the recommendations of the Board of Educational Finance. In our society, the experts are useful in illuminating choices, but the right and duty to make choices is an essential part of the political process. Vital issues relating to public higher education are, and must remain, within the arena of public debate and legislative decision.

Third, the review powers of the board—over budgets, new graduate programs, and building programs—are essentially negative. These powers were not intended to encourage active coordination of the educational enterprise—nor do they. The arsenal of weapons, therefore, may not be complete. All too frequently the Board of Educational Finance finds itself trying to close the barn door when it is too late. (Perhaps the horses should not have been purchased, fed, and fattened in the first place.) New Mexico needs specialized facilities at the graduate level in emerging fields such as "mental re-

---

[1] "How to Succeed as a University President Without Really Trying!" *Transactions and Proceedings of the National Association of State Universities in the United States of America*, Charles P. McCurdy, Jr. (ed.), LXVII (1962), p. 61.

tardation," "teacher training for exceptional children," "preparation of educational administrators." The Federal agencies offer a cornucopia of grants, all designed to entice institutions into new and important fields. Eager institutions deal directly with the various agencies, a practice which the Federal agencies generally encourage.

The Board of Educational Finance is then confronted with a *fait accompli*—since the opportunity for matching funds is hard to resist. But all too often, the new investment is a poor one, reflecting neither wise use of institutional resources nor a sensible coordinated approach to a problem essentially state-wide in character. (In some instances, the Federal Government dictates by law the direction of institutional growth within a state. The Water Resources Research Act of 1964 earmarks funds for the land-grant colleges, unless—and surely this is a remarkable provision—the legislature of the state arranges otherwise. In short, the Congress confers a monopoly privilege on one type of institution without regard to the profile of strength that may exist in the various states. In such circumstances, cooperative efforts are discouraged and "coordination" is a joke.)

Yet if energies are to be joined in areas where combined, interdisciplinary, and interinstitutional approaches are necessary—for example, water research, teacher preparation, and the like—the Board of Educational Finance is obviously the agency to take the initiative.

Questions for the Future

A decade of experience with the Board of Educational Finance indicates rather clearly what New Mexico is against. We are against public wrangling over the distribution of dollars, against "wasteful duplication" (where it is visible), and against low teacher-student ratios (too expensive).

But what is New Mexico for: This is much less clear.

Are we *for* a concerted drive on the causes of dropouts? Are we willing to spend money to salvage more young people and, incidentally, to diminish the waste of faculty energies? Are we *for* a talent search that would bring into our colleges and universities large numbers of Indians and Spanish-Americans now denied opportunity because of poverty, and the poverty of their education?

Are we *for* more and better continuing education programs, so that our doctors, lawyers, engineers, administrators can grow in professional competence? Are we to serve the needs of our citizens grudgingly or with full, spirited recognition that the dollar spent on public service opportunities is returned manyfold?

Are we *for* a joining of hands to exploit opportunities for combined programs in fields such as mental retardation, water resources research, work-training centers under the Economic Opportunity Act of 1964?

Are we *for* a rapid build-up of our graduate programs where it can be demonstrated that such programs are clearly justified?

Are we *for* education which is dynamic, which looks to the future, anticipates needs, and consciously, purposefully relates to the needs of our state?

If we are really *for* these things, the matter of coordination will fall into its proper place as neither the most important nor the least important of our concerns. In the educational household, enterprise counts for more than tidiness. It would be easy to stifle institutional aspiration with a querulous negativism; it will be extremely difficult to guide the institutions of higher learning, blending their aspirations into a larger harmony of purpose, graced with vitality. Yet this is the central task; one that will require the best efforts of the educational community as well as of the "coordinators."

The Coordination of State Systems
of Higher Education

T. R. McCONNELL

IN UNDERSTANDING the emergence of state-wide systems of higher education in this country it should be helpful to look briefly at the coordination of universities in Great Britain. Recently I studied British higher education, "post-Robbins"; prior to that I had looked at British postsecondary education when Lord Robbins was completing his studies and turning to the preparation of his report, which makes recommendations concerning the future pattern and coordination of higher education.

Another important document appeared almost simultaneously with Lord Robbins'—the report of the University Grants Committee on *University Development 1957–1962*. This is the account of the U.G.C.'s stewardship of the universities for the last quinquennium, and, I predict, it is the last report of its kind, for, although neither the U.G.C. nor the universities may more than vaguely realize it, a new era of university direction and coordination has begun.

The single really revolutionary element in the Robbins Report is that "courses of higher education should be available for all those who are qualified by ability and attainment to pursue them and who wish to do it." By unassailable statistical analyses, Robbins put to rest once and for all the notion that there is in Britain a highly limited reservoir of talent, and that anything more than a slight expansion in the number of university places would scrape the bottom of the pool of ability. Robbins showed conclusively that university enrollment can be greatly expanded without reducing the quality of entrants or endangering academic standards. However, the committee strongly opposed giving students of lesser ability access to the universities. As one of those at the highest levels of university policy expressed it, Robbins expanded the citadel but did not breach it.

Coordination through the U.G.C.

On the organization of higher education, Robbins made one significant recommendation. Before stating it, let me remind you that in 1961–62 a little more than 70 percent of the British universities' current income was from parliamentary grants. The present instrument of financial liaison between the universities and the government is the University Grants Committee. Until recently the U.G.C. was an arm of the Treasury; now it is responsible through the Ministry of Science and Higher Education to the Secretary of State for Science and Education. The U.G.C. is the agency which makes known to the government the financial needs of the universities, as it assesses them; negotiates the government grant with the ministry; and, finally, distributes among the universities individually the total amount provided by the government. The U.G.C., a large proportion of whose members are academics, has been a highly successful buffer between the universities and the main source of their support; it has effectively insulated the institutions from overt and, to a large degree, covert political influence. Although the British universities are almost solely dependent on the state for their support, they have maintained an amazing degree of autonomy. As a matter of fact, although they are also beholden to the U.G.C., they have even managed to hold it at a stiff arm's length.

Berdahl, who has written the authoritative volume on the autonomy of the British universities under the U.G.C.,[1] believes that the committee has welded the universities into a national system. I have always thought that this overstated the case. The U.G.C. brought about some concerted movement, it is true, but the amount of positive planning and coordination has been, in my judgment, minimal. Whatever direction the committee has given the universities has had to be exerted gingerly. As one official in a position to know expressed it, the coordination the U.G.C. *has* attained has been accomplished either through the most delicate negotiation and persuasion, earmarked grants (which the universities have disliked), or outright bribery. The result is a system of higher education far short of the nation's needs. Whether the government would have financially underwritten a bolder or more adequate national system of universities is admittedly doubtful, but in any event the universities themselves have never come forth with any such plan. It is doubtful that they would ever voluntarily do so.

Recent Growth and Change

The quinquennium 1957–62 began with 21 universities and three university colleges. It ended with 31 universities and one university college. Seven completely new universities were established during this period. In my view the only possible economic justification for

---

[1] R. O. Berdahl, *British Universities and the State* (Berkeley: University of California Press, 1959). Also, "University-State Relations Re-examined," in *Sociological Studies in British University Education*, Sociological Review Monograph No. 7 (Keele, England: University of Keele, 1963).

this expansion in the number of institutions was the probable cost of expanding already existing civic universities in the centers of large cities. At the end of the quinquennium all the older universities except Oxford, Cambridge, and London—and the last is actually a federation of relatively small institutions—were small by American standards. Excluding Sussex (which had just opened), Oxford, Cambridge, and London, eight of the remaining English and Scottish universities had fewer than 2,000 students, 12 fewer than 3,000, and 17 fewer than 5,000. Only four had more than 5,000 students and the largest had fewer than 6,500.

In this setting, it was an almost tragic expenditure of scarce resources to start seven new universities, most of them located in cathedral towns, and nearly all placed where residences must be provided for a large number of students. To provide the capital costs; to establish the research libraries and laboratories, not only for undergraduates, but also for the much greater number of graduate students the country must have; to create the administrative structure; and to supply the hierarchy of necessary staff will put an impossible strain on the amount of money any government, under the present British attitudes toward higher education, is likely to make available. Both the new universities and the others are unlikely to secure the transfusion of money that will make them progressive, virile institutions.

In spite of scarcity of resources, still more universities are to be created. The ten colleges of advanced technology established after 1956 to offer university-level courses in applied science and technology are to be transformed into technological universities, in accordance with a recommendation of the Robbins Committee. They will be brought under the aegis of the University Grants Committee in April 1965.

New Problems of Coordination

Not only does this sudden expansion in the number of universities strain the already inadequate exchequer still more; it immediately raises new questions of coordination. One of the new technological universities is in Birmingham, where one of the best of the older civic universities is also located. Problems of duplication of specialized efferings have already arisen, and the problem of coordination will be accentuated if the regional colleges of commerce and art, contiguous to the Birmingham College of Advanced Technology, are ultimately affiliated and perhaps other faculties join the new technological university complex.

Similarly, the Royal College of Science and Technology in Glasgow, once affiliated with the University of Glasgow, has become a separate autonomous university, as will Heriot-Watt College in

Edinburgh. A new Scottish university has been announced for Stirling. And so the voices clamoring for scarce resources multiply.

The necessary process of coordination is not merely one of allocation of scarce resources and avoidance of costly duplication. It is also one of expanding educational opportunity and of maintaining diversity in the system of higher education. The colleges of advanced technology have developed differently, for the most part, from the technological divisions of the universities. The former have responded much more sympathetically and directly to industry, both in teaching and research. Their particular educational innovation is the sandwich course—alternate periods in industry and in the college. There is evidence already that the colleges of advanced technology may abandon their distinctiveness and attempt to outdo the universities at their own game. Three of the four colleges of advanced technology in London have already decided to abandon their urban location—one is moving to the cathedral town of Guilford —and the others intend to move outside London. The technological university in the midst of its industrial complex may soon be a curiosity—if, in fact, any of them survive at all. There are also rumors that some of the new technological universities plan to give up their sandwich courses for more conventional curricula. The natural law seems to be that institutions will strive to be similar rather than different.

Further Recommendations

The Robbins Committee also proposed that, in order to meet enrollment projections for 1980, six more new universities be established in addition to those now in the process of formation. One of these would be a wholly new Special Institution for Scientific and Technological Education and Research, added to four other special institutions to be given preferential development—the University of Strathclyde (previously the Royal College of Science and Technology at Glasgow), the College of Science and Technology at Manchester, the Imperial College of Science and Technology in London, and one of the former colleges of advanced technology selected for this purpose. Wisely, if unconventionally, Robbins urged that the six new institutions be placed in urban settings. Robbins also proposed that certain regional technical colleges should have the opportunity to become parts of universities or universities in their own right.

Finally, Robbins recommended that the teacher-training colleges should be strengthened and greatly expanded in size and that they should be affiliated with universities through schools of education, which would serve as the agencies under which properly qualified students would be awarded degrees after four years of academic and professional study. At this writing the Robbins recommendation for the teacher-training colleges has not been accepted but, if adopted, it would bring them indirectly under the University Grants Committee, which by then might be an umbrella for sixty or so institutions, and, indirectly, for many more.

The U.G.C. has been a part-time body. Its major full-time officers have been a chairman and a secretary, who were supplemented by a small and, even for its recent responsibilities, an inadequate staff. A deputy chairman has just been appointed, and the staff will probably be increased. Yet one finds little conception, first, that there will have to be purposeful planning of a system of higher education that is most unlikely to take form through voluntary means; second, that there will have to be prudent allocation of resources in relation both to the number of youth qualified for higher education and to the needs of the economy and polity for specialized manpower; and third, that the basis for planning and allocation is continuing research.

There is some—although not widespread—recognition of the necessity for planning and coordination. A distinguished administrator said recently that the British universities "must regard themselves no longer as isolated units, but rather as parts of an articulated whole" and "some major academic issues which have hitherto been regarded as private matters for decision by individual university institutions must now be approached with national considerations in the forefront and that the successful solution of those problems calls for concerted action on an organized basis by universities going far beyond what has so far been achieved." [2]

But pressed to suggest means of coordination, this officer had little to propose. He certainly did not want the government to do the coordinating, and he apparently didn't want the U.G.C. to become a more aggressive planning and executive body. In my conversation with him, he fell back on the Committee of Vice-Chancellors and Principals, which, he had said in the paper just quoted, lacks the executive posture, prestige, and power to coordinate, but which he now said might at least have the informal authority necessary to do so if it were expanded by the addition of professorial members.

This, at last, brings me to the Robbins recommendation on organization. The committee proposed that the government should create a new Cabinet Minister of Science and Higher Education, and that this ministry should deal with the universities through a strengthened University Grants Committee, although little was said about how the strengthening was to be done. In making its recommendation on government organization, the Robbins Committee, for rea-

[2] Sir Douglas Logan, *Universities: The Years of Challenge* (Cambridge, England: Cambridge University Press, 1963), pp. 8, 34–35.

sons it is unnecessary to summarize here, rejected the alternative of a single ministry for all of education.

The government, however, adopted a compromise form of ministerial organization. It created a Secretary of State for Science and Education with two ministers—one for science and higher education, and one for the rest of the educational establishment—a scheme which the Labor government is not likely to change in any major way. The Conservative government retained the University Grants Committee as the liaison between the universities and the government, and the Labor government is expected to follow suit.

Probable Trends

Although action with respect to the governmental relations with the universities was limited pending the election, and the Labor government had not yet tipped its hand at this writing, certain changes in university-state relations are almost certain to occur. Some of these developments may be summarized as follows:

1. The degree of intervention and initiative by the government in university affairs will increase greatly. This is, in my judgment, both inevitable and necessary. It would have occurred irrespective of the political composition of the government, but it is likely to be greater under a Labor than under a Conservative ministry. There are many reasons to expect greater government initiative. One of them is that the universities and the U.G.C. have not done the necessary planning and have taken insufficient initiative in university development.

2. The University Grants Committee, as constituted and staffed at present, is seriously inadequate for the task ahead. The Labor government will almost certainly make at least a part of the membership of the U.G.C. full time and will give it a much larger, more professionally able, and more effectively organized staff. A Labor government may be expected to work with and through a more adequate U.G.C., but it will exert much more initiative and make many more final decisions in the process. I think it is fairly safe to conclude that the government will step into any vacuum left by the educational forces themselves.

3. Neither the Labor government nor a reconstituted U.G.C. will ride roughshod over the universities because both know that university autonomy is a rallying cry in Britain. The universities will be invited to participate in planning, but it is no longer possible for the nation to wait entirely for self-initiated collaboration, a collaboration which might never materialize on problems of far-reaching university and national policy. The future structure of higher education cannot wait for the measured and somewhat reluctant voluntary body of busy vice-chancellors, however fortified by the pro-

fessoriate. Neither can this structure take shape if individual universities continue to enjoy the right to go their own way, whatever the national needs of the present or future may be.

4. If the Ministry of Science and Higher Education and the University Grants Committee jointly succeed in shaping a university system more nearly adequate to the nation's needs, they will have to conduct much more research on university problems than anyone to whom I talked now realizes. The day of intuitive improvisation in university affairs is over if higher education is to give Britain the leadership and specialized manpower it must have to restore its falling fortunes. Where will the research be conducted? It could be done under the U.G.C. It might be done in the ministry. It may be done mainly in the former, and partly in the latter by a strong staff of civil servants.

5. The citadel will have to be breached. The universities will have to relate themselves in manifold ways to secondary and post-secondary institutions. The level of university support will have to be reckoned in relation to a great expansion in education beyond the ages of fifteen and sixteen—especially expansion in full-time general and specialized education outside the universities for youth between sixteen and twenty—just as the universities and four-year institutions in the United States will have to relate themselves to great expansion at the junior college level.

One of the serious side effects of the Robbins Report has been to strengthen rather than to weaken the stratification of education. The lines of demarcation between the universities and other institutions of postsecondary education need to be blurred, not accentuated. The problem of articulation of levels and institutions will become increasingly important.

One gets the impression that the new Labor government will be especially sensitive to the need to strengthen further education, and consequently that the universities, especially the new ones, may not prosper for a time as they would like. The exception may be the new technological universities; the Labor government is especially sensitive to the need for technological development.

Problems of U.S. Institutions

Let me turn now to some of the problems of state-wide coordination of higher education in the United States. I do not suggest that there is a close analogy between the coordination of British higher education and the development of our own state-wide patterns or systems of colleges and universities. The traditions and conditions in Britain and the United States are too different to use the one as a model for the other. Nevertheless, periodic studies of the coordination of British universities have helped to clarify, for myself at least, some of our own problems. What I now have to say, somewhat dogmatically, is the result of observations in Britain and of assessment of some of the results of coordination in several of our states.

I have long been an advocate of the voluntary coordination of higher education, but have now concluded that purely voluntary methods, at a certain stage of a state's development of facilities and resources for higher education, are almost certain to be ineffective. First of all, they are unlikely to produce the continuing and impartial planning on which a comprehensive and diversified system of higher education must be built. As pointed out above, in Britain neither the Committee of Vice-Chancellors and Principals, representing the universities themselves, nor the University Grants Committee has produced or planned a system of higher education adequate to the nation's needs. Neither, in my judgment, has any purely voluntary coordinating agency in the United States produced a plan for the orderly and comprehensive development of higher education in its state. Intuitive improvisation in providing resources for higher education is as obsolete in the United States as it is in Great Britain.

An adequate plan for educational development will propose constructive methods of mobilizing and coordinating a state's resources for higher education. To many people the term "coordination" has mainly negative connotations. Too often it is identified primarily with measures to avoid duplication of educational goals and programs and with other forms of restraint and control. It seems abundantly clear that, although effective coordination sometimes undeniably entails restraint, its results will be unfortunate if they are mainly negative. I have said elsewhere, and I repeat, that "the great need in public higher education" (and I would also now include private higher education) "is for constructive, collaborative, and comprehensive planning and for purposeful sharing, as well as purposeful division of responsibilities." [3] One of the most important purposes of a coordinating agency is to define new educational needs and stimulate present institutions—or, if necessary, new institutions —to meet them. A coordinating board can and should do its planning with widespread participation of institutions, professionals, and laymen, as the Board of Higher Education in Illinois has so recently and so well demonstrated.

Sources of Control

If those who are primarily and immediately responsible for the development of higher education fail to plan its orderly development, some agency less qualified to do so will almost certainly step

[3] T. R. McConnell, *A General Program for American Public Higher Education* (New York: McGraw-Hill Book Co., 1962), p. 169.

into the vacuum. The question is not whether to plan and coordinate. The real question is who will plan and coordinate. If coordination is inevitable, as most observers now think it is, the first choice to be made is between coordination by external agencies—legislatures or state departments of finance—or by responsible educational bodies. Nearly everyone connected with the government and administration of higher education deplores the former. The Committee on Government and Higher Education said that " . . . it is a certainty that if academic activities are not coordinated by the institutions themselves, the state will feel compelled to step in and do the job." [4] If the educational world defaults on its responsibility for planning its orderly development, the state finally will intervene. That will be demonstrated conclusively in Great Britain, if I am not mistaken, and it has already been demonstrated in some of the states of this country.

The president of a great state university recently warned against rigid master plans for the development of state-wide systems of public higher institutions. Everyone should oppose the engraving of a master plan on tablets of stone. Master plans need to be revised almost continuously. It is obviously impossible to foresee all contingencies, to anticipate all needs, or to predict human motivation with great accuracy. Therefore, an agency charged with planning a state's program of higher education must be staffed professionally to keep the development of higher education under continuing scrutiny, evaluation, and revision.

A list of some of the studies that have been undertaken during the short period the California Coordinating Council for Higher Education has been in operation is illustrative of the kinds of continuing studies that need to be made. The council has conducted, or has under way, investigations of medical and dental education; continuing education; year-round operation; faculty salaries and benefits; unit costs; student admission, retention, and transfer; the need for new campuses and colleges; space utilization; and methods of budgetary analysis—an extensive but incomplete list. Unless a coordinating agency is staffed for studies of such scope and significance, its usefulness will be inevitably limited. The California Coordinating Council for Higher Education is not a purely voluntary body because it was brought into being by legislative statute and is supported by legislative appropriations. However, its prerogatives are only those of analysis, report, and recommendation; it does not possess actual power over individual institutions or over the state college and university systems. Perhaps the council should be called a quasi-voluntary or quasi-formal coordinating body.

[4] Committee on Government and Higher Education, *The Efficiency of Freedom* (Baltimore, Md.: Johns Hopkins Press, 1959), p. 27.

Further Inadequacies of Voluntary Cooperation

Another reason why I consider purely voluntary coordination to be ineffective is that it is unlikely to assign functions and programs systematically among institutions or groups of institutions, or to make the efficient allocation of resources for educational expenditures and capital outlay that a coordinated and adequately financed system of higher education requires. Most voluntary coordinating agencies have found it difficult or even impossible to resolve the competitive propensities of major institutions, rival systems, or the imitative tendencies of "lesser" institutions striving to copy the structure, if not the substance, of the prestigious universities.

It seems axiomatic that no state now possesses or will acquire resources that would justify the unnecessary duplication of costly forms of specialized education. It is also increasingly evident that the unnecessary duplication of educational programs can only lead to educational enfeeblement. Unfortunately, many institutions would prefer being a pale reflection of some prestigious model rather than a more limited institution of academic excellence. It also seems true that by striving to be as much like one another as possible, institutions will fail to provide the diversity of educational opportunity our economy, culture, and polity require. It is still clear to me from my observations in Britain and in the United States that, as I have said before,

The diversity of students' attributes and the multifarious demands of the American society for educated manpower would seem to call for a reasonable division of labor among higher institutions; yet colleges and universities tend to converge rather than to diverge, to become more similar and less differentiated.[5]

I can only conclude that there should be some differentiation of responsibilities among public higher institutions and a distribution or allocation of programs relevant to these functions. This would, in turn, seem to entail efficient allocation of financial resources if educational opportunities of appropriate scope and quality are to be provided for the growing proportion of young people who will continue their formal education beyond the high school. Purely voluntary coordinating agencies are likely to be basically inadequate to this complex task. Five years ago there may have been some exceptions to this generalization. Today there are few, if any.

The Role of the Coordinating Body

It was pointed out above that the California Coordinating Council for Higher Education possesses statutory powers only to analyze,

[5] McConnell, *op. cit.*, p. 59.

review, report, recommend, and persuade. In my judgment, time
has proved that, however able and devoted the council has been in
discharging its responsibilities, its powers are inadequate to coordinate a pattern of public higher education as large and complex
as that of California. I have become convinced that a coordinating
board must at least have the power possessed by the Board of Higher
Education in Illinois, and by the new Ohio Board of Regents for
public higher education, to approve all new educational programs—
meaning any new unit of instruction, research, or public service
(such as a college, school, division, institute, department, branch,
or campus).

A coordinating board should also have the authority to discontinue educational programs. Such power may save the board from
being confronted, as is now often the case, with what amounts to a
fait accompli, that is, with a request to give approval to a *program*
or *curriculum* on the ground that the institution already offers all
or nearly all the necessary *courses*. If the authority to discontinue
programs does not control this sort of academic one-upmanship,
some continuing review of course offerings may become essential.

It is necessary, as in Illinois, California, and Ohio, for the coordinating agency to make recommendations to institutions and to
executive and legislative arms of the state government concerning
proposed operating budgets. The basic approach to budgetary
analysis should be the relevance of operating budgets to an institution's or a system's functions and programs. The process of
budgetary analysis, recommendation, and reporting, if it is to be
effective, must secure an appropriate response from both government and institution. One of the major functions of a coordinating
board is to effect a delicate accommodation between the financial
resources the executive and legislative departments believe they
can or should allocate, on the one hand, and the resources the institutions believe they require, on the other. If either the government
departments or the institutions lose confidence in the budgetary
recommendations of a coordinating board, its position becomes
untenable. In an extremity, a legislature may empower a new governing or coordinating agency to formulate and submit a single
appropriation request for the institutions or systems under its
supervision, and to allocate to systems or institutions, as the case
may be, whatever shares of the final appropriation may be just and
equitable. This power the University Grants Committee in Great
Britain now possesses and exercises, but in only two of our states
does a coordinating board for higher education have such authority.

It may be that some coordinating agencies will have to be given
the authority to approve or disapprove major proposals for the
construction or conversion of educational buildings, not merely to

make recommendations on institutions' proposals, if this authority is necessary in order to monitor educational programs effectively.

Conclusions

I have come reluctantly to the conclusion that voluntary coordination is inadequate and ineffective. I am in favor of the greatest possible degree of institutional autonomy, and I deplore the kinds of detailed regulations and controls that are increasingly being imposed externally on public institutions by governmental agencies and internally by their own administrations. Nevertheless, I am convinced that the essential outlines of the development of public institutions and public systems of higher education must be subject to the sanction of a coordinating body and responsive to an agency charged with planning a comprehensive state-wide educational program.

A comprehensive plan for public higher education must take into account the services of privately controlled institutions. The latter should participate fully in the development of state-wide master plans, as they did recently in Illinois, and as they did in California. The committee which produced California's master plan was actually chaired by the president of one of its private liberal arts colleges, and private institutions are represented on the statutory Coordinating Council. All resources for higher education will have to be developed and utilized if a state is to serve youth and adults adequately in the years ahead.

4

Voluntary Arrangements

Consortia and Related Interinstitutional Arrangements

JAMES C. MESSERSMITH

COLLEGES AND universities today are confronted with ever-increasing demands, obligations, and opportunities that carry the responsibility of finding material resources and manpower to meet the challenge of the present age. As one means, more and more of the institutions are turning to cooperative undertakings.

In the past, it was practically possible and perhaps educationally advantageous for colleges to operate unilaterally, each determining its own purposes, goals, and programs and promoting its own resources. This unilateralism was particularly influenced by three factors: (1) the ivory tower concept, which set colleges apart from the community; (2) the self-sufficient concept, which separated them from one another; and (3) the highly selective nature of single-purpose programs, which drew relatively few students to any one institution. Frequently, both the need and the desire to establish cooperative programs were lacking. Where the need existed, the benefits and potentialities of such undertakings were not always clearly envisioned.

Since World War II, three phases have marked the trend toward increased cooperative activity in higher education. Phase one, covering the period of heavy influx of returning veterans to colleges and other institutions of education and training, was a period of collaboration between the institutions and the Government; phase two, the period of ebb tide of veteran enrollments, witnessed a temporary return to intensive competition among higher institutions; phase three, the latest, has been accompanied by heavier college enrollments, rising educational costs, breakthroughs in science and technology, increasing demands upon higher education, and the establishment of cooperation and coordination among higher institutions.

Today many of the institutions recognize their inability, alone, to provide the necessary staff and facilities for more complex, costly, and increasing numbers of programs and services. Furthermore, there is widespread acceptance of the virtues of interdependence as well as those of self-sufficiency. An institution, when it enters into a

* Formerly specialist for state and regional organization, Division of Educational Organization and Administration, U.S. Office of Education.

cooperative arrangement, may surrender a degree of its autonomy and uniqueness; however, it is the diversity of unique qualities among cooperating institutions that enables them to become more useful and effective in concert. The prematurity stage, then, at least, has been reached in the use of cooperative undertakings as a means of achieving greater quantity, quality, and economy of "production" in higher education. In summary, the *raison d'être* of interinstitutional arrangements is the desire to provide improved and expanded opportunities for the clientele of higher education through the more effective utilization of facilities, programs, personnel, and other resources.

Explorations of Possibilities

An indication of the "coming of age" of the college federation movement was the National Conference on College and University Interinstitutional Cooperation at Princeton, New Jersey, in April 1962. The participants—directors and trustees of 24 federations, representing 223 colleges and universities—considered the following topics: Organizing the Cooperative Unit; Project Formation, Initiation, and Evaluation; and The Role of Executive and Policy Officers.

Concerning organization of a cooperative group, the discussants identified and reviewed: basic principles and guidelines for organization; the use of consultants; the question of incorporation; the nature of board membership; and problems of financing and implementing cooperative arrangements. Topics related to project formation, initiation, and evaluation included: devices to discover and initiate projects; types, areas, and patterns of cooperative projects; and the purpose, scope, and duration of project evaluation. The third session examined the nature of the executive officer, the board of directors, the relationship between the executive officer and the board, and the purpose and frequency of meetings. The conference identified thirty-two activities, most of them academic in character, as potentially appropriate for cooperative development.

Since this conference, executive officers of a number of the participating groups have had several meetings to review the current scene and consider the future course of the college federation movement. Three questions before them have been: (1) Where are we now? (2) Where do we go from here? (3) How do we get there? Such questions are rightly of concern to those who must provide leadership and service to multi-institutional groups. A pooling of their information on cooperative programs in operation can shed light on the scope and impact of such programs. Comparison of their viewpoints on problems can smooth the operation of existing programs and ease the launching of new programs.

Indication of the increasing significance being attached to this movement in higher education is to be found in special courses and related study activities. In the summer of 1964, for example, Catholic University of America held a ten-day Workshop on College and University Interinstitutional Cooperation. The workshop's objectives were: (1) to give participants a better appreciation of the nature and scope of cooperative arrangements in higher education through the use of representative examples of such undertakings, and (2) to give guidance in emphasis, planning, and methodology in establishing, administering, and evaluating cooperative programs.

Two other developments in the trend toward greater cooperative efforts are the growth in number of cooperative groups and the increase in the literature on interinstitutional cooperation. At the 1962 Princeton conference some persons represented groups that were not then formally established; other groups present were in various stages of pre-organization. Since then, these and other federations have been formed.

A 1957 report [1] on interinstitutional cooperation contained a bibliography of 79 items. Four of these items were published between 1930 and 1939; nine were published between 1940 and 1949; and the remaining 66 (84 percent) were published between 1950 and 1957. A 1961 report [2] on the same subject identified 70 items published between 1957 and 1961—almost as many as the number reported for 1930–57.

Patterns of Agreements

Cooperation among higher institutions has encompassed a variety of arrangements, agreements, contracts, and other relationships, ranging from the informal to the highly formal.

In some instances, the institutions involved in a cooperative arrangement have been able to administer their joint programs without a separate staff agency. Why? Traditionally, such undertakings have been informal in nature—characterized by simplicity in design and structure. Also typically, the arrangement has been rather narrowly conceived, both in scope of program and number, type, and location of institutions participating. The most prevalent patterns have been the bilateral arrangement and the multilateral arrangement among a small number of institutions located relatively near each other. In the informal arrangement there may be no recognized or exhibited need for a contract or other document of establishment

[1] Merton W. Ertell, *Interinstitutional Cooperation in Higher Education* (Albany: New York State Education Department, 1957).

[2] S. V. Martorana, James C. Messersmith, and Laurence O. Nelson, *Cooperative Projects Among Colleges and Universities*, U.S. Office of Education, Circular No. 649 (Washington: Government Printing Office, 1961).

or control. Programs thus conceived have operated successfully for the purposes set for them. In other situations, however, more formalized plans have been required.

Past practices indicate that colleges frequently set out to establish cooperative ventures largely on a mutual determination-and-consent basis. (This is not meant to imply the arrangements have not been preceded or accompanied by adequate planning, including the identification and analysis of the important issues and problems likely to be encountered and the provision of means of dealing with them.) However, as cooperative programs have grown in scope and complexity and as the number of institutions participating has increased, the trend, especially in recent years, has been to employ more formal procedures and practices in their establishment. Obviously, the greater the scope and complexity of the arrangement, the greater the need for written agreements covering terms and provisions. Formal contracts committing institutions to participate in cooperative ventures are now frequently used to consummate such undertakings.

Patterns of Federation

The varied nature and design of the interinstitutional federations are truly remarkable. Some have involved only two institutions; others have encompassed many times that number. Undertakings have involved public institutions only, private institutions only, and both public and private institutions. Sometimes the contracting agents have been the institutions as a whole. Again, cooperative arrangements have evolved from efforts of separate departments within the institutions. The simplest pattern is, of course, the bilateral arrangement, which is likely to involve two institutions located near each other, but many join the effort of a U.S. and a foreign institution. A recently employed technique, which is growing in significance, has been the creation of an agency or corporation that draws upon the facilities, programs, personnel, and other resources of the higher institutions available to its purposes and needs.

Present conditions are demanding a broadening of interinstitutional arrangements in higher education. On this matter, the Committee on University and World Affairs observes:

> Improved mechanisms for cooperation among the universities, and between universities and other agencies (including those of government) that contribute to and draw upon their resources can greatly assist the difficult process of relating individual efforts to nationwide needs. A healthy pluralism demands not only a diversity in the programs of individual universities, but also the active cooperation of universities in a concerted approach to problems that face the nation as a whole.[3]

[3] *The University and World Affairs* (New York: Ford Foundation, 1961), p. 16.

It is likely that many cooperative arrangements of the future will be characterized by broad geographic distribution of the participants and increasingly will be state-wide, interstate, regional, national, and even international in scope.

Multilateral Arrangements

Multilateral arrangements vary from those found within an individual community or locality to those which are regional or national in spread. Two patterns of organization have characterized multilateral federations of higher institutions. One of these, the *association* pattern, consists of a number of institutions of relatively similar purpose and stature. The Associated Colleges of the Midwest and the Great Lakes Colleges Association, both in the Midwest, are illustrative of this type of federation among liberal arts colleges. The Committee on Institutional Cooperation, the Associated Rocky Mountain Universities, and the District of Columbia Joint Graduate Consortium are representative of this pattern at the university level.

The *center* pattern of federation is characterized by a number of smaller institutions grouped around a larger institution, or university, for purposes of mutual benefit and assistance. The Atlanta University Center, the University Center in Georgia, and the University Center in Virginia are examples.

RESEARCH CENTERS

Recent developments have produced significant variations of regular patterns of cooperative arrangements. One of these is the graduate research center, an agency which draws upon the resources of the higher institutions in the area. The Graduate Research Center of the Southwest, established in 1961, is an illustration. Located in Dallas, Texas, the center is a private nonprofit institution chartered by the State of Texas for the purpose of conducting research and advanced graduate education in the public interest.

Certain of the center's purposes and objectives involve cooperative commitments with the higher institutions in the region. These commitments include: (1) encouraging, promoting, and arranging, through formal or informal agreements for research and teaching, the interchange of staff and advanced students among the universities and other institutions in the Southwest and elsewhere; (2) promoting the opportunity of the universities and other institutions in the region to enlarge their graduate faculties and to make such positions more attractive by virtue of the research and other facilities afforded by the center; (3) increasing the graduate-level teaching competence of the Southwest by providing opportunities for faculty members at the center to spend certain periods of time teaching at the universities and other institutions in the region; and (4) establishing working arrangements with graduate research centers located at universities and other institutions in the region.

Since the establishment of the center, cooperation with the universities in the region has resulted in the development of several new doctoral programs at area institutions. Joint teaching arrangements have also been effected in a number of curricular areas.

Current members of the center's thirty-five member Board of Directors include administrative officers from the following institutions: Rice University, University of Oklahoma, Tulane University, Austin College, University of Arkansas, University of Texas, Texas Christian University, Southern Methodist University, Oklahoma State University, and Stanford University. In addition, the University of Dallas and Hendrix College are represented on the center's Advisory Council.

The center is able to develop arrangements with industry under which its research facilities, faculty, and research personnel, separately or in affiliation with those of the universities in the region, afford opportunities for industrial scientists to engage in laboratory and advanced course work. The center is also associated with the Inter-University Council, a federation of five universities in the Dallas–Fort Worth–Denton area, in an arrangement that makes the combined resources of all the institutions available to any graduate student of any of the five schools.

Counterparts or variations of the Graduate Center of the Southwest have been established in other areas throughout the country. In North Carolina, for example, the Research Triangle Institute is a subsidiary property of the Consolidated University of North Carolina and Duke University. RTI is the outgrowth of efforts begun in the 1950's by a committee of university and business leaders to establish a research program that would take advantage of the combined assets of the university community (University of North Carolina, North Carolina State, and Duke University) in accelerating industrial and economic growth. The institute uses consultants from the three institutions, works jointly with them in the execution of specific projects, and furnishes adjunct faculty.

Another research center, in the Midwest, is the product of efforts of the Midwestern Universities Research Association (MURA). MURA, which was formally organized in 1954, has among its membership fifteen of the principal universities of Illinois, Indiana, Iowa, Kansas, Michigan, Minnesota, Missouri, Ohio, and Wisconsin. Its major purpose is to provide research and instruction facilities in the field of high energy nuclear physics for all scientists who can make appropriate use of them. Its activities have been supported financially by its members and by such Federal agencies as the National Science Foundation, Office of Naval Research, and the Atomic Energy Commission. MURA and the member institutions cooperate in staffing the MURA laboratory, on a leave-of-absence basis, with personnel from the universities.

These illustrations of the graduate research center pattern of cooperation in higher education show the heavy emphasis on programs in science, technology, and engineering. However, cooperative undertakings in the social sciences and other areas are also becoming increasingly significant.

The Inter-University Consortium for Political Research (ICPR), barely two years in existence, was established by twenty-one universities spread from the eastern seaboard to the Pacific Coast. Since its formation, at least five additional institutions have become members. A principal objective is to establish, maintain, and service a data repository of such materials as comprehensive national election statistics in a form that will make them readily usable for purposes of analysis; United States census data of political pertinence adapted to analytical use; Federal congressional and senatorial legislative records; decisions of the Supreme Court of the United States; and data collected from special research studies and investigations. Charges for services of the consortium to graduate students, faculty members, and scholars—in addition to those selected, specified participants from the member institutions—will be nominal. The consortium also has a clearinghouse function of publicizing other sources of similar research data. Negotiations have been undertaken to obtain data from major survey studies conducted over the past twenty years, to be incorporated in the repository, and plans are under way for developing an information retrieval system. The consortium, which has its headquarters in Ann Arbor, Michigan, has established a working arrangement or partnership with the Survey Research Center of the University of Michigan, under which a Committee of Representatives, consisting of individuals from interested universities, works with the Survey Research Center staff in planning consortium activities.

INTERSTATE AND INTRASTATE PROGRAMS

The University Council for Educational Administration, an inter-university cooperative organization of forty-six institutions, with offices at Ohio State University, has as its stated objective the professional preparation of principals, superintendents, and other public school administrators. Its program has been supported, since its inception, by the Kellogg Foundation, in addition to which member institutions pay annual service fees. Member institutions are widely dispersed geographically, with one principal criterion for membership being that the institution have a doctoral degree program in educational administration. Another function is the promoting of research through interuniversity cooperation.

An intrastate program with similar objectives is the Inter-University Program in Teacher and Administrator Education in New York State, sponsored by the State University of New York at Buffalo, Cornell University, the University of Rochester, and Syracuse University. This program has been primarily concerned with two specific projects: (1) professional preparation of teachers, and (2) the internship in educational administration. Initiated in 1961, after four years of studies and conferences, the projects are being supported during a six-year phase by a substantial grant from the Ford Foundation.

The Regional Council for International Education is a recently established cooperative arrangement designed to expand and strengthen activities of the twenty-eight member institutions in international education and cultural exchange. The council arrangement has enabled the participating institutions—which consist of both small colleges and large universities, located (with one exception) in the states of Ohio, Pennsylvania, and West Virginia—to pool their resources and, thereby, undertake many programs which would be impossible on a unilateral basis. Projects under way or planned include: curriculum development and cooperative research; faculty seminars; a regional orientation center for foreign students; junior year abroad; and interfaculty exchange. The council maintains an office at the University of Pittsburgh.

URBAN AREA COOPERATION

An urban area cooperative arrangement, which is unusual from the standpoint of its membership, is the Higher Education Coordinating Council of Metropolitan St. Louis. Council members include public and private secondary schools, junior colleges, senior colleges, and universities in the city of St. Louis, St. Louis County, and St. Charles County (all in Missouri), and Southern Illinois University. Business and industry are also represented on the council.

A primary objective of HECC is the improved coordination of program offerings, plans, and facilities, to avoid unnecessary duplication of effort among member institutions. A second objective is better communication of community needs and educational trends among secondary schools, institutions of higher education, and business, industrial, and professional groups in the St. Louis metropolitan area. The council is also concerned with continuing studies of population trends and types of education needed by organizations and industry; planning programs to increase the numbers of highly qualified faculty members in the area; and finding ways of making higher education available to more area students with exceptional ability.

HECC is an illustration of higher institutions in an urban setting attempting to meet more effectively the needs of their community through a coordinated effort not only of the institutions themselves, but of other community agencies as well. What this points up is that cooperative programs in higher education, to be most effective, should not be planned and executed within the isolated environment of the institutions concerned, but, rather, coordinated with related programs of other agencies within the local, state, regional, or national matrix.

Urbanization has a strong impact on higher education today; higher education must make a reciprocal impact upon urbanization. Through cooperative action, groups of urban higher institutions such as those in HECC, working in a coordinated and sustained effort with other agencies and organizations having related interests and concerns, can promote achievement of their common objectives.

Like the patterns of interinstitutional organization and federation, the types of cooperative activities being promoted by these groups are also increasing in number and variety. Approximately five years prior to the establishment of the District of Columbia Joint Graduate Consortium in 1964, a survey was made to identify specific examples of cooperative endeavor then existing among the institutions of higher education (universities) in the Washington, D.C., area. The survey disclosed eighteen such activities, practically all very informal in their arrangement and, with one exception, academic in nature. (As mentioned above, the Princeton conference of 1962 had identified about thirty-two activities.)

Cooperation of Institutions with Outside Agencies

Working arrangements and relationships between higher institutions and industry constitute another growing type of cooperative effort. An excellent example is that of Williams College and Sprague Electric Company in Massachusetts. This program provides for supplementing the teaching resources of Williams College in the fields of physics and chemistry; it also aids Sprague Electric Company in upgrading its personnel and in recruiting new employees in scientific fields. Under the terms of an informal agreement, Williams College offers a master of arts program in physics and chemistry to which Sprague Electric Company contributes funds, students, and teaching personnel. Over-all administration is assigned to the chairman of the board of Sprague Electric Company and the president of Williams College.

All indications today point toward greater cooperative activity between higher institutions and government. Federal, state, and local levels of government are becoming larger consumers of the products of higher education and larger users of its services. In some instances, these products and services will be furnished on an institutional basis. In other instances, a *group* of institutions, under an established cooperative arrangement, will be the supplier. For example, the Foreign Language Program of the Associated Colleges of the Midwest, instituted in 1960, has been principally supported under terms of a three-year contract with the U.S. Office of Education. This contract has made possible the employment of a full-time coordinator to direct the program and of part-time coordinators to work on individual campuses of ACM institutions. It has also provided funds for office and travel expenses and for certain other items which the program has required.

One growing area of cooperation between higher institutions and government is that of public service training. Local, state, and Federal government service personnel constitute one of the largest segments of the total labor force. As their duties have become more complex and demanding, the need has arisen for additional training and upgrading of government service personnel. Working in collaboration with government, colleges and universities have provided various types of training programs for improving the quality of governmental employees at all levels. Programs have included extension courses, short courses, special conferences, staff services, and other forms of training opportunities. Maximum effectiveness of these programs is promoted when the university, the government agency, and professional organizations cooperate in their sponsorship, planning, and execution.

In the field of research in public administration and service, the university will be primarily interested from the standpoint of adding to knowledge, while the government agency will be principally motivated to do research as a basis for action. Despite these differences, however, varied research studies and projects can well be jointly undertaken by higher education and government.

Technical assistance is another area of university-government cooperation. University functions in this capacity are: direct consultative service; assistance in the development of staff manuals and guides on public administration and management; and the supplying of professionally trained personnel for technical assistance programs in government. In Federal Government technical assistance programs abroad, cooperative efforts of universities may include: furnishing technical assistance under terms of a contract; conducting studies of Government technical assistance programs in foreign countries; and supplying staff members for the operation of specific programs abroad.

The Need for Reporting

Although the concept of interinstitutional cooperation is not new, only recently has it been given any considerable degree of recognition and publicity. Indeed, there is demonstrated need today for a more systematic, regular, and detailed reporting of cooperative programs, including their nature, scope, planning, administration, financing, and evaluation.

Conversely, administrators, board members, faculty, and other persons involved in the establishment of new interinstitutional programs should be encouraged to examine documents relating to the planning, establishment, and development of programs that have proved successful. The purposes and objectives of cooperative programs can often be found in the documents of specific interinstitutional federations. The following are illustrative:

> The purpose of the Associated Colleges of the Midwest is to contribute to the educational effectiveness and operating efficiency of the member colleges.[4]

> The goal of the C.I.C. (Committee on Institutional Cooperation) is to improve educational and public services while minimizing costs by (1) encouraging cooperative efforts among the eleven institutions, (2) identifying specialized areas of teaching and research in which cooperative arrangements may be desirable, and (3) initiating cooperative activities in instruction and research, particularly in graduate areas, among the universities.[5]

The preamble to the bylaws of the Mid-America State Universities Association states:

> Being mindful of the increased costs of higher education in all of its phases, including but not limited to the ever-increasing requirements for expensive equipment to properly conduct research programs, the competition with other segments of society for competent staff members, and the explosive increase in student enrollments, the state universities of Mid-America have entered into this agreement to achieve the following goals: (1) to promote the improvement of specialized facilities and programs at the several institutions and to prevent wasteful duplication in order that each university may achieve a high degree of excellence in all of its programs, (2) to make the specialized or unique educational programs of these universities available at resident fee levels to students on a regional basis, (3) to promote the cooperative use of unusual research facilities among the member universities, and (4) to cooperate wherever possible in providing a unified voice in bringing major research and advanced educational facilities and programs to the region.[6]

The pressures for innovative, joint approaches to expanding higher education services do not automatically ensure the establishment and successful operation of interinstitutional ventures. Not

---

[4] Algo D. Henderson, "The CCC of College Relations," *Educational Record*, January 1962, p. 48.
[5] *Loc. cit.*
[6] *Ibid.*, pp. 48–49.

every institution of higher education will be in a position to participate in such an undertaking. These facts, however, do not lessen the
need for adequate reporting of the accomplishments and potentialities of cooperative arrangements in conserving institutional resources and promoting effectiveness in meeting mutual goals.

Guidelines

In the actual stimulation and initiation of interinstitutional programs, administrative leadership should be recognized as the single
most important element. As such, the administrator must demonstrate a willingness to: (1) examine closely the purposes conceived
for his institution by its constituency, board of control, administration, and faculty; (2) search for gaps in the program of his own
institution and admit the presence of weaknesses when identified;
(3) recognize and accept the strengths of other institutions which
will be participants in the cooperative arrangement; (4) create an
atmosphere of mutual trust with administrators of the other participating institutions in the discussion of institutional strengths
and weaknesses in specific areas; (5) plan jointly for greater effectiveness of the total higher education offering to the community being served; (6) share the resources of his own institution, as well as
use the resources of the other institutions; and (7) initiate and encourage carefully conceived plans of interinstitutional cooperation.
Without this willingness of institutional administrators to provide
true leadership for the larger task, cooperative efforts are not likely
to succeed.

The following guidelines for establishing interinstitutional arrangements grow out of, and build upon, the principle of administrative leadership just stated:

1. Using appropriate criteria, administrators should determine
which institutions can conceivably benefit from participation in a
proposed cooperative arrangement.

2. Representatives of the institutions and other agencies which
have expressed an interest in the joint undertaking should meet as
soon as possible to consider various areas of cooperation. Inclusive
representation at this meeting is of extreme importance.

3. A record should be kept of expressions of willingness to share
resources on a mutual basis.

4. Plans for initiating a specific cooperative arrangement should
be formulated tentatively and restudied at subsequent meetings of
institutional representatives.

5. Communication lines to all the institutions concerned with
establishing and participating in the program should be continuously open. Intrainstitutional communication is likewise important

and should be encouraged, particularly in the early stages of project development.

6. The roles, responsibilities, and commitments of each of the institutions participating in the undertaking should be clearly and completely indicated.

7. The actual establishment and development of a cooperative arrangement should be followed by a continuing, objective, and complete appraisal of the project in all its aspects.

8. Reports of the progress of the venture, including both its strengths and its weaknesses, should be made periodically to all who are involved in its operation.

Samuel B. Gould has pointed out that scarcely a double handful of colleges are capable of going it alone on their own resources during the next twenty-five years. "We can," says Dr. Gould, "survive and grow in strength by intelligent interaction or many of us will ultimately perish separately as our offerings become steadily more inadequate. I do not say this to be dramatic or sound the voice of doom; I say it because it is the simple truth."

The future holds much promise for improved and expanded interinstitutional programs in higher education. The need and the demand for these programs will in all probability continue to grow. This means that colleges and universities will be breaking more and more with tradition and will be increasingly engaging in new and different collaborative ventures. It means, also, that sufficient time and effort will have to be devoted to program planning, organization, administration, evaluation, and modification, when necessary, to ensure the optimum success of these undertakings.

Coordination of Higher Education in Missouri

ELMER ELLIS

UNTIL RECENTLY the only avenue through which all segments of Missouri higher education had an opportunity to work together was the Higher Education Division of the Missouri State Teachers Association. Perhaps it would be more nearly correct to say "meet together" rather than "work together." This organization did not have a continuous program of activities, but it did sponsor, at the annual convention of the State Teachers Association, one divisional session devoted exclusively to college and university interests. Its only state-wide project in recent years was a Missouri college enrollment projection study in 1956–57.

Early in 1958 the governor of Missouri set up the Governor's Committee on Education Beyond the High School. Total membership of the committee was 36, including 11 public and private college presidents, one public school superintendent, and 24 other professional and business people. The work of the committee covered a three-year period, closing with a report to the governor in November 1960. One of the several recommendations in the report was that a continuing commission on higher education be established and that state financial assistance be provided for the public junior colleges.

In October 1959 the governor established another group which was called the Governor's Council on Higher Education. It was composed entirely of representatives of public higher education—the presidents of the state colleges and universities, the presidents of their governing boards, the state commissioner of education, and the state budget director. The governor enumerated several matters to which the council should give attention, including more effective *coordination* of state-supported higher education. In its report to the governor in December 1960 the council summarized certain researches and accomplishments aimed at better coordination. These studies and agreements had to do with greater uniformity in credits and honor-point systems, greater uniformity in fiscal accounting forms and procedures, greater uniformity in reporting enrollment statistics, and more efficient space utilization.

155

Area Studies and Organizations

In 1957 a report on the metropolitan area of Kansas City resulted from a higher education study sponsored by the Kansas City Association of Trusts and Foundations and conducted by Dr. Dean McHenry, then of the University of California, Los Angeles. In 1959 a St. Louis area study of higher education needs was sponsored by the Committee on Education Beyond the High School. The study, directed by Dr. Edward B. Shils of the University of Pennsylvania, was put into final report form in January 1960. Among the several recommendations was one calling for a state commission on higher education and a similar commission for the St. Louis Metropolitan area.

Following each of these reports, area committees—not confined to Missouri—have been established to coordinate higher education by voluntary means in Missouri's two large urban regions. For the Kansas City area the organization, set up in 1962, is the Kansas City Regional Council on Higher Education. Its membership includes eleven colleges in Missouri and three in Kansas. In March of 1963 the Higher Education Coordinating Council of Metropolitan St. Louis was created.

Early Work of the Councils

The Kansas City and the St. Louis area councils have not been in existence long enough for their full effectiveness to be assessed, but they have fostered a number of valuable projects, such as: the sharing of outstanding speakers, coordinating class listing of evening courses, cooperation in student recruitment and admission, encouragement of research and travel on the part of faculty members, exchange of library materials, coordinated calendar of events, coordination of plans for advanced placement of certain freshmen, and, of course, the more comprehensive exchange of information between institutions.

In April 1962 the University of Missouri sponsored a two-day Missouri Assembly on Higher Education. Twenty-five educators and fifty prominent business and professional people participated, including members of the state legislature. One of the ten statements in the "consensus report" of the assembly was that "Missouri should create a permanent state Commission on higher education . . . to plan and coordinate the future needs of both public and private higher education in Missouri." It also approved state aid for public junior colleges.

The Governor's Council on Higher Education, mentioned earlier, employed three out-of-state educators in 1962 to come to Missouri and make a study of the entire state system of higher education.

These three special consultants were Robert J. Keller of the University of Minnesota, Raymond C. Gibson of Indiana University, and Allan O. Pfnister of the University of Michigan. Their report, submitted in December 1962, contained a dozen or more recommendations, one of which proposed a state council on higher education, such council to be a structure through which to "coordinate purposes, plans, and institutional research for higher education in Missouri."

Two Developments in Coordination

I mention these various organizations, studies, and reports to show that Missouri has had some awareness of its growing needs for expanded and better-coordinated higher education services and has been at work to find solutions. In 1961, state aid for public junior colleges was provided, much as proposed by the Committee on Education Beyond the High School. And in 1963, out of this preliminary work came two developments which we believe will be of considerable value to higher education in Missouri, particularly in respect to more effective coordination among our more than fifty colleges and universities.

The first of these two developments was the enactment of legislation creating the Missouri Commission on Higher Education. According to the language of the act itself, its purpose is "for planning and coordination of higher education in the state." The commission, composed of four educators and six laymen, appointed by the governor, is advisory to the governor, the General Assembly, and the educational institutions themselves. It is not a governing body, but a planning, research, and coordinating agency, whose advice may well become very influential. It reports to the governor and General Assembly prior to each regular legislative session. Its report includes: a plan for the coordination of higher education; a review of institutional enrollments and programs; a review of requests and recommendations the commission has made to the institutions and the responses which the institutions have made to such requests and recommendations; and its recommendations regarding the budget requests of the institutions.

The other development of 1963 was the creation of a new association in which all of the colleges have membership. Formerly we had, in addition to the Higher Education Section of the State Teachers Association (which I mentioned at the beginning of these remarks), an organization for the liberal arts colleges, one for the state teacher education institutions, and one for the junior colleges; we now have *one* organization for *all*. The new one is called the Missouri Association of Colleges and Universities.

While it is too early to make a meaningful evaluation at this time, we believe that with our new Missouri Commission on Higher Education, and with our new Missouri Association of Colleges and Universities, we should be able to direct the structure of higher education in our state so as to make its growth orderly and its services both appropriate and effective in meeting its increasing responsibilities to our state and the nation.

The Pennsylvania Way

MILLARD E. GLADFELTER

IN THE AMERICAN tradition of publicly supported higher education, state and municipal boundaries generally prescribe the geographical area from which local aid is received and within which policy is defined. Accordingly, we find almost as many patterns for support and control as there are states, and the extent of local effort is closely related to the corporate nature of the institutions declared eligible to receive it.

In early New England the influence of the private colleges and universities dominated. Only in recent times have some state universities emerged in that region. The state-owned and state-managed approach had its early roots in Virginia and the Northwest Territory. All the states to the west and south of these areas placed great dependence for higher education on the land-grant institutions—with their northern, western, eastern, or southern state counterparts—or on the multiversity concept which is as distinctively Californian as is her sunshine.

Pennsylvania Institutions and Support

The pattern for public support of higher education in Pennsylvania is a hybrid of all plans. Like New England, New York, and Ohio, the Commonwealth has an unusually large number of degree-granting institutions whose entire support comes from private sources. Of the 95 colleges in Pennsylvania chartered to grant baccalaureate degrees, 32 are state-owned or state-aided:

Independent colleges receiving state aid	6
Independent universities receiving state aid	4
Independent medical and veterinarian schools receiving state aid	7
Land-grant university	1
Publicly owned state colleges	14

The General Assembly approved the following allocations for each group for use during the 1964–65 academic year:

Independent colleges receiving state aid	$ 594,150
Independent universities receiving state aid (exclusive of university-affiliated medical schools—$4,500,000)	13,671,340
Independent medical and veterinarian schools receiving state aid	9,560,909

159

Land-grant university.   24,197,700
Publicly owned state colleges.   19,381,893

This unusual practice has placed a responsibility upon each of the private institutions receiving aid to assess firmly and to accept the educational trust it holds, particularly as it relates to the educational needs of the state, and to pursue with diligence, care, and integrity all sources for financial support in the discharge of that trust. Even so, every commission appointed by governors or legislatures to study higher education in the Commonwealth has detailed the low financial effort at the state level without specifically proposing a plan for its improvement. Two paragraphs from the 1960 report read as follows:

A review of the literature and statistical information relative to the State's role in supporting higher education financially does not present an impressive picture when compared with other states.
It is quite possible that Pennsylvania's unique way of distribution of State monies is often responsible for Pennsylvania's unusually low position. Nevertheless, available statistics show Pennsylvania significantly low in the amount of state aid and local aid going to institutions of higher education.[1]

This discussion will relate principally to procedures followed by the private state-aided universities for the advancement of their interests in the Commonwealth program of higher education. Statutes and school code prescribe the method by which budget, appropriation, and educational policy are determined for the state colleges. For several reasons the Pennsylvania State University follows a procedure which has single application, although meetings are held jointly with the State University and the state-aided universities for discussion of new issues and legislation for which there is common concern.

Voluntary Cooperation of State-Aided Institutions

For thirty years the state-aided universities—the University of Pennsylvania, University of Pittsburgh, and Temple University—have held voluntary conferences for the discussion of pending legislation, their individual purposes, and issues on which joint action is useful.

These meetings are attended by institutional presidents and officers and are held in turn in eastern, central, and western parts of the state. They are convened by the chairman president, an office which rotates every two years. The agenda vary, but never omit

---

[1] *Financing Higher Education in Pennsylvania*, a report prepared by the Bureau of Research, Department of Public Instruction, Harrisburg, for the Task Force Committee on Higher Education Meeting, July 25, 1960.

discussion of any issue considered important by any member. It has been my privilege to attend since the meetings began in the middle '30s, and during this span institutional interdependence has increased with easily recognized benefits to the Commonwealth.

Any list of the results of this voluntary association would include the following:

1. The need for diversity among the institutions has been recognized and diversity in purposes and programs has been encouraged.

2. Mutual confidence in and understanding of the educational purposes of each university in the Commonwealth have been established.

3. When geographically advisable, the undertakings of one institution have been used as examples for others to expand and improve their own offerings in similar or related areas.

4. Each institution, in varying degrees and ways, has been encouraged to direct its attention and resources toward the needs of the Commonwealth.

5. The recognition of strengths in others has encouraged each to develop the areas that had been weak in relation to total institutional strength.

6. A united front and a single voice have been developed in appeals to the governor and the General Assembly, so that each university has been able to interpret its needs to legislative committees, confident of interinstitutional support.

7. The universities have developed a formula which is now the basis used by state budget officers and legislative committees to apportion appropriations.

8. The presidents of the three state-aided universities have twice traveled across the Commonwealth to address joint meetings of their alumni and important citizens on the merits of the Pennsylvania way for support of higher education.

9. This voluntary association has provided a means by which the governor, the legislature, and nongovernmental bodies could easily secure representation on state-wide committees and judgment on critical issues from an important segment of the state's higher educational resources.

Development of a Formula for Apportionment of Funds

Probably the most significant recent accomplishments are represented by statements seven and eight. In 1955, at the request of the governor, the three institutions set about to devise a formula which could be used by state budget officers in the allocation of the total amounts recommended to the General Assembly for appropriation to each of the state-aided universities. The formula, as developed, provides for a merit evaluation that recognizes the quantitative dimensions of the educational job each of the universities is performing and the qualitative factors which distinguish the excellence of one educational program from another. The recognition of a formula as a basis for the apportionment of funds provides not only a reliable yardstick for performance, but also minimizes the likelihood of the universities competing among themselves for legislative favor.

Under the formula, each of the three universities is credited with *(a)* two points for each $1,000 spent on faculty salaries; *(b)* one point for each full-time student or equivalent enrollment of part-time students; *(c)* one point for each full-time graduate student or equivalent; *(d)* one point for each $1,000 of gross tuition income; and *(e)* one and one-half points for each $1,000 spent for libraries and research supported by the university itself. The points earned by each institution are determined and added together. The percentage of the points that each institution has earned against the total points earned by the three institutions is ascertained. This percentage becomes the basis on which the total funds appropriated to the three universities are allocated to each institution.

For three sessions of the General Assembly the relative claim of each institution upon the total legislative grant for the three has not varied more than one percentage point. This practice has indicated to people in government a reasonable basis for cooperation and distribution and set before the institutions weighting factors with particular reference to quality in areas relating to instruction. It also gave recognition to institutional efforts to acquire income beyond the state appropriations.

Adjusting the Formula

After a three-time experience with the 1955 formula, there was a desire to widen its scope and flexibility so that it would easily be applied to the land-grant university and also to the bringing in of Drexel Institute of Technology, which has recently been included among the state-aided institutions. The revised formula rests basically on the belief that, although support of the state colleges is an urgent obligation of the Commonwealth, utmost flexibility and economy in state expenditures can be achieved through an extension to them of the partnership between the Commonwealth and institutions not wholly dependent on the state for their support.

These institutions vary in the scope and emphasis of their programs, in their relationship to the Commonwealth, and in obligations imposed by the state. The formula classified them as *land-grant,* *state-related,* and *state-aided,* and established certain considerations for relating the amount of state subsidy to these classifications. The formula suggests that the subsidy considerations applying to the land-grant institution could also apply to the state colleges.

A second fundamental of the formula is the assumption that the purposes of state support of general maintenance are to aid in improving the quality of higher educational programs, to enable enrollment opportunities—particularly for Pennsylvanians—to be expanded, and to assure that high tuition costs do not deny educational opportunity to able and deserving Pennsylvania students. The revised formula now stands ready for use by the next session of the General Assembly.

Support of Medical Schools

Pennsylvania has another tradition which is fortunate. Each of the medical schools in the Commonwealth receives an annual state appropriation based on student enrollment. For the current year the grant is $3,000 per student. Even though this method has shortcomings, it is a great improvement over the former practice whereby an institutional grant was made to each college on the basis of individual plea and pressure. The medical school deans now meet as a body, agree upon budget requests, and submit their appeal in unison.

"The Forward Look"

To help the Governor and the General Assembly, the presidents of the three state-aided universities—the University of Pennsylvania, University of Pittsburgh, and Temple University—in 1956 and again in 1959 held joint meetings with alumni and friends in ten cities across the state. During the evenings, each of the three university presidents spoke on the "forward look" for higher education in the state and each institution's relationship to it. These meetings accomplished several purposes. They brought to a large and representative audience, directly and through the press, the urgency for increasing support for higher education, the advantages that exist for the taxpayer and the Commonwealth in state financial support for private universities that have physical and endowment resources, and the values that come to the public welfare from grants to complex universities that concentrate on graduate and professional education. In this association with each other, the universities also strengthened their statements of purposes that are in the common good and sharpened their projections for future service.

Whatever disappointments have come in efforts to develop a rationale for subsidy have been well offset by the confidences gained among governmental officials in the facts and figures used to chart our educational futures.

Until the spring of 1964 there was no official state board or agency charged by statute with the responsibility of charting and advancing the Commonwealth's interests in higher education. But at that time the General Assembly established a State Board of Education within which is the State Council of Higher Education. This new body, to which we look hopefully, is the result of our united efforts. We confidently believe that we would not have come to this important day in our state's educational history without the influence of our voluntary association.

Voluntary Cooperation and Coordination of Higher Education in Michigan

JAMES W. MILLER

IN FALL 1963, Michigan's 68 institutions of higher education enrolled approximately 195,000 students. The ten degree-granting, publicly supported colleges and universities, including four branches, enrolled 118,000 (60.5 percent) of this total. Another 39,000 students (20 percent) were enrolled in the 18 publicly supported junior and community colleges. The remaining 38,000 students—19.5 percent of the total college and university enrollment—were in private institutions of higher education, with better than 25 percent of this total enrolled at the University of Detroit.

The six voluntary coordinating organizations existing in Michigan in 1963–64 for some or all of these 68 institutions included the Michigan Council of State College Presidents, the Michigan Coordinating Council for Higher Education, the Michigan Association of Colleges and Universities, the Michigan Association of Catholic Colleges, the Michigan Association of Church-Related Colleges, and the Michigan Association of Junior and Community Colleges. In addition deans, registrars, directors of admissions, field service directors, and other college and university administrators have formed voluntary organizations of their own professional groups, and most recently there has been an active campaign to establish a voluntary interfaculty council among the ten degree-granting public institutions.

Michigan Council of State College Presidents

The oldest of the above organizations was formed in 1950 under the title of the Michigan Council of State College Presidents. It consists of the presidents of the ten degree-granting, publicly supported institutions in the state. In addition to providing opportunity for discussion of joint approaches to the problems facing state-supported colleges and universities, M.C.S.C.P. organized and directed the preparation of a series of studies which were subsequently published by the council in the period 1953–56 and then distributed to state legislators, executive officials, educators, and, to a limited extent, the general public. The series was initiated in 1952 and financed by member institutions of the council through assessments based on each institution's enrollment. The actual research and writing were performed by teams of three to nine faculty members from among the institutions.

From 1950 to 1960 the M.C.S.C.P. operated on the basis of minimal organizational arrangements, with the chairmanship of the council rotating annually and without permanent staff. It became increasingly clear in the late fifties that some form of permanent staff was needed if the council was to pursue a sustained and systematic course of activity leading to a program of cooperation and coordination which would satisfy the member institutions as well as state legislators, executive officials, and the public.

In the academic year 1960–61, the M.C.S.C.P. took a significant step in the direction of preparing itself for effective voluntary cooperation and coordination by establishing and providing adequate financing for four "task force" studies: a study of unit cost reporting, a study of uniform accounting classifications, an investigation of enrollment and instructional load reporting, and a study of plant facilities and space utilization.

In June 1961 appointment of the first full-time executive director for the council, Dr. M. M. Chambers, was announced. In the letter of appointment to Dr. Chambers, the chairman of the M.C.S.C.P. stated:

The Council views the Executive Director as a professional associate having responsibility to give leadership and assistance in their [the Council's] committed purpose of developing an evolving program of voluntary coordination among the public colleges and universities of the state.

It was further stated that the council envisaged among other emphases:

(1) A basic information gathering research analysis activity dealing with essential operating data which . . . will form the bases for many policy judgments of the Council; (2) The direction of studies which deal with the instructional and service development and coordination among the institutions; (3) The development, through analyses, of positional statements of the Council which properly reflect the efforts of the Council in voluntary coordination on precise matters; (4) The analyses and presentation to the Council of apparent problems and suggested approaches on matters of continuing . . . concern in higher education in Michigan; and, (5) Giving leadership and direction to various aspects of interpretation of higher education in Michigan through various programs and contacts agreed to by the Council.

Finally the letter of appointment stated that:

It should also be clear for the record that we are not selecting the Executive Director to be a lobbyist operating at the legislative level, or a "professional drum-beater" for narrow, vested interests of the public colleges and universities.

In late fall 1962, following Dr. Chambers' return to the University of Michigan, Dr. Ira Polley, a former state budget examiner for higher education and for two and one-half years state controller of Michigan, assumed the position of executive director of the council. Dr. Polley has devoted the major portion of his effort and that of his small staff to eliciting from the business and academic officers of member institutions agreements which might fruitfully lead to the presentation of a unified or integrated budget for the degree-granting, state-supported colleges and universities in Michigan. The central office of the council has at hand information concerning Michigan's large, complex, and diverse enterprise of state-supported higher education in well-organized form and understandable language, available not only to state legislators and executive officials but also to other interested persons and organizations. Dr. Polley is frequently called on by legislators, the governor's office, citizens' committees, and business organizations in Michigan to present the over-all needs of state-supported higher education in Michigan.

It seems fair to say that the M.C.S.C.P. has served its member institutions well as a forum within which to discuss openly and frankly problems and issues of concern to more than a single institution.

The council, through a series of publications, initiated, directed, and distributed under its auspices, has brought a considerable amount of information concerning higher education to the attention of both public officials and interested lay citizenry. Important, too, is the fact that each of the council's publications has brought together significant numbers of the professional staffs of the member institutions. The regular meetings of the business and academic officers over the past two years have not only made each member institution better acquainted with the academic programs and the accounting procedures of the other member institutions, but have also produced classifications for cost accounting which now have a very high degree of comparability. It should be noted that, on an issue which is most difficult for institutions of higher education—particularly state-supported colleges and universities—to handle adequately by themselves, M.C.S.C.P initiated the preparation of a common policy in regard to outside speakers which was subsequently approved by the Coordinating Council for Higher Education.

The role of M.C.S.C.P. hopefully will evolve in the direction of adding to the activities mentioned above a determined effort to present the member institutions' budgetary needs in a single unified budget which will, in substance and in form, be easily understood by each and fully and enthusiastically supported *in toto*. If this role cannot be performed, it will not be because we are lacking in the know-how or the techniques of developing reasonably comparable data for our budget requests, but rather because we are lacking in the will to pursue our fiscal needs jointly rather than individually. The heart of a successful program of voluntary coordination, in my opinion, is the willingness of each of the members to have new programs and significant expansions of existing programs subjected to the scrutiny of all institutions to the end that whatever is included in the final unified budget will be supported equally and vigorously by all institutions.

The council, meeting on June 12, 1964, directed the development of a unified budget on an experimental basis for fiscal 1965–66. In the judgment of the council members, this problem is now of manageable proportions and, although procedures in the development of unified budgets will need to be refined in subsequent years, there is no time like the present to develop the basic concept.

The Michigan Coordinating Council for Public Higher Education

The Michigan Coordinating Council for Public Higher Education is an outgrowth of a meeting held on January 22, 1961, by members of the Michigan Association of Governing Boards. The Coordinating Council was officially launched on February 12, 1961. Its first chairman, Eugene Power, regent of the University of Michigan, said the purpose of the organization was to form a "single educational district" of Michigan in the field of higher education. The constitution of the Coordinating Council establishes membership on the basis of a delegate from each of the ten governing boards of the degree-granting, state-supported colleges and universities, the ten presidents of such institutions, the state superintendent of public instruction, and two delegates from the community and junior colleges. According to its constitution, the Coordinating Council has as one of its main purposes the dissemination of "information regarding financing and operation of public higher education, with advice and recommendations thereon, to the people and to the appropriate governmental authorities." As one of the trustees said to the press following the organizational meeting, the Coordinating Council is an outgrowth of the "need to forego the individual institution approach" to educational problems.

The Coordinating Council, which was originally set up to meet four times a year, has actually been meeting each time that M.C.S.C.P. meets, and uses the Executive Director of M.C.S.C.P. as its secretary. No specific budget has been established for the Coordinating Council other than to have its financial needs met from the budget established by the M.C.S.C.P. To date, the Coordinating Council has organized and directed a task force of medical authorities and professional consultants throughout the nation to study and make recommendations relative to Michigan's need for a third medical school and make recommendations on a possible location.

The Coordinating Council has organized special presentations to legislators and to the governor relative to the needs of all higher education in Michigan. In addition to the oral presentations, there was prepared for the Governor's Citizens Committee on Higher Education a special publication entitled *Remember the War Babies.* Over 30,000 copies of this publication were distributed, beginning in September 1963, and the content of the publication was presented orally, accompanied by slides, to many thousands of community leaders throughout Michigan.

When the Governor's Citizens Committee on Higher Education presented a summary of its recommendations to cover the minimal needs of publicly supported higher education in Michigan, both in the areas of operation and capital outlay, it was the Michigan Coordinating Council for Higher Education which directed that copies of the Citizens Committee's report be mailed to the 260,000 alumni of Michigan's ten publicly supported colleges and universities. This report, incidentally, called for an increase in appropriations for operating funds of no less than $25 million for the year 1964–65. In addition, the report called for the expenditure of at least $48 million for new construction each year for the next several years.

The Coordinating Council has the advantage of involving individual board members in its deliberations and decisions. In Michigan the members of the governing boards of our three largest universities are elected at large. These board members are extremely conscious of the need to bring to their respective publics a better understanding and appreciation of the finances and academic programs of the state-supported institutions of higher education. It may be that the Coordinating Council will expedite the adoption of the concept of the integrated or unified budget.

Michigan Association of Colleges and Universities

For some years there has been a Michigan Council of College and University Presidents consisting of the state college presidents, the presidents of church-related colleges, and presidents or deans of the community or junior colleges. In the past this council has met at an annual dinner for a program of speeches.

It was felt that there was a need for a vigorous organization, and one was formally organized recently as a nonprofit, unincorporated educational association to be known as the Michigan Association of Colleges and Universities. The purposes of the M.A.C.U. are the promotion of educational advancement and efficiency of member institutions and the utilization of every opportunity for such institutions to act and serve their mutual interests in concert. The new constitution further provides that, in the pursuit of these objectives, the M.A.C.U. shall: hold conferences of representatives of the teaching faculty and administrative staff of the member institutions; make studies of educational and administrative problems; serve as a clearinghouse for the exchange of information; promote projects of educational experimentation; and provide a common and clear voice for the institutions of higher education in the State of Michigan. It may also undertake, by common agreement, cooperative programs in teaching, research, publishing, educational evaluation, college finance, and administration, the promotion of student extracurricular activities, and the fostering of lectures, concerts, and exhibits. And it may provide the vehicle for undertaking related items and programs compatible with the spirit and purposes of the organization.

The M.A.C.U. will be financed by contributions from the institutions accepting membership on the basis of an annual assessment not to exceed five cents per full-time-equivalent student. It is much too early to say what may be accomplished in the way of voluntary cooperation and coordination by M.A.C.U., but there is no denying that it is the one voluntary organization in Michigan which currently encompasses all institutions of higher education, both private and public, both degree-granting and terminal degree institutions.

Conclusions

Voluntary cooperation and coordination of educational institutions in Michigan is in a period of evolution which may be affected by any number of circumstances peculiar to this state. Michigan adopted a new constitution in the spring of 1963, the provisions of which became effective on January 1, 1964. The newly created State Board of Education (consisting of eight members nominated by party conventions and elected at large for staggered terms of eight years) came into being on January 1, 1965. One provision states that this board "shall serve as the general planning and coordinating body for all public education, including higher education, and shall advise the Legislature as to the financial requirements in connection therewith."

It is interesting to note that the new constitution provides for the establishment by the Legislature of a state board for public community and junior colleges to advise the State Board of Education concerning the general supervision and planning of such colleges and requests for annual appropriations for their support. This board, too, will consist of eight members serving staggered terms of eight years and will be appointed by the State Board of Education. It is clear that the members of the Constitutional Convention who drew up these provisions in the new constitution were anxious to establish a central coordinating body for higher education in Michigan. They, the general public, and Michigan's public state officials were acutely aware of the statement by John Dale Russell in his final report in 1958 of *The Survey of Higher Education in Michigan* to the effect that ". . . little or nothing has been done to coordinate the total program of publicly controlled and privately controlled higher education in Michigan." [1]

All the publicly supported, degree-granting institutions are now granted the constitutional status enjoyed by the University of Michigan for more than a century. The need for voluntary organization appears to be no less now than in the past because, even with vigorous action by the State Board in the areas of general planning and coordination, the question of whether the ten publicly supported colleges and universities submit their budget requests individually or jointly is vital. Whether all institutions of public higher education in Michigan will act in concert, in special groupings, or individually is still moot.

Michigan desperately needs sustained, systematic, objective, and critical analysis of how its 68 institutions of higher education can best serve the youth of Michigan who want, need, and are qualified for a formal education in these institutions. Henry Adams once pointed out that the mark of an educated man is to react sensitively to those lines of force that most dominate the age in which he lives. Surely the mark of any successful organization in the area of higher education is not different, and if our institutions are to survive in the decade ahead we must react to those lines of force which will most dominate this age.

As we go about our task of serving these demands, planning our programs of research and extension, and attempting to cultivate in our students a desire to shape beneficially the democratic enterprise in whatever field they may enter, we must have far greater public support than we currently enjoy. To get this support, it is imperative that we organize our efforts in such a manner as to establish confidence that we are making all reasonable effort to pursue our individual goals, while we remain acutely mindful of what our sister institutions are doing and explore all avenues of possibilities for doing certain things together better than we can do them individually. Finally, we need to convince our several publics that we are definitely committed to maximizing the contributions our dollar support can make in serving society through the preparation of young people for competent and cultivated citizenship, capable of responding to those forces which dominate this, the twentieth, century.

[1] John Dale Russell, *The Survey of Higher Education in Michigan*, Final Report, 1958, p. 110.

5

Interinstitutional and Interstate Agreements

Interstate Cooperation and Coordination in Higher Education

ROBERT H. KROEPSCH

M. STEPHEN KAPLAN

WHAT IN the West is WICHE? The typical Westerner may never have heard of it. Nor, perhaps, has the typical Southerner heard of the SREB—nor the typical New Englander of NEBHE!

Yet, in the past decade, these three public interstate compact agencies have become well known to governors, key legislators, state officials, and college and university administrators—as well as to leaders in medicine, dentistry, nursing, mental health, juvenile delinquency programs, special education, public administration, and other specialized fields. Through regional cooperation these three organizations help states and institutions pool their resources to solve certain problems in higher education.

This statement describes their birth and evolution, legal mandate, organization, and financing, and gives examples of their programs—and the issues they raise—so that others may become cognizant of their functions and contributions in advancing the cause of higher education in their member states.

Forerunners of Regional Compacts

Despite the tradition of autonomy and imperialism of colleges and universities, interinstitutional cooperation has long been evident in higher education. A trend toward voluntary collective action began to appear in the late 1920's, and by the mid-1930's, 230 institutions are reported to have been involved in 115 cooperative arrangements to reduce unnecessary duplication of facilities and services and to extend and improve instruction. The pressures prompting these arrangements included the depression and the growing criticism of overzealous competition, needless duplication, and excessive institutionalism.

Interstate agreements to share educational resources came into being prior to the establishment of formal educational compacts. One of the earliest plans was developed in 1943 by Virginia and West Virginia. Since West Virginia had only a two-year basic medical science school, it contracted with Virginia to provide places for fifteen to twenty students a year in the Medical College of Virginia. Under this plan, the students were charged resident tuition, and West Virginia paid $1,000 in addition for each student to help defray the cost of his education. The Virginia–West Virginia precedent was later adopted to meet the needs of the Southeast for veterinary education, when in 1948 Alabama Polytechnic Institute (now Auburn University) made its veterinary school facilities available to other Southern states on a contract basis.

In the West the first interstate agreement for sharing educational facilities was developed in 1949 between the University of Colorado and the states of New Mexico and Wyoming. Through this arrangement the University of Colorado agreed to reserve places in the School of Medicine for New Mexico and Wyoming students at instate tuition rates, for which the sending states would help defray the cost of education by paying a fee of $2,000 for each student.

Evolution of Interstate Compacts

The compact device was so well established in the early days of the Republic that the Founding Fathers provided for the formation of compacts in both the Articles of Confederation and the Constitution. According to the Constitution, congressional consent to interstate compacts is required. However, because the compact clause fails to spell out how consent is to be given, or under what conditions it is necessary, it has been the topic of much congressional debate and a number of court cases. In general, Congress has given consent to compacts by act or joint resolution. The Supreme Court has ruled that in some cases consent can be given by implication, and that only certain types of compacts—those which affect a power delegated to the national government or which affect the "political balance" of the Federal system—need congressional consent.

Before the twentieth century, compacts were used infrequently and for limited purposes such as settling boundary disputes between states. Since 1900, the use of interstate compacts has broadened to include such diverse areas as the allocation, conservation, and pollution of water; management and development of ports and harbors; regional cooperation in higher education; and others. Nearly half of the more than one hundred compacts concluded since the turn of the century provide for interstate agencies and staffs.

Birth of Interstate Compacts in Higher Education

The forces that produced interstate cooperation in higher education in the South, West, and New England arose from post-World War II crises that placed tremendous demands on the states to supply graduate, professional, and technical manpower and to provide greater educational opportunity for an unprecedented influx of college students. All institutions, throughout the nation, faced serious shortages of facilities, staffs, and funds for operating expenses. At the same time, mounting demands on state budgets for a variety of needed public services left a critical shortage of public funds to devote to institutions of higher education, whose costs were rising each year at a dizzying rate. However, the Southern, Western, and New England regions faced particularly acute problems in developing adequate, let alone high-quality, public higher education. And in each region unique ecological, economic, and educational factors affected the nature of the problems. It was in this atmosphere that the three regional higher education compacts were created. The interstate cooperation they represent offered—and still offers—these regions a means of increasing both the quality and the quantity of educational opportunities for their citizens.

SOUTHERN REGIONAL EDUCATION BOARD (SREB)

SREB, the oldest and largest of the educational compacts, was established in 1948. It arose out of a complex set of forces operating in the South in the postwar years. A strong tradition of regionalism and interinstitutional cooperation, acutely felt needs to upgrade the educational and economic level of the region, serious shortages of trained manpower, and the race issue—all contributed to the creation of the Southern Regional Education Compact.

Southern educators had discussed over a period of years the need to improve higher education in the region and the possibility of building centers of strength. In the immediate postwar period the problem of quantitative inadequacy occupied much of the educational discussions of the Southern Governors' Conference. The idea of a regional compact was first formally discussed at the 1945 and 1946 meetings of the governors. The serious financial plight of Meharry College in Nashville, Tennessee, which had produced one-half of the nation's Negro graduates in medicine and dentistry, was called to the attention of the Southern governors in 1947, and it was proposed that the medical, dental, and nursing programs at Meharry College become the first object of interstate cooperation in higher education.

In 1948, at a special meeting, the Southern governors decided to enter into an interstate compact designed primarily to establish, support, and operate regional educational institutions on a joint basis. Nine governors signed the agreement with the provision that it would become effective when ratified by the legislatures of at least six states. A director was appointed, and a regional office was established in Atlanta, Georgia.

An original emphasis on the acquisition and operation of regional institutions was soon abandoned, and the bylaws adopted in 1949 make no reference to operating regional institutions. Instead, a council of governors and educators developed an interstate student exchange program in veterinary medicine and established a committee on medical and related training to study other possible contract arrangements. Shortly after, it formally urged the establishment of contract programs in medicine, dentistry, and veterinary medicine.

On June 11, 1949, the Southern Regional Education Compact became operative, with ten states as members. All sixteen Southern states have joined. They include: Alabama, Arkansas, Delaware, Florida, Georgia, Kentucky, Louisiana, Maryland, Mississippi, North Carolina, Oklahoma, South Carolina, Tennessee, Texas, Virginia, and West Virginia.

WESTERN INTERSTATE COMMISSION FOR HIGHER EDUCATION (WICHE)

WICHE, the second largest and oldest of the regional education agencies, was in large part the creation of Western governors in cooperation with leading educators and physicians in the region. The Western states faced the same postwar dilemma confronting Southern and Northeastern states: growing demands for trained manpower and greater educational opportunities for youth, but insufficient financial and educational resources in some states to meet these needs. To help resolve this dilemma, the political and educational leadership of the Western states turned to the still-novel device of interstate cooperation in higher education.

Although needs were apparent in many areas, shortages were particularly acute in the health sciences. For example, with only eight four-year medical schools in the Western region, states without these facilities were experiencing difficulty in attracting needed physicians and other health science professionals and in providing medical education for their youth. At the same time the have-not states lacked the financial resources, the number of potential medical students, and the clinical resources to justify the heavy expense of building and operating medical schools. Similar dilemmas prevailed in dentistry and veterinary medicine.

In 1948, the manpower crisis in the health sciences was the main topic of a Governors' Conference on Education for the Health Services. As a result of the meeting, the governors of New Mexico, Utah, Colorado, and Wyoming appointed a regional committee, comprised of three representatives from each state, to study the feasibility of providing educational facilities on a regional basis in medicine, dentistry, and veterinary medicine.

Meanwhile, as noted above, the University of Colorado School of Medicine consented to admit to its 1949–50 freshman class, on a cost basis, five students each from Wyoming and New Mexico. A few months later, the Wyoming legislature authorized the University of Wyoming to contract with out-of-state schools for the training of Wyoming students in health science fields, and appropriated funds for grants-in-aid to the medical students already enrolled at the University of Colorado.

In 1949, the Western Governors' Conference unanimously endorsed the principle of close interstate cooperation in higher education, and appointed appropriate committees. A plan for interstate cooperation was formulated, and a compact, closely patterned after the Southern Regional Education Compact, was drafted. Both were submitted to the Western Governors' Conference in 1950 and, with minor changes, adopted unanimously.

In 1951, the Western Regional Higher Education Compact became effective, following ratification by the legislatures of five states (Colorado, Montana, New Mexico, Oregon, and Utah). In 1953, the commission established its first office in Eugene, Oregon, and appointed a director. Also in 1953, Arizona, Idaho, and Wyoming became members, and the compact was approved by Congress and signed by President Eisenhower. By 1955, Alaska, California, and Washington had joined. In that year, the headquarters was moved to Boulder, Colorado. The full complement of thirteen Western states was reached in 1959 when Hawaii and Nevada joined.

NEW ENGLAND BOARD OF HIGHER EDUCATION (NEBHE)

The New England Board of Higher Education, operating under a compact ratified by the six New England states, was created in response to postwar conditions similar to those in the South and West, with one radical difference. Higher education in the region was dominated by privately controlled colleges and universities, many with restricted enrollments and national orientations. In comparison with facilities in other parts of the country, public higher education was underdeveloped. Prior to World War II, the region had no state university comparable to the comprehensive state universities of the Midwest and elsewhere; in professional and graduate education, there were no public dental or veterinary schools, only one public medical school, and only embryonic doctoral-level graduate programs in other fields. After the war, the situation began to improve as state universities were strengthened and professional and graduate programs established. But the shortage of facilities for the health sciences remained critical, and neither the public nor the private institutions were prepared to meet the tremendous needs imposed by the postwar enrollment boom.

In the late forties and early fifties, New England state officials and educators began to consider interstate cooperation as a way of meeting the region's pressing educational needs. State university presidents first discussed the idea at their 1947 meeting, and shortly thereafter the New England Association of Colleges and Secondary Schools created an *ad hoc* committee on regional education.

A first formal attempt was made in 1951 to establish broad interstate cooperation in several areas of state responsibility, but it was unsuccessful. The second formal effort was restricted to higher education. In 1953, the legislatures of New Hampshire, Maine, and Vermont passed legislation enabling the state universities to contract with other institutions to provide educational programs they themselves did not offer. Only two contracts, both between New Hampshire and Vermont, resulted—one in medicine and the other in vocational education. The final impetus for the establishment of the New England Education Compact came from Massachusetts. In reaction to growing pressure to establish a public medical-dental school, the Massachusetts legislature appointed a study commission, perhaps as a means of deferring immediate legislative action. Out of studies and regional conferences sponsored by the commission came model legislation which proposed a compact establishing the New England Board of Higher Education. Massachusetts adopted the compact in 1954.

After receiving congressional approval in 1955, the compact was ratified in the same year by Connecticut, Maine, New Hampshire, and Vermont. A director was appointed, and a headquarters was established in Winchester, Massachusetts, in 1956. Rhode Island joined in 1957.

The Legal Mandate

Legal mandate for the activities of the regional education agencies is found in the interstate compacts ratified by the member states, their bylaws, and in the program decisions made by their respective boards or commissions. The compacts and bylaws constitute what might be called the fundamental law of regional education, while commission or board decisions form the common law of interstate cooperation in education. Although the analogy between Anglo-American common law and the law of interstate compacts is not exact, it illustrates the evolutionary character of modifications in the meaning of the broadly stated provisions of the compacts.

The charters of all three agencies are similar. Each agency is charged with two primary functions: (1) fact-finding and research into the needs and problems of higher education within the region, and (2) developing and administering interstate or interinstitutional arrangements to provide adequate facilities and services for graduate, professional, and technical education. By implication, each agency is also charged with searching for new methods of interinstitutional and interstate cooperation in higher education in order to improve the quality and quantity of educational opportunities for the youth of the region.

Legally, politically, and financially, the interstate agencies are creatures of the compacting states. They were authorized by the legislatures of the member states; they receive their basic financial support from the states; and they must depend upon the states for their continued existence. Moreover, none of the agencies has any authority or control over the educational policy of individual states or institutions. No legal coercions or sanctions are available to enforce their views. As regional agency officials have often stated, their only compulsion is the compulsion of facts. Lacking coercive power, they must work by building consensus among affected groups, using persuasion to secure agreement among states and institutions on mutually advantageous projects.

Contrary to popular belief, individual colleges and universities are not themselves members; however, without the continued interest, support, and cooperation of the academic community, the efforts of the regional agencies would be completely ineffectual.

Although the three compacts are basically similar, differences in legal authorization do exist. For example, both the Southern and New England compacts specify that the agencies operating under them shall provide consultative services to states and institutions on the improvement of higher education. The Western compact lacks such a provision, although WICHE is called upon to draft and recommend to the governors uniform legislation dealing with problems of higher education in the region. All three agencies have, in fact, provided consultation, upon request, to state and university officials on such subjects as state-wide coordination, medical education, and the location of, and planning for, new institutions of higher education.

The provisions and bylaws of the compacts are framed in language that permits a variety of interpretations. In this respect, they resemble the United States and state constitutions and, like them, must be interpreted anew as new problems, needs, or demands arise. The task of interpretation falls to the board or commission governing each compact agency. As the agency is called upon by staff, board members, or constituents to perform new functions or enter into novel programs, the governing board must decide, case by case, whether the proposal conforms to the purposes and objectives of the agency.

Legal authorization is, of course, only one of the factors entering into board decisions, but is an important one. Given the broad statement of purpose in the compacts, the question whether a particular program does or does not conform to the spirit of the compact often becomes a point of controversy. Some feel that the regional agencies have exceeded the charter provisions in their activities. Others examining the same set of facts feel that the programs in question are authorized by the compacts, which must be viewed in the light of changing needs and problems. In the case of concrete programs, the debate between these two views—and shadings in between—is eventually settled by the decisions of the board, which tend to become precedents for future decisions, but not, however, irreversible precedents, given the changing composition of the boards over the years.

Administrative Patterns

In each compact agency, major responsibility for policy making is vested in a board or commission consisting of representatives of the member states. The composition of this body varies from agency to agency, but in each case the major constituents of regional education —state government, higher education, and the general public—are usually represented.

ORGANIZATIONAL STRUCTURE

The Southern compact specifies that board membership shall consist of the governor of each member state and four other persons appointed by him, at least one of whom must be a state legislator and one an educator. SREB is the only regional agency that has governors as ex officio members; it is also the only agency whose charter requires appointment of at least one legislator from each state. Board membership numbers eighty.

Under the terms of the Western compact, the Western Interstate Commission consists of three representatives from each of the member states, appointed by the governors. This compact specifies that at least one of the commissioners from each state be an educator engaged in the field of higher education. In many cases, the presidents of the state universities have been appointed as commissioners, but this is not a uniform practice. Commission membership numbers thirty-nine.

The New England compact specifies that the board shall consist of three members from each compact state, chosen in the manner and for the terms provided by law of each state joining the compact. In practice, the governors appoint the members of the board, but in several states the president of the state university is an ex officio member. Board membership numbers eighteen.

All three of the regional agencies have administrative staffs, headquartered in one of the member states. Because of the varied programs of the agencies, staff members are either administrative generalists, with specialized training or experience in one or more fields, or they are qualified specialists in selected program areas such as nursing, medicine, psychiatry, clinical psychology, and others. Advisory groups and councils aid in planning programs, obtaining vital information, providing grass-roots support, and implementing programs. For example, the most recent SREB annual report listed thirteen such groups totaling more than seventy individuals.

FINANCIAL SUPPORT

The basic administrative costs of the agencies are met by appropriations from the member states. In addition, all receive grants from private foundations and public agencies to finance projects in specialized areas. They also serve as fiscal agents for interinstitutional and interstate contracts and other cooperative arrangements involving the exchange of students and the transfer of funds across state lines.

SREB's basic support comes from the sixteen member states, each of which currently appropriates $25,000. SREB receives an additional $8,000 per year from each state that participates in its regional mental health program. Since SREB began operations fifteen years ago, it has brought into the region over $3 million from private foundations and public agencies for the support of cooperative projects.

WICHE's basic support comes from state appropriations from the thirteen Western states. As of 1963, the amount was increased from $10,000 to $15,000 per state. The Western states do not provide separate appropriations for a mental health program, as is done in the South. During the past ten years, WICHE has received more than $3 million from sources outside the region for programs in specialized areas.

Unlike SREB and WICHE, the New England compact does not provide for equal appropriations from each of the member states; instead, the annual budget, as set by the board, is apportioned among the six states according to their population. Moreover, the board may adopt a different financial formula if it chooses. In 1963, the total amount appropriated by the member states was $81,500, of which Massachusetts paid the greatest share. NEBHE, like the other compact agencies, has many regional programs financed in whole or in part by funds from nonstate sources.

During the current year more than $2.5 million flowed across state lines in the three regions to help support instruction for nearly sixteen hundred students in highly specialized professional programs in forty public and private colleges and universities. This is one of the most dramatic manifestations of interstate cooperation in higher education.

Program Activities

Because kindred problems and needs exist in all three regions, the programs bear marked similarities. Significant differences do appear, of course, since each agency operates within a distinctive environment and must react to a different set of needs, demands, and conditions. In general, the programs can be summarized under the following headings: Interstate Contracts; Regional Common Market Programs; Needs and Resources Studies; Higher Education Planning and Research; In-Service Training and Continuation Education Programs; Curriculum Development Projects; Promotion of Inter-institutional Cooperation; and Public Information.

INTERSTATE CONTRACTS

All three agencies administer interstate agreements through which member states share high-cost professional school facilities, particularly in the health sciences. Although administrative and fiscal details vary, the arrangements are similar in purpose and design. A member state which does not offer a certain type of professional program in its public institutions may purchase places in public or private institutions in other states. The sending state provides funds to reimburse the receiving institution for part of the cost of education for each student, and the institution in turn enrolls the student on a resident basis, waiving out-of-state tuition or, in the case of private schools, charging a reduced fee. In this way, students so registered secure professional education for considerably less than they would pay as ordinary out-of-state students, and the sending states fulfill part of their responsibility for educating their citizens, but at a cost much lower than would be required to build and maintain their own professional schools.

The most extensive of the contract programs is operated by the SREB. In 1963, more than one thousand students from fifteen states attended twenty-four regional institutions to study medicine, dentistry, veterinary medicine, public health, social work, and special education. SREB disbursed $1,539,923 from the states under this program. Since 1949, more than $15 million has been channeled by SREB to institutions in the region.

SREB also administers student aid contracts, through which Southern states send students to schools in other states and defray part of the students' costs. Student aid contracts are in operation in actuarial science, architecture, forestry, and library science.

More than 600 physicians, dentists, and veterinarians have been prepared under WICHE's student exchange program, which began in 1953. In that year five states sent a total of forty-one students to professional schools in other Western states; in 1963, eleven states sent nearly five hundred students under the program. During the past decade, total state appropriations for the program have risen from $70,000 to over $800,000 annually.

Under the medical contract plan conducted by NEBHE, four New England states (Rhode Island, Maine, New Hampshire, and Massachusetts) send students to the University of Vermont College of Medicine. Initiated in 1960, this plan has provided medical school places for approximately one hundred students from the four contracting states, at $2,500 each.

NEBHE also serves as fiscal agent for a contractual agreement in industrial arts between Vermont and New Hampshire, under which prospective teachers of industrial arts from Vermont enroll at Keene State College in New Hampshire.

REGIONAL COMMON MARKET PROGRAMS

NEBHE and WICHE conduct regional student programs which provide that participating public institutions open specialized professional curricula to regional students on a preferential-admission and resident-tuition basis. Unlike the contract programs, these plans do not involve exchange of funds. A wide variety of curricula are offered, including forestry, hydrology, journalism, nursing, electronics, astronomy, and pharmacy. This type of regional cooperation, pioneered by NEBHE, expands the number and variety of educational opportunities available to students, promotes more efficient utilization of existing educational resources, reduces expensive duplication of specialized facilities and staffs, and increases the supply of highly specialized manpower. More than three hundred students are enrolled under the NEBHE plan. The WICHE plan—the Western Regional Student Program (WRSP)—became operative in 1964-65.

NEEDS AND RESOURCES STUDIES

All three agencies are called upon periodically to study the manpower needs and resources in shortage areas critical to the development of their respective regions. For example, WICHE and SREB have conducted surveys in medicine, nursing, dentistry, special education, and mental health. In addition, each of the agencies has surveyed other shortage fields—at the request of governors' conferences, professional associations, and other groups. For example, WICHE recently completed a regionwide study of manpower needs and resources in juvenile corrections; SREB has made studies of such fields as architecture, city planning, forestry, and social work; and NEBHE has examined the field of agricultural education.

These studies typically ask the following questions: What is the need of the region and of individual states for trained personnel? What is the supply and demand? What training programs exist within the region? What is the student demand? What are the gaps between needs and programs? And (in some cases) how and where should needed programs be developed?

Following such regional manpower surveys, institutions have established new facilities, made arrangements for sharing existing facilities, and, in a few instances, changed their plans so as to avoid unnecessary and wasteful duplication. It is sometimes difficult to identify the links between regional needs-resources studies and changes and adjustments in institutional programing. However, the studies appear to serve a catalytic function: they define and analyze the dimensions of manpower problems, point out their urgency and the consequences of inaction, and suggest the requirements and possibilities for constructive solutions.

RESEARCH, PLANNING, AND CONSULTATION

As noted above, two of the regional agencies provide, as part of their mission, consultative services to the states and their institutions, and the third agency has, in fact, also provided such services. In this capacity, they are called upon to help the compact states and the institutions solve problems associated with expanding and improving higher education—the nation's leading "growth" industry. To this task the regional associations bring unique resources and competencies—extensive communication links with both public and private sectors of higher education, national education associations, and the Federal and state governments, coupled with their own regional perspectives.

Improvement of current operations and the making of plans for the future require that colleges and universities know more about themselves, about their educational objectives, the characteristics of their faculties and student bodies, and the extent to which their programs do or do not achieve stated goals. In short, they need to study themselves with as much vigor and ingenuity as they display in studying the universe and the world around them. The regional agencies have been positive forces in encouraging such studies. WICHE initiated its efforts with a regionwide survey of the status of institutional research or college self-study in 1959. It has since cosponsored annual institutes on college self-study, which have dealt with research on college students, college faculty, campus cultures, academic administration, and long-range planning. Hundreds of college administrators and faculty members have enrolled in these workshops, and other interested persons throughout the region and nation have shared in the contributions of the workshops through institute proceedings and other publications. SREB and NEBHE also hold similar annual institutes on college self-study.

For use in planning and research, the compact agencies, as clearinghouses of information, collect and distribute comparable data on the states and institutions within their regions. All three publish fact books on regional population, current and projected college enrollments, institutions of higher education, migration of students, tuition and fees, and the like.

The states and higher education officials within the states, in carrying forward long-range planning, have increasingly called upon the agency staffs for consultation on state-wide surveys of higher education, development and location of new institutions and expansion of existing institutions, planning of medical education facilities, development of educational television, and mental health planning. NEBHE has, in addition, assisted a number of small New England colleges with management problems by obtaining foundation funds for the services of consultants.

In the areas of state-wide and institutional planning and administration, the agencies have offered research studies and regional seminars and conferences. SREB and NEBHE have sponsored regional projects on the college teacher shortage. SREB's research unit has sponsored a series of studies on faculty recruitment, preparation, in-service development, and utilization. Most of these were conducted by researchers in Southern colleges and universities under SREB study fellowships. NEBHE has undertaken similar studies, and has also held regional seminars and conferences on increasing the supply of qualified faculty members. Other topics of studies conducted or sponsored by the agencies include: Guidelines for State-wide Coordination and Planning Agencies (SREB); Guidelines for the Establishment of Community Colleges (SREB); Why Educational Costs Are Rising (WICHE); and Yardsticks and Formulas in University Budgeting (WICHE).

IN-SERVICE TRAINING AND CONTINUATION EDUCATION

Surveys conducted by the regional agencies have uniformly revealed gross deficiencies in the supply of trained manpower, particularly in the health and welfare fields. Even with the increased efforts being made to recruit young people into these shortage areas, serious supply-demand gaps are likely to continue. To assure high-quality public services, despite shortages, the regional agencies have undertaken experimental in-service training and continuation education programs for professionals already on the job.

Both WICHE and SREB sponsor in-service training and continuing education programs for personnel employed by institutions for the mentally ill and mentally retarded. Regional training sessions—called "visitations"—bring selected groups of mental institution personnel to "innovating" rehabilitation centers to observe their programs, administrative organization, and research facilities.

For the past four years, WICHE's nursing council has provided short-term courses at eight universities in the West for full-time nurses desiring new skills and knowledge. Staffed by experts from nursing and allied disciplines, these programs have given training to more than eight hundred nurses whose jobs or personal obligations make formal academic study impractical or impossible. Similar training programs in nursing are sponsored by NEBHE and SREB.

Continuation education programs are currently being conducted by one or more of the regional agencies for personnel working in the fields of juvenile corrections, mental health, public school administration, and adult education. Through WICHE's efforts, evening courses in psychiatry are made available to physicians who practice in areas remote from mental health training facilities. In addition, it sponsors a summer work-study program in half a dozen states for students interested in careers in mental health. NEBHE has been a leader in developing a regional program for improving education of school administrators.

CURRICULUM DEVELOPMENT

Even though higher education is called upon to provide an ever widening range of specialized manpower, university curriculum and field agencies have often failed to keep abreast of research advances. Moreover, the traditional organizational structures of some colleges hinder the development of programs requiring interdisciplinary and interdepartmental perspectives and collaboration. To meet these problems, the regional agencies have pioneered in programs of interinstitutional planning of new curricula and educational programs.

WICHE's nursing council, for example, is attempting, by means of seminars of nursing educators, to improve nursing curricula and education at all levels in the light of new knowledge and needs. Representatives from sixty-two Western colleges and universities are participating.

SREB, by pooling the resources of groups of colleges and universities, is advancing curriculum development and new knowledge in statistics, forestry, plant virology, nematology, and many other areas.

PROMOTION OF INTERINSTITUTIONAL COOPERATION

Most of the programs of the regional agencies are designed to encourage interinstitutional, as well as interstate, cooperation. The best example of formal interinstitutional cooperation under compact auspices is represented by SREB's memoranda of agreement, by means of which institutions carry out a joint effort in a specific field. Examples include recruitment of students, joint curriculum or research planning, and summer graduate institutes. Projects carried on under the terms of an agreement are guided by a regional committee, composed of representatives of each institution and of SREB. WICHE and NEBHE do not employ formal agreements, but rely on informal cooperative arrangements among institutions.

Both SREB and WICHE have encouraged the establishment of other regional agencies, and have assisted in their birth and development. SREB was instrumental in the creation of the Southern Interstate Nuclear Board, which now has its own compact. WICHE helped to create the Association of Rocky Mountain Universities

(ARMU), which is seeking to coordinate the scientific education and research activities of universities in the Rocky Mountain states. WICHE was also responsible for establishment of the Western Association of Graduate Schools and served as its secretariat during its early years.

PUBLIC INFORMATION PROGRAMS

Higher education, especially its public sector, depends heavily on the understanding and support of the public, and particularly of its elected representatives and influential community leaders. For this reason, the regional agencies engage in a wide variety of activities designed to clarify public understanding of major issues in higher education and to improve communication among educational and political leaders.

The public information programs employ a number of media and techniques. The most comprehensive program, conducted by SREB, attempts to reach the general public and leadership groups through quarterly newsletters, weekly editorial columns in Southern newspapers, films and tapes, a monthly editorial service for alumni magazines, special newsletters on higher education issues (particularly in the area of finances), and special reports on state legislation affecting higher education and mental health.

The SREB, with the assistance of its Legislative Advisory Council, has also developed the most comprehensive program for communication between educators and legislators. The council advises the board on legislative matters pertaining to education and serves as a steering committee for an annual legislative work conference at which educators and legislators discuss problems of mutual interest. NEBHE and WICHE have employed similar techniques, but on a less regular and structured basis.

Some Problems and Issues

Any complex organization which affects the aspirations and expectations—and fears—of a large number of individuals and institutions must also cope with complicated problems and issues. It must expect to be subject to criticism, both deserved and undeserved. Each regional agency has its critics, friendly and otherwise. Indeed, legal questions have been raised in the courts, but the decisions have been in favor of the agencies.

Interstate cooperation is most successful when every segment involved feels that it will gain from the involvement. This utopian situation is difficult to achieve. Although a policy decision may appear to work to the advantage of the region as a whole as well as to that of most of its states and institutions, it may backfire in a specific situation, causing concern, frustration, and even animosity.

Again, a set of facts that argues for one line of action in most states can be politically disastrous if followed in a particular one.

With such variety of interacting interests, consensus is slow and sometimes painful to achieve. The regional agencies, unlike local, state, and Federal governments, would be doomed if they were to formulate policy based on slim majority votes. Instead, a firm commitment of most of the important power factors is necessary for the successful implementation of any project of major significance.

As stated above, the major issues in regional education concern determination of program activities. The basic documents setting forth the legal mandate have at different times meant different things to different people: to all those educators and state officials who participated in the formulation of the three compacts; to those legislative leaders in the thirty-five states who sponsored the enabling legislation and encouraged its adoption; to the original commissioners appointed by their governors as well as to their successors; and to those staff members who have placed their professional careers on the line to further the cause of interstate cooperation in higher education.

Following are ten questions that have been debated in one or more of the regions and are likely to be debated further:

1. What is the proper scope of interstate cooperation in higher education?

2. Should the compact agencies exert positive leadership in approaching problems of higher education, or should they act, rather, as passive instruments of the member states, reacting to requests which come to them?

3. What criteria should regional agencies apply in selecting, sustaining, or discontinuing programs?

4. To what extent should they concern themselves with the problems of high-cost, specialized types of professional education, in contrast to the problems of all types of education above and beyond the high school?

5. To what extent should the agencies be responsive to the needs of the member states vis-à-vis the needs of particular institutions within those states?

6. How can the agencies respond to the increasing legitimate requests from various publics and yet avoid the charge of empire-building?

7. What is the proper role of the individual commissioner or board member? Under what circumstances should he don his "state" or "institutional" hat in contrast to his "regional" hat?

8. What is the proper role of professional staff members in policy development and implementation? Under what circumstance may

they speak for the commission? When may they express themselves as qualified, professional individuals?

9. How can the agencies best interpret their programs to their constituents so as to ensure continued support, financial and other?

10. What are appropriate sources of financial support for regional agencies? What is the optimal pattern of support from these sources? How much should come from state appropriations?

REFERENCES

The primary sources used in preparing this paper were: the published reports of the three regional compact agencies in higher education; Redding S. Sugg, Jr., and George Hilton Jones, *The Southern Regional Education Board, Ten Years of Regional Cooperation in Higher Education* (Baton Rouge: Louisiana State University Press, 1960); and an unpublished doctoral thesis by Victor J. Danilov, *The Western Regional Education Compact.*

The Southern Regional Education Board

ROBERT C. ANDERSON

THE SOUTHERN Regional Education Compact became effective as a legal instrument for interstate cooperation in 1949. Its operating agency, the Southern Regional Education Board, was organized informally in 1948, and it has had a working staff and headquarters in Atlanta for over sixteen years. Sixteen Southern and border states are now party to the compact. As the first interstate agency to be created by compact for a "social" purpose, as opposed to such purposes as regulation of natural resources, it received the early attention and support of national organizations, Federal agencies, and foundations.

From the beginning the Southern Regional Education Board included in its membership the governors of the cooperating states and, later, at least one legislator from each state. SREB's greatest strength, perhaps, stems from its close relationship with two power groups: the educators and the political leaders. SREB has been able to maintain good communications with each of these groups and, indeed, has served as an agency of communication between the two.

Much has been written and said about the similarities of the three regional educational compact agencies—the Southern Regional Educational Board, the Western Interstate Commission for Higher Education, and the New England Board of Higher Education. There are similarities, of course. I submit, however, that SREB is a different animal. It bears little basic resemblance to either WICHE or NEBHE.

The major difference lies in the unique position of SREB as an extension of the governmental function of each of its member states. While WICHE was established by the Western Governors' Conference, the governors of that region do not actively participate in its policy making. NEBHE has even less governmental relationship. SREB is an agency of the states, not an agency of the universities of the South. Its philosophy is to serve the states, and, to do so, it works closely with state government, as well as with the universities of the region.

SREB has managed to keep itself close to the higher education community, although in its early years there were fears and concerns about its purposes and directions. There were those who feared that the board might assume the role of accrediting agency. SREB's bylaws prohibit such a function, and the board has scrupulously avoided any project which might tend to push it in that direction. There were those who feared that the board's program of regional contracts might be used to perpetuate segregation. Time and the board's legal position in that matter have shown that fear to have been groundless. There were those who were concerned that SREB might become another bureaucracy, a superstate agency interposed between higher education at the state level and higher education at the national level. Time has shown this concern, too, to have been unrealistic.

SREB Today

Today the Southern Regional Education Board appears to be accomplishing its purposes with success and with efficiency. Its operating budget will approach $1 million during 1964–65. It has a staff of some twenty professional persons, and an equal number on its clerical and service staff. It occupies its own modern head-quarters building, provided through an arrangement with the State of Georgia. It continues to receive the support of national organizations, Federal agencies, and foundations. Less than half of current operating funds are derived from state appropriations.

Current guidelines for SREB's program are to be found in the report of a Commission on Goals for Higher Education in the South, published in 1961. This report has become a truly vital part of educational thinking and planning in the region. The result of two years of study and discussion by a commission of seven distinguished Southern lay and professional leaders, supported by the research of the staff and some fifty consultants, this report spelled out broad new goals and objectives for the future of higher education in the region.

The South's continuing commitment to those goals and objectives is reflected in the notable advances made in higher education in the region in 1963 and 1964, and the promising signs of more progress in 1965. According to the director of SREB, Winfred L. Godwin, "the Board's own varied activities remain directed essentially at helping states and institutions achieve [those] objectives through better planning and increased reliance on cooperative university programs."

Planning

SREB approaches its role as a planning agency through continuing appraisal of educational needs and resources to meet those needs and through provision of information about changing issues and problems. SREB continues to provide consultant services to states and institutions engaged in planning for the future. Such services have involved the organization and carrying out of state surveys of higher education and studies relating to the development and location of new institutions or expansion of existing institutions. In 1963–64 alone, SREB provided major consultative services to the States of Arkansas, Georgia, North Carolina, Oklahoma, and Texas.

SREB's editorial services and its continuing periodical publications are valued by educators, legislators, and other public officials alike. A weekly editorial column of information about higher education is used by more than one hundred daily newspapers in the South. A continuing series of research reports relates to the financing of higher education. Recent and forthcoming issues deal with faculty salaries, student costs, research, revenue potentials, state appropriations, and voluntary giving.

SREB provides research data and information to the public through a periodic summary of state legislative action affecting higher education, a special feature series for major dailies, an editorial service for weeklies, and a taped series for the region's radio stations.

University Cooperation

Southern institutions have joined together and with SREB in a wide variety of efforts to strengthen university staff, faculty, and programs. One effective device for such interinstitutional cooperation has been that of the regional institute. Groups of institutions with common interests in changing problems and techniques join together with SREB to sponsor such institutes. Another such device is that of the regional summer session. Regional summer sessions for faculty and advanced graduate students continue to provide an effective service for the pooling of teaching talent in various subject-matter fields. Such sessions have been held in the areas of statistics, nematology, plant virology, industrial engineering, and others.

Nine regional university committees operate continuing programs in cooperation with SREB in nine major fields. One of these, Regional Council on Collegiate Education for Nursing, was established in 1963, as a logical development of SREB's long-time cooperation with regional nursing schools. Some fifty institutions will participate in a five-year council program.

SREB's first major program effort, which began in 1949, continues to provide for more efficient use of the region's educational resources through contracts for services. In 1963–64 more than a thousand students from fifteen states attended twenty-four public and private regional institutions to study medicine, dentistry, veterinary medicine, public health, social work, and special education. SREB's annual report for 1963–64 shows disbursements of over $1.5 million from the states to the institutions under contract. Through a related program, tuition aid for students from several states studying forestry, architecture, actuarial science, and library science was transmitted to regional universities through SREB.

SREB continues a strong interest and program in the special field of mental health training and research, which began in 1954. This was the first broad field, involving many academic disciplines, which had received regional attention under the compact program.

Review of the Program

As the Southern Regional Education Board completes its first sixteen years of operation, it is recognized as a successful and efficient agency for interstate cooperation in higher education. Its record of service, of financial success and solvency, of support by the higher education community and by the political leadership of the region are witness to a job well done and a job being well done.

SREB has been fortunate through the years in its choice of chairmen. Traditionally the chairman of the board has been a governor, and the list of chairmen is impressive. All were "education governors" and all gave greatly of their time and effort in behalf of the regional program.

These regional political leaders and the many capable and dedicated legislators of the South who have participated in SREB programs have provided a spearhead of political action for improved higher education. Working closely with educational leaders, they have been able to assist in providing the funds and governmental support necessary to educational progress.

SREB has had the advantage of continuity of staff, and yet occasional infusions of new blood which have helped to keep up enthusiasm, energy, and creative imagination.

Extending Activities for the Future

Within Our Reach, the report of SREB's Goals Commission, provides strong and forthright guidelines for the board's present and future program, at least for the next several years. As an agency for planning, consultation, and the dissemination of information, SREB is making a real contribution to the educational progress of the region. It has become recognized by the regional and national press and by the political leaders of the South as an authoritative source of accurate and useful data on higher education.

In the area of interinstitutional cooperation, SREB has proven its effectiveness as a catalyst and a secretariat. It should and must continue to develop new techniques, new devices, new methods for university cooperation. And it must continue to explore possible new fields for such joint effort. One area which needs immediate attention at the regional level in the South is that of interlibrary cooperation on a broad basis. Several years ago the board sponsored a significant pilot project in interlibrary cooperation involving a subregion. This effort should be updated and expanded. The board should make a major attempt to convene librarians and university administrators to develop specific plans for library cooperation.

SREB has achieved notable success in lowering some of the barriers to cooperation across state lines. Its contract programs, tuition aid plan, regional institutes and graduate summer sessions, and regional committees have all contributed to that success. It has not succeeded in two areas of endeavor to which attention should be given in the future. Both the New England and the Western agencies have developed programs for interstate cooperation in specialized undergraduate curricula which make it possible for students to cross state lines to study without payment of non-resident fees.

Summary

In summary, perhaps SREB can best be understood by an analysis of some of the things that it is not.

SREB has never been party to an attempt on the part of any Southern university to avoid its responsibilities to the citizens of its states, regardless of race, creed, or color. In its early years one university did so attempt to use the compact. The director of SREB, and its attorney, appeared before the court concerned as *amicus curiae*, to state the board's position on the matter—to the effect that there was nothing in the compact or bylaws of SREB which was intended to provide for an evasion of a state's responsibility to its own citizens.

SREB is not an accrediting agency—and has carefully pursued a policy designed to prevent any effort to force it into that role. SREB is not a regional supereducational governing board. In spite of the active participation of state governors and legislators, no action of SREB is binding on any state or any institution. SREB is not concerned only with public institutions. Representatives of private colleges are members of the board; private institutions receive the bulk of monies funneled through the board's contract programs; and private institutions participate, if they have reason to do so, in all of SREB's regional committees, institutions, and memoranda of agreement. And finally, SREB is not an agency which attempts to dictate educational policy for the region, but rather one which attempts to help states and institutions, upon invitation, to clarify their own policies and programs and to help the public understand them.

Within the framework of the Southern Regional Education Compact, Southern colleges and universities are able to maintain an optimum degree of autonomy, while taking advantage of a regional arrangement designed to promote and encourage optimum inter-dependence.

The New England Board
of Higher Education

JOHN T. FEY

IN A TRADITIONAL background of New England individuality and Yankee reserve, the New England Board of Higher Education (NEBHE) was conceived in 1955 for the purpose of providing greater educational opportunity through regional cooperation among all institutions of higher education in the area. Each of the six New England states is represented by three members chosen in accordance with the procedure established by each legislature. In some states the president of the state university is automatically a member; in others, he is not.

Unlike its two sister boards in the South and the West, the New England Board has not enjoyed the active participation of its state governors, although it generally has had at least their passive support. Nor has it been concerned primarily with public institutions. On the contrary, throughout its existence it has striven to include all colleges and universities in the area—both public and private— junior colleges, community colleges, liberal arts colleges, technical institutes, teachers colleges, university graduate schools, and professional schools of all kinds—which, if realized, would mean an encompassment of almost 200 institutions in the area offering education beyond the secondary school. Unfortunately, however, the board cannot claim to have been entirely successful in this effort, and full participation by private institutions has been and continues to be a goal rather than an achievement.

In its operations, the New England Board has no authority or control over state activities or over educational institutions. In every sense the board has been nonpolitical, and its range of activities has depended entirely on voluntary cooperation. And here I hasten to add that the extent of cooperation varies widely with the subject being considered.

Goals and Activities

To summarize briefly, the activities of the NEBHE include the collection of facts and figures; the identification of problems and needs of higher education within the area; the communication of these problems and facts to educators, legislators, and the public; and the conduct of research and study programs in special areas of regional concern. In carrying out these functions, the board serves as a clearinghouse for information; as a research center for the procurement and administration of special grants for regional programs; and as a fiscal agent for interstate educational programs.

One of the first concerns of the New England Board was a study of regional manpower needs in the medical, dental, and nursing professions. To meet these needs, an agreement was made with medical and dental schools in the region to provide an incentive payment for increased enrollment of students from each of the New England states. Unfortunately, this system was not widely approved nor enthusiastically backed by the schools, and its impact was not significant. Subsequently, the board has encouraged the development of a contract plan between the individual states and the University of Vermont, which has the only public medical college in the area, whereby the state contracts for a certain number of spaces in the university's College of Medicine. Certified residents of the state who meet the academic qualifications of the university are then admitted at in-state tuition, and the state makes a payment of $2,500 for each student so admitted. Each of the states except Connecticut has now entered into such a contract with the university, and the system is operating to the benefit of the participants.

A second activity which has characterized the work of the board from an early date has been the Regional Cooperation Program of the New England state universities. Under this plan, each of the six universities offers certain professional subjects to students from other New England states at in-state tuition. The exchange may be made for the full undergraduate program, for some portion of it, or at the graduate level, depending upon the course involved. The objective of this program is to extend educational opportunities without duplication of costly facilities and scarce faculty in specialized fields. For example, to build and staff a program to train pharmacists would cost each state initially $1.5 million, and over $200,000 annually for operation. Under the cooperative program, two university schools of pharmacy can serve the whole region.

Of course, the story of cooperation and elimination of duplication is not always one of success and achievement. For instance, some years ago, it was generally felt that one program in oceanography could serve the region's needs. Today, three of the six states are offering programs and a fourth is about to be pressured into the field—or water—by commercial and political interests. With no ocean, I can predict with some assurance that Vermont probably will not institute such a program, but it is an example of the pressures exerted from both inside our institutions and from without which prevent fully effective regional planning and action.

Conclusion

After nine years of operation, I can fairly say that the work of the New England Board has been successful and that there is every reason to believe that its impact on the region will increase. It has stimulated regional cooperation through the state universities; it has provided manpower studies and programs in medicine, dentistry, nursing, teaching, agriculture, and school administration; and it has extended information services to educators, legislators, and the public.

Although its forcefulness is limited by its role of persuasion rather than coercion, it has had a favorable influence on higher education in New England, and the demonstrated advantages of the cooperative effort which it has fostered should make the New England Board of Higher Education an important agency in planning for the future.

College Groups and the Claremont Example

LOUIS T. BENEZET

IN THE GROWING body of experience among associated college plans, some classification system is overdue. One system could reflect the nature of control, and two main classes then emerge. The first is control at the center, which becomes also the creative source of new colleges for the group. The second is controlled by the college group itself, with certain executive functions given to central officers under the group's direction.

A simpler way to state this might be that some associated college plans start with the plan and create the colleges to carry it out; others start with the colleges, and the plan develops as the colleges mutually decide to associate for various reasons. The second plan is more typical of the earlier college groups, such as the Associated Colleges of the Midwest; the first, or centralized, plan will probably become more common as new college clusters are created around the country. Wesleyan University and the University of California, Santa Cruz, illustrate that both private and public sponsors can plan in this way. However, the second, or decentralized plan, is rarely found among public institutions.

Origins of the Claremont Plan

All categories are made to be broken, and let Claremont cast the first stone. The Claremont Colleges follow the first plan in that when their group idea was born in 1925, only one college, Pomona, existed. The initial step taken was to create a central institution, now called Claremont Graduate School and University Center. This institution was to do the planning of new colleges and the central servicing, such as business accounting, for the group.

Yet Claremont is also like the second plan in that its central institution is itself one of the six Claremont Colleges; and although it is the source of many central functions for the group, it is not the source of control. Control remains a matter of group consent, arrived at through a republican system of central committees of officers and board members. Each of the colleges—Pomona, Scripps, Claremont Men's, Harvey Mudd, Pitzer, and Claremont Graduate

School and University Center—has its own president, dean, and board of trustees. The six trustee boards meet jointly at least once annually for review of the Claremont Group's progress, and the presiding officer then is the board chairman of the Claremont Graduate School and University Center. At biweekly meetings on joint operating policy, one of the six presidents, as provost for a year's term, presides. The provost also presides at public occasions of the Claremont Colleges as a group.

President James Blaisdell, founder of the Claremont plan, said in his retirement years that the Claremont Colleges were designed to emulate Oxford less than they were meant to emulate the United States. Here, too, comparisons break down, for the executive center in the Claremont Colleges is much more limited; suffice it to say, no White House exists at Claremont. Liberal education has requirements quite unlike those of civil government. Autonomy and local initiative supply hemoglobin for the lifeblood of individual teaching. Dr. Blaisdell would have been closer if he had said that we emulate the U.N. with a limited secretariat. It might be presumptuous even to suggest comparison; but I assure you the president of Claremont Graduate School and University Center feels not at all like Lyndon B. Johnson, even in miniature, and considerably more akin to Mr. U Thant.

What, then, is the corporate nature of the Claremont Colleges? It consists in two bodies of precedent—"law" being perhaps too strong a word. One is written, the other unwritten, reflecting perhaps our mixed American and British ancestry. The corpus is the Articles of Affiliation, a series of agreements reached by the colleges in 1961. Among the agreements are the specification of enrollment size for each college; the general methods of operating central services, such as the Honnold Library and the common business office; the form and function of central committees such as the Intercollegiate Council, our top policy group; and the procedures for the establishment of a new college to be added to the Claremont Group.

Voluntary Coordination

The unwritten body of precedent may be phrased in a simple statement: voluntary cooperation shall be the norm. In planning educational programs and administrative services for those programs, each college is moved to seek group cooperation from one or more sister colleges to carry out its plans. It does this, not automatically, but whenever such group cooperation shows prospects of greater effectiveness, either educational or economic. Thus over the years the Claremont Colleges have developed fifteen central budgets for common services and facilities, including Health Service, Faculty House, Printing Shop, Campus Security, and Shops and Stores. The colleges have combined in twos, threes, and fours to develop a common admissions office, ROTC, student newspaper, drama group, athletic teams, bookstore, and so on. And their respective faculties annually work out with each other instructional exchanges and collaborations almost beyond count. Students take courses throughout the six campuses. Instructional exchange reaches its highest point in the Graduate School. There, a small graduate faculty carries out master's and doctor's programs in which undergraduate professors participate. The several graduate faculty members in turn offer undergraduate seminars, usually open to students from all the colleges.

The exchange of student class registrations among the colleges is to a large extent the function of particular fields and subjects which the respective faculties feature. Pomona, as the oldest and largest college, offers a rather complete faculty in the liberal arts and sciences. It goes on to offer, for the group's benefit as well as its own, certain fields such as botany, geology, Russian, and Chinese. In various economics courses, on the other hand, Pomona students will seek additional work at Claremont Men's College, with its strong curriculum in political economy. Harvey Mudd centers its program in physical science and general engineering. Scripps emphasizes the humanities and fine arts. Pitzer, our new member, will stress the social and behavioral sciences.

The Concept of Community

The enrichment of instruction which several co-adjacent good colleges make possible is one of two basic arguments for the college group plan. As specialism grows in the undergraduate college, so will the economic necessity for faculties specialized according to college, which can then complement each other. Such a deliberate interweaving of faculties, to provide the breadth of offering of a university while avoiding duplication of specialist professors, is indeed the driving force behind the national trend toward association among small colleges. It moves those with campuses a hundred miles apart as insistently as it does us, a hundred yards from each other.

Yet without the other basic argument for the college group plan, the group idea is a waste of time and effort; for, after all, a centralized, departmentalized university can probably manage a lower unit cost. What moved the founders of the Claremont group was a belief in *community as an active ingredient of college teaching and learning*. To be effective with most persons in this respect, a college community needs to stay relatively small.

During the past decade the idea of community in college education has been under major attack. The attack has come from several sides: the pressure of mass enrollments; the isolating effects of specialism and the knowledge explosion; vocationalism and status drive among the professoriat; and the postwar revolt of youth against community restraints of all kinds except against pressures for academic performance measured by grades and quantity of assignment. Currently, various educators downgrade community by telling us that the small instructional group does not increase learning, at least objective learning; and that too much individual attention to students is a heritage from the misreaders of John Dewey. College education in the 1960's to many has come to mean nothing more or less than the temporary acquisition of quantities of knowledge. Certain clear evidence of growing student reaction to this has not thus far lessened the trend.

If such is to be our norm for some time to come, then one can argue that to preserve some community for the student during his years of acquiring knowledge may be more important than ever. For the demands of world society there is not much promise ahead in the value-free scientist, the social scientist who builds models but little else, or the humanist who is without compassion. One antidote for these tendencies, many have believed over years past, is the college community as an intimate personal experience. That experience is not automatic or inevitable. There should be enough structure in the college community and enough leadership so that the student is moved to accept his part as active citizen. The community, furthermore, must be small enough for the student to feel that he is more than a face in the crowd. The personal influence professors have with individual students is still going on, in upper-class years; yet it is needed even more in the first two years. A college community ought to make it possible for a student to know his fellows and his teachers well enough so that they may help him come to know himself. The student's "identity crisis" has become a modern cliché; still it reflects a true and serious situation for young people in college today.

Conclusion

To preserve community as a working principle in education is the reason the Claremont Colleges, among others, prefer not to merge their identities for efficiency's sake into one institution. Some universities also are moving toward the group pattern, against a certain public question about the prospective costs involved. We do not have the answers yet on how college groups can be run with a minimum of bureaucracy and cost. But if through college group plans we can help restore undergraduate education in the liberal arts and sciences to its former dimensions, the costs may prove worthwhile.

The college group idea, to repeat, rests upon two points: one, the enrichment of education at a decreasing rise in unit cost; two, the valid place of community in higher learning. To enrich education while controlling unit costs makes sense, and it points at a pressing college need. To preserve community during the learning experience, some of us believe, is more important.

Cooperation among American Universities in Technical Assistance Programs

JAMES A. McCAIN

TWO STRIKING and relatively new trends in American higher education have found a common ground in programs of technical aid to universities in underdeveloped countries. I refer to the deep involvement of our colleges and universities in international activities of many types, and formal arrangements which have been developed since World War II for interinstitutional cooperation and coordination.

Many of the scores of projects supported by the Agency for International Development and private foundations for assisting foreign universities involve consortia or systematic cooperative agreements among two or more American higher institutions. Two AID programs in which my own university, Kansas State, is participating —in India and Egypt—illustrate the two different types of interuniversity cooperation.

Agricultural Development Programs

Since 1956 Kansas State University has been one of five land-grant institutions assisting India in agricultural development. The predecessor to AID in cooperation with the Indian Government divided the country into five regions and assigned an American university to each area of responsibility: the University of Illinois was assigned the North; the University of Missouri, the East; Ohio State University, the North Central; Tennessee, the South; and Kansas, the South Central. In the early stages of this program most of the assistance was scattered throughout a variety of existing agricultural colleges and research programs within India. A basic objective, however, was the establishment of a new institution of the land-grant type in each area, a goal now near realization.

Although the American universities are not parties to a formal consortium, they have cooperated closely since initiation of the program. Each fall the campus coordinators meet for two or three days to share mutual concerns, meetings which have been rotated among the home campuses. AID personnel from both Washington and New Delhi participate in these conferences.

The five university contracts make provisions for annual executive visits to India. The university administrators (in one instance four of the five presidents) have made these trips together and have met as a group with the AID/New Delhi personnel and representatives from the India Government both before and after visits to their respective regions. This arrangement has enabled the American teams to speak in accord, and has impressed Indian leaders with the cooperative relationships among the universities.

Several specific benefits have accrued from these meetings. Agreements were reached on program objectives. The strengths of the five institutions were mobilized to secure decisions resisted by both AID and Indian officials. The morale of university staff members in India was enhanced by bringing them together periodically to meet with one another as a means of sharing accomplishments and frustrations. Through such coordination, the universities have been able to draw upon one another's staff and equipment resources both at home and in India.

Under these five university contracts, 95 American faculty members have served a total of 2,298 man-months in India, and 477 Indian scientists, teachers, and administrators have pursued graduate study in the United States.

A Technical Assistance Program

The Egyptian program is an example of the formal consortium of several universities engaged in a technical assistance program. In April 1964, Kansas State University signed a contract with AID on behalf of engineering schools in ten Midwestern state universities for a program of assistance in engineering education to the University of Assiut. This newest university in the United Arab Republic, located on the Nile about two hundred forty miles south of Cairo, is expected to play a significant role in the industrial and technological development of Upper Egypt. The project is expected to run for seven years, contingent upon AID support and evaluation by the participating universities of the success of the program, and will phase out beginning in 1970.

The major effort of this program lies in appointing American professors to serve on the faculty at the University of Assiut in order to introduce the American philosophy of engineering education to the Egyptian faculty. The more practical American approach, in contrast to the classical European method, should be better adapted to preparing engineering graduates to meet the challenges of an expanding technology in a developing country.

Five American faculty were at Assiut in September 1964. This number will double in 1965, and the level of ten engineering professors will be maintained until the program is phased out. Textbooks and laboratory apparatus will be purchased for the Assiut University. Beginning with the second year of the program, there will be an exchange of students, both at the graduate and undergraduate level, between Assiut and the American institutions.

The ten engineering schools cooperating in this consortium are located at the following universities: Colorado State University, Iowa State University, Kansas State University, Oklahoma State University, Rolla School of Mines, University of Colorado, University of Iowa, University of Kansas, University of Missouri, and University of Oklahoma.

Included within these rather homogeneous engineering schools is a broad spectrum of engineering programs, which provides an excellent variety of curricula and resources for the students from the U.A.R. Also, greater flexibility in faculty recruiting to fill special needs at the University of Assiut is provided. In fact, a major advantage of the consortium approach to a program of international assistance is the excellent vehicle provided, through which the group of universities can bring their total resources to bear to meet a specific need.

Conclusion

Finally, the consortium arrangement makes it possible to carry on a successful program without seriously depleting the resources of any given institution. It would be extremely difficult to spare the ten required professors from a single engineering school, but distributed over the consortium membership, this is far less of a problem. Similarly, several universities are able to share in the benefits derived from the cultural exchange aspects of the program.

I have no doubt that their participation in foreign technical assistance programs will rank among the most notable accomplishments of this century by our American universities. The extent and manner of interuniversity cooperation in these programs reflect the dedication and unselfishness with which these responsibilities have been accepted.

Cooperation by Small Groups
of Liberal Arts Colleges

BLAIR STEWART

COOPERATIVE programs and consortia are being organized in relatively large numbers at the present time. Hardly a week passes in which there does not appear a new list of colleges planning to combine in some manner. Although the purposes these organizations serve and the form of the association may, in many cases, be quite new, it should not be forgotten that cooperation between educational institutions in the United States is very common and has a long tradition. The American Council on Education is an illustration of such cooperation, and others will come readily to the mind of anyone who is familiar with higher education in this country. The type of association with which I shall deal, however, does have certain distinguishing features.

Common Characteristics

First, it involves a relatively small number of institutions. Most of the associations I have in mind consist of not less than five nor more than twenty-five institutions. Second, these member institutions are liberal arts colleges. (This restriction is not to be taken as involving any value judgments with respect to complex universities, teachers colleges, or technical institutes.) Third, the foci of association activities are in educational programs and business operations. The objectives are increased effectiveness and lower costs. Fourth, the colleges belonging to the group will be located in some proximity to each other. This is a rather flexible criterion. In some cases the colleges will be quite close together and in others very considerably dispersed. The Associated Colleges of the Midwest, with ten colleges in four states and an average distance between colleges of 200 miles, probably approaches the limit of dispersion.

The Current Need

It is not easy to answer the question of why these small associations of liberal arts colleges are being organized at the present time. One might answer that a group of colleges working together can do some things that the individual colleges could not do by themselves, and can also do some things better than could the individual colleges acting alone. This is true, but it has always been true, and it gives us no clue to why colleges should be organizing in this manner at this particular time. The needs of colleges for expanding resources are particularly pressing today, but the associations I am talking about do not raise money for their member colleges. This is a function being performed by the state foundations of independent colleges, a quite different and valuable form of cooperation. Recently most liberal arts colleges have acquired considerably increased financial resources both through the Ford Foundation programs and otherwise. Although desperately in need of money, they are generally financially much better off than they were a few years ago. Furthermore, most liberal arts colleges are now receiving increased numbers of applications for admission and, in spite of higher tuitions, are enrolling larger classes of better-prepared students. They have also been receiving substantial sums of money from the Federal Government for construction of self-liquidating facilities and for other types of construction and scientific equipment. In a number of very real senses "they never had it so good," but nevertheless, they feel the urge to join together with their fellows in relatively small, cohesive clusters.

Rise of the Universities

It may be that Clark Kerr, in *The Uses of the University*, has provided a clue. He points out that during and since World War II there has been a revolutionary development in American higher education. This has been the rise of the "Federal grant universities." This relatively small group of universities graduates a large percentage of the Ph.D.'s produced in this country and has received an overwhelming proportion of Federal grant monies in recent years. This has resulted in many changes in higher education. Its impact on the research activities and financial expenditures of this relatively small number of universities has been great. The repercussions for other universities, and particularly the liberal arts colleges, have been significant, but are as yet not fully apprehended. Kerr concludes that by and large, also, the results of this revolution have been deterioration in undergraduate education at a considerable number of universities.

Although the liberal arts colleges have not shared proportionately in these revolutionary developments, they have not been unaffected. The new emphases on research, grantsmanship, and lighter teaching loads have been felt on most liberal arts campuses. There is a clear tendency for these colleges to move in the direction of the university through increased emphasis on research, but generally with much less adequate facilities for research than are available at the university. It is also clear that as the universities tend more and more to neglect undergraduate teaching, the liberal arts colleges have a competitive opportunity if they can offer greater educational opportunities to their undergraduate students to justify their high tuition charges.

Associated Colleges of the Midwest

A number of programs of the Associated Colleges of the Midwest combine, in varying degrees, increased research opportunities for faculty members and enhanced educational opportunities for students. The Argonne Semester Program provides fifteen-month research experiences at the Argonne Laboratory for faculty members in biology, chemistry, and physics and one-term experiences in these fields as junior members of research teams at Argonne to undergraduate majors from the member colleges. The A.C.M. Wilderness Field Station in northern Minnesota makes summer opportunities for research and study in geology and biology available to faculty members and students. The field study program in Central America in cooperation with Central American universities offers field experience for faculty members and students in biology and the social sciences. Starting in 1965 a program in cooperation with the Newberry Library in Chicago will provide research and independent study opportunities for faculty members and students in the humanities. The A.C.M. Urban Semester Program of student teaching through cooperation with the Board of Education of the City of Chicago presents unusual opportunities for undergraduate teacher-training experiences. Our program of video-taping actual classroom situations is also designed to improve undergraduate learning opportunities.

One of the topics discussed by Clark Kerr is the conservative atmosphere of the institution of higher learning and its resistance to change. A good deal of recent change in the large universities has been unplanned and has been the result of the presence on their faculties of persons to whom large grants of Federal funds have been made. Also at the university level, consortia have been formed to carry on projects that went beyond the scope of individual institutions. In some cases these consortia were a means of introducing change which could not have been effected by the members of the faculty of a single university. In a similar fashion cooperative activity can provide opportunities for change at the undergraduate level. Faculty members who may be in a minority at a single college can, by combining their efforts, carry on activities which would not have been possible had they remained isolated at their respective institutions. The program of experimentation in the field of foreign language study at A.C.M. colleges is an illustration.

To some extent the association is a means of bringing the resources of foundations and Federal granting agencies to the support of the constituent colleges. Of the approximately $2.2 million received by the Associated Colleges of the Midwest in its first five years of existence, $466,000, or 21 percent, came from the Federal Government and $1,733,000, or 79 percent, came from private sources, mostly foundations, but also member colleges, earnings on investments, and student fees.

The illustrations drawn so far have come exclusively from educational activities. It is also possible for small-group associations to perform functions that are useful on the side of business operations. With the Associated Colleges of the Midwest these have been confined to joint purchase of insurance consulting services, some joint purchase of insurance, and the development of a centralized program for the collection of National Defense Student Loans.

Other groups of colleges in other situations have developed programs quite different from those of the Associated Colleges of the Midwest. I am sure that these programs have evolved out of the needs of the member colleges and that the range of such needs and the opportunities for meeting them through joint efforts are very great. It may be that other forces than those I have mentioned here have been of prime importance. I am sure that, in our efforts to perceive how social inventions of this kind come about, we all "see through a glass darkly."

6

Unified Approaches
to National Problems

Nationwide Standards and Accreditation

WILLIAM K. SELDEN

HISTORICALLY, this country was developed and has thrived in the past on the philosophy of *laissez faire*. The forests were felled, the land cultivated, the mineral resources explored, and business and industrial enterprises created through individual initiative seldom restricted until near the end of the past century by governmental regulations and legal controls. It was only after flagrant abuses of the public welfare became widespread that the United States Congress officially recognized the situation and adopted legislation providing for some governmental regulations. The first independent Federal agency created for this purpose was the Interstate Commerce Commission (1887), followed many years later by others, including the Federal Trade Commission (1914), the Federal Power Commission (1920), the Federal Maritime Commission (1933), the Federal Communications Commission (1934), and the Securities and Exchange Commission (1934).

Although we may disagree with and argue vehemently over some decisions of these and other governmental agencies, not even the Republican party in its conservative tangent of 1964 proposed that this country could afford, at a time of increasing complexity and a multiplying population, to rely solely on self-regulation and consumer control. The recent scandals in cotton and olive oil, the price fixing in the electrical industry, the income tax frauds of judges in Oklahoma, the bribery of judges in New York, and the convictions of the president of the teamsters union attest to the continuing need for some collective control and supervision. The abolition of those agencies of the Federal Government that assist in the governance of our society is unthinkable despite the fact that there is widespread yearning for the simple and readily comprehended days of the past untrammeled by governmental controls.

Freedom for Higher Education

Parallel with the economic and industrial development of the country, higher education expanded as numerous colleges and universities were established and freely chartered by the various states to offer education in nearly any town or hamlet that could raise sufficient funds to induce a church body or other groups to found a college in it. As in business and finance throughout the nineteenth century, higher education was permitted—even encouraged—to expand with few external controls or restrictions. In fact, the Tenth Amendment to the Constitution has consistently been interpreted to prevent the Federal Government from exercising control over education in a manner commonly practiced in other nations with ministries of education.

In the United States, education has truly been a local responsibility, and higher education has been permitted generally to decide for itself how large it will grow, what quality of students it will admit, what requirements it will establish for graduation, and which programs of study it will offer. This freedom of operation has permitted colleges and universities to meet, although sometimes quite belatedly, the needs of our society at the local and regional levels and, incidentally, at the national level. But this freedom has also permitted many institutions to offer programs of instruction for which they were ill-prepared in personnel, in financial resources, or in physical facilities. By the end of the nineteenth century the result was a pronounced unevenness in academic quality in which a number of colleges offered little more than an advanced secondary school course of study, and in which the majority of the professional schools were operated with attention being given more to the profits for the owners than to the education of the students.

In the case of business, when abuses became too excessive for society to withstand, the Federal Government enlarged its scope of activities to counteract these excesses. When good government became threatened by political bosses, the reform movement during the early part of this century burst into bloom. When higher education required standardization, the public with its small percentage of college graduates was not competent to initiate the task, and the Federal Government, despite an attempt of the United States Bureau of Education to issue a public classification of colleges during President Taft's administration, was limited primarily to issuing reports. Since the various states with which legal responsibility for education actually rests were, and still are, most uneven in the execution of their responsibilities, the only hope for the development of standards in higher education rested exclusively with the institutions themselves and with the various professional bodies whose ranks were increasingly being replenished by the graduates of the colleges and the professional schools.

To meet the social needs for improved higher education and the individual needs of the better colleges and universities for protection from the competition of unqualified, even dishonest, institutions, associations of the colleges and agencies of the professions initiated the process of accreditation. Ever since, these voluntary, nongovernmental, extralegal organizations have grown in number and influence. As in the case of the regulatory commissions of the Federal Government, the accrediting agencies have been subject to much criticism, some of it highly justified. The bases of these criticisms have encouraged some individuals to condemn all external regulations and to claim, as in the case of business, that the nineteenth-century concept of the completely free marketplace should again prevail. Similarly, in the case of accreditation, there are claims uttered often enough to warrant rebuttal; namely, that higher education is now sufficiently mature no longer to require any external control and that accreditation should be abolished because, among other factors, it frequently inhibits the institutions from adequately meeting the demands of society.

Whenever controls are established for the purpose of improving minimum standards, regrettably but inevitably there is some restriction on those who are fully capable of employing appropriate judgment and who would conduct excellent programs regardless of the demands of regulating agencies. Such restrictions can be minimal, but even if they are not, this fact does not imply that society would benefit if educational institutions were subject to no external supervision and both the weak and the dishonest, as well as the excellent, institutions were permitted to operate unmonitored. The consumer in the marketplace in our complicated society cannot protect himself from those organized to perpetrate frauds or to distribute goods of shoddy quality.

There is Gresham's law of economics, dating from the sixteenth century, which states that coins of good value are driven out of circulation by coins having equal monetary value but less intrinsic value. A similar principle can be applied to education: *as a society places greater value on the attainment of academic degrees, the degrees from colleges and universities whose academic programs are superficial and shoddy will undermine the value of similar degrees from institutions whose educational offerings are excellent.* A nation can no more afford to permit the operation of unqualified colleges and universities than it can permit the circulation of counterfeit money. As one of the two present leading powers in the world, the United States cannot afford to allow either its coinage or its academic degrees to be debased. And the United States public, which has heretofore relied primarily on higher education to enforce its own minimum standards, will soon begin to question this reliance if higher education does not improve its methods of self-governance.

What Is Accreditation?

In the United States, accreditation is the primary method by which higher education provides its own self-governance. It is an extralegal operation conducted by educational organizations and professional associations of different types of composition whose decisions and lists of approved institutions are generally accepted by legal bodies in lieu of lists which some of these legal bodies, such as state licensure boards, are empowered to prepare.

Aside from the programs of accreditation conducted by the states, which programs are with few exceptions not especially effective, there are two types of accrediting bodies. First, there are the six regional associations of colleges and schools, each responsible through parallel commissions for the accreditation of secondary schools and postsecondary institutions. The latter include universities, four-year colleges, junior colleges, and separate specialized colleges, such as theological schools, conservatories of music, art schools, and technical institutes. With regard to the accreditation of these specialized institutions, there has been some hesitation in the past in their acceptance by the regional associations just as there was marked delay in earlier years in the regional accreditation of teachers colleges. Although the regional associations vary considerably in geographical size, in the number of member institutions, and somewhat in policies and procedure, each will accredit only an entire institution and make no public distinction in the quality of any single institution's individual programs of study. However, regional accreditation is never intended to imply that all programs are equally strong or that all the individual programs have attained minimum quality. This fact has frequently encouraged the unknowing members of a profession to be disappointed when they notice on the lists of the regionally accredited institutions the names of several colleges that may be offering programs of study in professional fields that are below minimum standards. This fact has lent encouragement to the creation of accrediting agencies for professional or specialized fields of study.

Accrediting agencies of the second type are called "professional," since they are involved in such fields as chemistry, dentistry, engineering, law, medicine, social work, theology, and others, totaling between 20 and 30. They are not limited to particular geographical regions of the country but are national in operation. Their primary concerns are to see that society is well served by adequate provision for the education of the future members of the respective professions, and that the professions will not be debased by the addition of incompetently educated members. In exercising these concerns through accreditation, the professions rely on the regional associations to judge the total institutional quality and limit their attention to the specific programs of study. Among the factors reviewed by the professional accrediting agencies are administration of the programs, financial support, faculty competence, physical facilities, library and other educational resources, quality of entering and of graduating students, research, and curriculum.

In contrast to the regional associations, which are composed entirely of institutional members, the national professional agencies vary in composition of their committees responsible for accreditation. Some comprise only practitioners; some, only representatives of the professional schools; some, a combination of both; and others, a combination of both plus representatives of state licensing officials. In only two cases—pharmacy and teacher education—are representatives of the central administrations of colleges and universities intentionally included.

Hindrances to Improvement of Accreditation

From this description of accreditation it is readily apparent that society has assigned to the colleges and universities and to the professions the primary responsibility for the governance of higher education. However, for the institutions and the professions to continue to warrant this confidence of society, they must fulfill their obligations among other steps by improving accreditation—the institutions' primary method of collective regulation.

The improvement of accreditation, and thus the fulfillment of these obligations, has been hindered by several major factors.

First, with the exception of the desires of some professors for controls that will protect their respective fields of study, there is a widespread attitude in academic circles that most regulations of universities are barnacles to educational development. Professors who might strongly support the extension of governmental controls over business, the banks, or the securities exchanges have argued without hesitation that the establishment of regulations for colleges and universities is an intrusion into academic freedom. The revulsion of the academic person to regulations, even those established by his own colleagues, is being duplicated in the nostalgic idealism which insists that only by a marked reduction in Federal regulations will the country be diverted from its present path to ruin.

Second, the presidents and other major officials of the most influential colleges and universities have shown in the past several decades decreasing interest, if not antipathy, to accreditation as an important function in the governance of higher education. Such institutions as Columbia, Harvard, Michigan, and Vanderbilt, whose earlier presidents were significant figures in the creation and orientation of the Middle States, New England, North Central, and Southern regional associations of colleges, no longer set an example to the less widely known institutions in their support, let alone their acceptance of, accreditation as a part of self-governance.

Third, as institutions have grown in size, as they have become more numerous and diversified, as their programs of study and their services to the public have multiplied, confusion about the purposes of accreditation have correspondingly increased. Originally established to identify those institutions that met certain predetermined standards and presumably offered education of fine quality, accreditation as conducted by the regional associations of colleges and schools has, according to the claims of many educators, now been redirected to place its primary emphasis on stimulation for further improvement on the part of the individual institution. Although this emphasis allows considerable flexibility and partially counteracts by intent the tendency of regulating agencies to insist upon conformity to a more rigid design, it does not basically satisfy the outstanding universities and many educational analysts; nor does it satisfy the public that is seeking more information about the relative quality of educational institutions. The outstanding colleges and universities need no regional accrediting association to stimulate them to improvement; and they are frequently quite unhappy to observe the names of institutions which in their view are markedly inferior being added to the lists of accredited institutions undifferentiated on the basis of any quality. Those undifferentiated lists of regionally accredited institutions have provided additional support to the national professional organizations in their contentions that they must undertake accreditation of the specific programs of study in their respective areas of concern. The fact that the professions are naturally more interested in minimum quality than in stimulation for improvement has added to the confusion about accreditation on the part of both educators and the public.

Fourth, because of the diversity and numbers of institutions of higher education, because of the great variation in their programs of study, because of the personal nature of education, because of the many purposes which it is intended to meet, and because of the present elementary stage of development of educational evaluation, there are wide differences of opinion with regard to the factors that should be judged in measuring the quality of an institution or a specific program of study. Lacking adequate indexes and proven techniques of measurement, and occasionally lacking adequate concepts of educational effectiveness or excellence, accrediting agencies have been forced to rely more than is ideally desirable both on personal judgments, which are fallible, and on quantitative factors, which do not always have a direct or proven correlation with excellence. As a result, accreditation has been subjected to harsh but sometimes justifiable criticisms, on the one hand, by institutions barely able to qualify for initial accreditation or reaccreditation and, on the other hand, by colleges and universities of known excellence that no longer feel the threat of the shoddy or dishonest institutions and accordingly feel less individual need to support accreditation as a vital force in the self-governance of higher education.

Fifth, basic to all of the factors that have hindered accreditation from fulfilling its total potential has been the very human and understandable characteristic of educators to be more concerned with their own fields of study or their own institutions than with the total governance of higher education. As they conduct their program of accreditation, the chemists are indifferent to the accreditation of clinical and counseling psychology or social work education. At a time when all engineering education is undergoing a fundamental transformation, engineers are apparently focusing their attention on the accreditation of their individual specialties—such as chemical, electrical, mechanical, mining, or petroleum—instead of viewing the accreditation of the total field of engineering in the larger expanse. The lawyers have supported the concept that law schools should be integral parts of universities but have simultaneously appeared to act in their programs of accreditation on the concept that their schools should be operated as completely autonomous units of universities. The medical profession, in its insistence upon attainments that have helped to make it the envy of all other professions, has all too frequently overlooked the fact that its demands on the universities, which have provided great assistance to the improvements of medical education, have frequently been met at the expense of other equally important schools in the universities.

For their part the officials of many colleges and universities have tended to regard accreditation as little more than a nuisance that they were willing to countenance for the apparent benefits and protection it offers; and they have been reluctant to recognize that the operations of their own regional associations are more than locally or regionally important. Historically oriented toward liberal arts colleges, the regional associations were collectively slow to grant recognition to teachers colleges; and, partially as a consequence, some years ago a national agency to accredit institutions and programs in teacher education was established. In the case of schools of art and conservatories of music the same situation prevailed, and separate accrediting agencies were established for these fields of study.

Although all regional accrediting agencies will now consider for accreditation institutions primarily concerned with teacher education, art, music, and a few other specialized fields, they have not yet attained consistency with regard to the burgeoning field of postsecondary technical or vocational education. Likewise they have been inconsistent in their requirements that institutions be nonproprietary and that they must be in operation a stated number of years before being eligible for accreditation. Their approaches to the increasing numbers of institutions offering graduate work vary greatly. One regional association accredits and publicly identifies specific programs at the graduate level that it has accredited, in contrast to the other regional associations that simply grant general accreditations to the total institution.

In addition to these inconsistencies among the regional associations, there are marked variations in their standards for accreditation, in the type of information elicited from the institutions by their different questionnaires, in the influences these questionnaires exert on the self-studies expected of the institutions, in the composition and size of the visiting committees and in the use of generalists, in their plans of coordination with the many professional accrediting agencies, and in their policies and procedures for the reaccreditation of institutions previously accredited. Is it any wonder that the professions, government agencies, foundations, and other groups and individuals whose concern for academic standards is national in outlook are dubious about reliance on regional accreditation for identification throughout the country of quality in education!

Needs for Improvement in Accreditation

If higher education is to be permitted to continue its own self-governance, and if higher education is to continue to rely on accreditation as the primary means of self-governance, accreditation needs to be made a much more effective instrument than it is at present. Among the concerted efforts that must be made to accomplish this improvement are the following:

1. The presidents and other officials of the outstanding universities can no longer afford to be indifferent to accreditation, as many have been in recent years. Continued indifference to its effectiveness will further undermine its influence and lead eventually to the development of other forms of educational governance. These leading educators should recognize that our society has granted a privilege to higher education to conduct its own self-governance, that accreditation is the primary method by which this self-governance has been conducted, and that they—more than any other individuals in education—have a definite social responsibility to assist in the improvement of accreditation and to see that it effectively fulfills its public obligations.

2. Despite obvious difficulties in reaching a consensus, the purposes of accreditation need to be redefined in the light of contemporary and future social demands. The accrediting agencies must be prepared to *prove* to the public, including congressional committees, that accreditation is fully meeting social needs and not merely following the desires and convictions of those who are conducting the many different accrediting programs. Can the public, especially prospective students and their parents, be expected indefinitely to be satisfied with such a statement, for example, that regional or

general accreditation "applies to the entire institution" and "it indicates that each constituent unit is achieving its own particular aims satisfactorily, although not necessarily all on the same level of quality"?

3. For many years there has been much talk of the need for improved methods of measuring and identifying quality in education. This need still exists. It is high time that a cooperative and significant effort be made on the part of all accrediting agencies to find ways to improve their techniques of measurement and to refine the indexes that will indicate quality of education.

4. In order that higher education may fully meet its obligations to society through self-governance, *common policies* and *common practices* in accreditation must be adopted by all of the regional associations. These common policies and common practices should be applied by the appropriate regional associations to all institutions seeking initial accreditation or reaccreditation.

Failure of the regional associations to adopt common policies with reasonable promptness, and eventually common practices, will have many consequences. Among the most significant will be the reaction of the Federal Government—forced indirectly by the educators themselves as they continue to seek further Federal funds—to extend its activities in identifying institutions that are eligible for grants for construction and for other specific programs and projects. For example, grants by the Federal Government cannot be made even partially on the basis of regional accreditation to institutions offering vocational instruction if there are conflicting policies in six different sections of the country regarding the accreditation of this type of institution.

Conclusion

Higher education—now so vital to the national welfare—will not be permitted to enjoy a privileged position in its self-governance unless it regularly and consistently places the welfare of society ahead of interest in the individual institution or the individual profession. When any segment of society fails adequately to monitor itself, a public clamor for governmental controls develops. The drug, television, and tobacco industries are obvious, current examples. With the increased importance of higher education, with a larger percentage of the growing population enrolled in universities, colleges, and specialized schools, and with a correspondingly larger percentage of the population possessing academic degrees and certificates from these institutions, the public no longer considers itself incapable of proposing and requiring changes and improvements in higher education. I am predicting that the public will eventually insist upon an external monitoring of higher education unless the regional associations are able collectively to reinvigorate general accreditation and to do so with an emphasis on its responsibilities to national welfare.

Fortunately the regional associations have demonstrated within the past year their realization of this larger national responsibility by creating the Federation of Regional Accrediting Commissions of Higher Education. Among the responsibilities assigned to the federation are those of codifying and developing "general principles and procedures for institutional evaluation and accreditation and generally for strengthening and increasing the effectiveness of higher education in appropriate ways."

The federation, which has been supported and assisted by the National Commission on Accrediting, has shown an awareness of the importance of local initiative and appropriate institutional autonomy within a framework of improved self-governance based upon nationally oriented policies regionally applied. The future of accreditation—our primary method of collective institutional self-governance—largely depends upon the success of the federation, its relationship with the National Commission on Accrediting, and the constructive initiative and enlightened influence that the commission can exert throughout higher education.

Developing Nationwide Standards: Admissions

RIXFORD K. SNYDER

THE YEARS 1964 and 1965 have been widely publicized as the time when the tremendous number of babies born in the immediate postwar years would be reaching college age and knocking at the doors of college admissions offices. In 1964 the first wave knocked precisely on schedule, with the resulting increase in application volume for colleges ranging from 8 to 200 percent. In 1965 comparable increases can be expected. But no amount of comment about numbers can convey accurately the amount of work added to already overworked admissions office staffs by this rise in numbers. An office receiving 750 additional applications will have to file and process 6,000 additional forms, consisting of letters, blanks, recommendations, transcripts, and test reports. It also means 250 additional hours of evaluating and decision making. In addition, of course, there are the endless hours of interviewing involved. These are the statistics, then, that become meaningful in terms of the rise in births of a generation ago, and these are the statistics that are compelling admissions officers to work cooperatively and diligently for nationwide standards of operation that will make their monumental task less difficult and less repetitious.

There are seven discernible areas where college admissions officers are or should be working together to bring about common standards: (1) common forms and credentials; (2) common criteria for selection; (3) uniform closing dates for admission of candidates; (4) a uniform and universal candidate's reply date; (5) standard procedures in handling multiple applications; (6) greater cooperation in handling and selecting foreign students; and (7) coordination of admission of American Negro students.

Standardizing Forms: With the constantly increasing volume of credentials, the problems created for high school counselors and principals in filling out secondary school report forms becomes very important indeed. The Ivy League colleges have devised a common school report form in order to lessen the burden of the high school counselors. It has been so successful that it is being continued and twenty additional colleges and universities are adopting it. Each college gives up little in the way of autonomy and gains much by way of information. They lose some of their pet questions and their location on forms, but they gain much information because overworked counselors can now make out one form and theoretically give each college twenty-eight times as much information.

There is another area, however, where common standards have yet to be developed. This is in the reproduction of academic records on transcripts. Both high schools and colleges have long indulged in an anarchy in this area which cannot continue. High schools frequently send unique transcripts, and only too often they are illegible. Colleges are equally remiss in this area, because in sending transcripts to other colleges either for transfer or graduate study, they are perpetrating the same crime. Educational institutions cannot long continue this arrogant evidence of autonomy, and interdependence must be effected if the channels of transfer from school to college and from one college to another are not to become hopelessly clogged.

Selection Criteria: A second area where more uniform standards must be developed concerns criteria for selection of students for admission to college. Traditionally, the high school diploma and the high school record on which the diploma was awarded were the standard bases for selection. More recently, however, competition and autonomy have led to the consideration of candidates on the basis of seven semesters only. And many colleges, in an effort to gain a time advantage, are now moving to the junior-year record as the basis for early decisions, and in some cases for all admissions. This leads to a state of confusion in the minds of secondary school counselors and, indeed, in the thinking of the candidates themselves. Such lack of common standards may lead to chaos, and there, too, colleges are going to have to cooperate and give up some of their sovereignty in the interests of greater efficiency.

Admission Dates: Another area in which autonomy has too long been maintained and where difficulties are arising is dates of admission. Traditionally, students were notified of the decision on their application in June following graduation. Within the last twenty-five years, however, notification dates have moved into the eighth semester of high school, and April 15 has now become the generally accepted date, with May 1 as the date when candidates should reply. Early decisions, however, for candidates for single-choice colleges, are now moving into December and even earlier. These plans benefit the candidate only if he does not change his mind about the type of education he wants and where, geographically, he wants to receive it. The entire procedure is one designed to protect the college rather than the candidate, and thus gives expression to a distasteful philosophy that the college is more important than the candidate. In fact, colleges should base their philosophy on the position that the college is bigger than the candidate and therefore can afford to take more chances.

Reply Dates: A candidate's reply date is a fourth area in which the universities of this country need to give up autonomy and develop greater common standards. Through the College Entrance Examination Board, members may voluntarily agree to a program where candidates need not give a decision to a college until a certain prescribed date. At one time it was May 20, then it moved to May 15, and currently it is May 1. Colleges with early decision programs may exempt these candidates from the agreement, and many member colleges do not subscribe to the plan at all. Further, there are scores of colleges outside the College Board which make no pretense of adhering to any reply date. These latter two groups are literally playing havoc with candidates and with colleges who do subscribe to the date. This year, Stanford received more than fifty calls and telegrams from candidates being pressured by a single Midwestern university for a decision and a substantial deposit prior to the common reply date to which Stanford subscribes. This is a situation which cannot continue.

Multiple Applications: Multiple applications are becoming ever more frequent as the pressure to gain admission to colleges increases. This trend has created the so-called fallout problem for colleges, whereby they must estimate how many of the top candidates accepted will actually enroll. It is apparent to all admissions officers that this group is gaining admission to the other colleges where they have applied, and so, in effect, it becomes a game of gambling in which the more experienced directors have a distinct advantage. What is needed are standard procedures for exchanging information and perhaps a clearinghouse where colleges can know in advance what their acceptance rate is going to be.

Handling Foreign Students and Negro Students: Finally, the decade of the 1960's has seen the emergence of a new problem of admission involving foreign students and the admission of American Negroes to integrated colleges. Applications from both groups have been increasing rapidly, and they present problems which can be better solved if the colleges give up autonomy and proceed on certain common standards. Great progress has already been made in the admission of foreign undergraduate students from the continent of Africa, through the African Scholarship Program of American Universities. What is now needed, however, is an extension of this program to other overseas areas. In the admission of American Negroes, colleges need to work together so that they do not appear to be competing for the top Negro students, much as many colleges have for years competed for the so-called blue chip athletes. The competition is doing no service to the Negro minority group, for it tends to concentrate the efforts of colleges on the top students only, leaving the rest with inadequate academic opportunities.

In conclusion, then, it is clear that in college admissions autonomy can profitably give way to greater interdependence in the interests of both students and the colleges.

Testing: Wise Restraints

GEORGE H. HANFORD

IN THE AWARDING of degrees in law at Harvard, reference is made to "those wise restraints which make men free." What catches the ear is the contradiction between freedom and restraint. What catches the mind is the consonance of freedom with restraint. Similarly, in considering nationwide standards for testing, what catches the eye is the contradiction between autonomy and interdependence. What catches the mind is the problem of maintaining an equitable balance between local control of, and nationwide standards for, education.

Recently, much has been said of the restraints that external tests impose on secondary schools; too little has been said about the freedoms which nationwide tests preserve. Some redressing of the balance is overdue, for there is more than a touch of irony in the recollection that the first standard college entrance examinations were established at the insistence of schools to restrain colleges.

The Need for Uniformity

In the latter half of the nineteenth century, local autonomy in higher education had bred chaos and confusion in college admissions requirements. Not only did college prerequisites for the necessary mix of courses vary; what was more, so did college prescriptions of individual course content. As a result schools were forced to offer about as many different courses as there were different colleges to which their students aspired. In response to this situation, the College Entrance Examination Board was founded in 1900 to supply standard examinations based on published descriptions of course content. This deliberate move to bring some kind of uniformity into college entrance requirements succeeded also, of course, in standardizing the college-preparatory curriculum. Schools and colleges alike, recognizing the need for interdependent action, gave up a large measure of autonomy and mutually accepted the restraints that a standard system of entrance examinations imposed.

For sixty-four years the story of the board's college entrance examinations has been one of trying, in the face of changing circumstances, to keep the restraints on curricular autonomy in balance with the need for nationwide admissions standards. The first fifty years of that history were characterized by a gradual easing of the

restraints which the board's examinations had suddenly imposed on
the secondary school curriculum and college entrance requirements
in 1900. The original, rigorously restrictive instruments gave way
to the written Comprehensive Examinations in the 1920's, which in
turn yielded during World War II to the multiple-choice tests we
know today.

From Aptitude to Achievement

Since the end of the war, the positive contribution of the "College
Boards" has been thought to be their usefulness as a common
currency, a nationwide standard for the measurement of academic
ability amid a welter of grading systems and requirements. Their
influence on the curriculum has been considered at best a necessary
evil. Despite this attitude, however, college admissions tests have
for the past few years been moving back from a passive to an
active role in their effect on the secondary school curriculum. They
have done so in response to the explosions of population and
knowledge.

Growing pressures for admission have forced many colleges to
higher ranges of selectivity and hence to the use of subject-matter
tests. While the number of candidates taking the Scholastic Aptitude Test has grown two and a half times since 1959, Achievement
Test volume has better than tripled. Whereas the decade of the
1950's might be termed "the aptitude era," the first five years of
the 1960's could be called "the return to achievement." The most
dramatic demonstration of this trend has been in the Advanced
Placement Program, where the numbers have increased fivefold in
five years. A throwback in a sense to the syllabus-based comprehensive tests of the 1930's, the Advanced Placement Examinations
have served to reimpose restraints on the secondary school curriculum directly through the course descriptions for them and indirectly through the prerequisites to advanced placement work.

Testing and Curricular Change

The explosion of knowledge has manifested itself in a curricular
revolution in the secondary schools. There is the old math and the
variety of new maths, the conventional approach to the sciences
and the concept approach, the traditional study of foreign languages
and the audio-lingual. In such circumstances, the problem for the
teachers who are responsible for a nationwide testing program such
as that of the College Board is to maintain a proper balance in
examination content between the old and the new, between following and leading, between responding to curriculum change after the
fact and supporting it before the fact. Whatever it does cannot help

but influence the curriculum; and whatever that influence is, it cannot help but appear unduly restrictive to someone.

My thesis is that the board's tests are more than the necessary evils or undesirable influences that my analysis along traditional lines might thus far suggest. I hold that the curricular restraints which the tests impose constitute a positive factor in maintaining a precious measure of correspondence between what schools teach and colleges require; and that such restraints, wisely imposed, are more than ever appropriate in the face of today's curricular ferment and increased admissions pressure.

Most countries of the world have nationally prescribed secondary curricula. Logic would suggest that there is a close correspondence between their programs of study and requirements for college entrance. But this is not usually the case. The diverse requirements of different universities are imposed through examinations which often vary from one faculty to another within a particular institution for the same subject. In response, a secondary school must embellish the national curriculum with special courses designed to meet a variety of university requirements. Or, as often happens, its graduates must take a year of special tutoring to prepare for the university entrance examinations.

Conclusion

That these chaotic conditions do not exist in the United States today can be traced in no small measure to the presence of nationwide, standardized college entrance examinations. Because the restraints which they impose are mild, locally autonomous school districts can feel free to experiment with new curricular developments. Because the restraints they impose are present, a college can consider a candidate from any school—and a candidate from anywhere can consider any college.

As the controversy about the influence of external tests rages on, as I suspect it inevitably must, I would ask that this important and oft-forgotten role of college entrance examinations be kept in mind. Just as laws may be considered "those wise restraints that make men free," so may admissions tests be considered "those necessary restraints that make our schools, our colleges, and our students free."

Efforts of the Mathematical Community To Improve the Mathematics Curriculum

MINA REES

THIS DISCUSSION will focus on the efforts of a professional community to affect goals and standards on the nation's campuses relating to its own discipline. The attempt to achieve distinction rather than minimum standards must rely, I believe, on the professional identification of faculty members and on national cooperation within a discipline. Activities of mathematicians over the past decade illustrate practices for such national efforts. I am concerned here only with the mathematical content of school and college curricula, not with pedagogical problems.

Though I believe the activities of mathematicians may suggest courses of action for other disciplines, I recognize that mathematics and English share characteristics which distinguish their educational problems. Both are concerned with education from the cradle at least through graduate school, as well as with adult education; their concern is not only with the training of specialists in their own disciplines, but with service to a very broad spectrum of users. In mathematics the past decade has seen the development of a sweeping effort that has, to a marked and increasing degree, won the support and participation of research mathematicians as well as teachers at all levels and has resulted in a noteworthy rise in the morale of many teachers across the country. The resulting community of interest gives us a strong base for continuing improvement.

Attempts to Set Goals

There have been several efforts in the past to set curricular goals in mathematics and to call on the profession to recognize the need to reflect new unifying principles in the curricula of the lower schools. But the rapid expansion of mathematical research and the decisive new insights of the thirties and forties had left the schools behind, while the elementary schools were increasingly staffed by teachers who, lacking any understanding of mathematics, tended to empha-

228

size manipulation based on rote learning. The current efforts in elementary and secondary schools have, therefore, been concerned not only with setting goals, but with writing sample materials, in the hope that textbooks reflecting the new material and produced commercially would soon be widely available. In 1964 the result began to manifest itself. The materials produced aimed to provide the students with understanding based, in many instances, on advances in mathematics during the nineteenth and early twentieth centuries. But in no instance has manipulative skill been sacrificed. One concomitant of the reorganization of material is the possibility of making available in the lower schools several subjects that were formerly in the college curriculum. Another is the clear need for better-prepared teachers. Both effects imply a redefinition of curricula at the college level.

Although I will not have time to dwell on activity on the secondary and primary levels, I must mention it in passing. Probably, the first substantial effort in this direction was undertaken at the University of Illinois in the early 1950's, when the School of Engineering announced that it would not continue to teach its students mathematics that should have been learned in high school. With the support of the Carnegie Corporation and, later, the National Science Foundation, the Illinois mathematics project was begun and achieved distinguished results. Shortly afterward, the CEEB embarked on a study that resulted in recommendations aimed at introducing modern concepts into secondary mathematics and at changing its scope. These recommendations were subsequently used as the starting point of the curriculum discussions of the School Mathematics Study Group. Since 1958 this nationwide effort, along with several other projects concerned with the improvement of elementary and secondary school mathematics, has had a tremendous impact—so great that many students entering our colleges may now be expected to come with considerably improved preparation.

Effort at the College Level

Concurrent with these developments, an effort involving hundreds of mathematicians grew up under the auspices of the Mathematical Association of America, the organization of mathematicians concerned with collegiate-level instruction. Possibly as an outgrowth of interest on the part of the Office of Naval Research and the National Research Council, aimed at encouraging the development of mathematics in regions not identified with the leading mathematical research centers of the country, the Committee on the Undergraduate Program of the Mathematical Association was formed in the early 1950's, and assisted in the first summer institute for college mathematics teachers. It also recommended the establishment of a program of visiting lecturers to establish contact between leading university mathematicians and the faculty and students at some of the smaller colleges. Both the institutes and the visiting lecturer program have flourished under the sponsorship of the National Science Foundation.

The committee's early work included the writing of six books embodying new ideas for undergraduate mathematics and new approaches to old ideas. In 1957–58, in response to a general recognition that more intensive work was needed to increase the vitality of undergraduate curricula and to ensure more substantial coverage of modern mathematics, a new program was formulated. The acute need for additional qualified college teachers led to a long discussion that resulted in the proposal for a Doctor of Arts degree to be granted after course work of the same level now expected in Ph.D. programs but with an expository, rather than a creative, dissertation. After widespread discussion, this proposal was dropped—though some universities are accepting a changed emphasis in some Ph.D. dissertations. New ideas for increasing the supply of qualified teachers of college mathematics are now under discussion.

Teacher Training and Program Improvement

The continuing problem of making better use of existing college teachers has occupied the C.U.P.M.A. The committee has conducted a survey of mathematical curricula, particularly at small colleges, and a survey of teacher-training curricula. All its major findings have been published and given wide distribution.

The committee operates through four subcommittees: on teacher training, on mathematics for the physical sciences and engineering, on mathematics for biological, management, and social science, and on pregraduate training. There is also a consultants bureau, established in response to suggestions made at some of the regional meetings held to discuss those recommendations of the committee aimed at assisting colleges interested in upgrading their undergraduate programs. The panel of consultants consists of thirty mathematicians from colleges and universities all over the United States who, on invitation, visit colleges for a two-day period and assist with recommendations on a variety of issues. These consultants have been used by about fifty colleges a year. Special efforts are now being made to reach junior colleges, whose responses have thus far not been good. The basic materials used by the consultants, and more generally by colleges across the country, have been produced by the panels, each of which has published recommendations outlining courses appropriate for the mathematical education of the group of students with which the panel is concerned. Course guides and library lists which help teachers to prepare the recommended courses have also been published.

The most extensive work has been done by the panel on teacher training. A critical issue is the fact that efforts to change elementary and secondary curricula can be effected only through extensive in-service training, including National Science institutes for teachers. At the same time that this is going on, however, the teacher-training institutions (including, of course, the liberal arts colleges) are turning out large numbers of new teachers who are no better equipped to handle the new material than those who are already in the schools. Because of this situation, the panel on teacher training has given the highest priority to immediate work with colleges throughout the country in the hope that changes can be made quickly in the mathematical preparation of teachers for the secondary and elementary levels.

Preparing Elementary Teachers

The panel has recommended courses appropriate for the training of teachers at all levels and has produced a set of course guides for these courses. For the purpose of discussing the recommendations and learning how best to implement them, five regional conferences were held in the spring of 1961, with participation by chairmen of mathematics departments, state education officials, and professors at teacher education institutions. The National Association of State Directors of Teacher Education and Certification, in cooperation with the American Association for the Advancement of Science, has now adopted the C.U.P.M.A. recommendations for the education of future elementary school teachers, and these recommendations are reflected in the publication *Guidelines for Science and Mathematics in the Preparation Program of Elementary School Teachers*, published in August 1963.

The panel has also cooperated with the University of Minnesota project which is producing science and mathematics material for both the elementary school and the undergraduate preparation of future elementary school teachers, and in the future may embark with the Minnesota project on efforts to produce and test teacher-training materials. This collaboration will afford an excellent opportunity to study the effects of improved preservice education upon the classroom performance of teachers. The panel has encouraged the writing of suitable textbooks for teacher-training courses and has recommended more NSF institutes for college teachers to provide opportunity for teachers in teacher-training institutions to become qualified to handle the new materials. It has cooperated, too, with the panel on educational films of the Mathematical Association of America and with the National Science Foundation summer institutes and conferences.

Programs for Undergraduates in Science and Engineering

The second panel, concerned with recommending materials for college students in the physical sciences and engineering, has been working in cooperation with the Commission on College Physics, and with the Commission on Engineering Education. It has also held conferences with computer specialists and has developed a detailed program for undergraduates interested in automatic data processing. Collaboration with the Commission on Engineering Education has been particularly fruitful, having produced what mathematicians typically find extremely difficult to get—a considerable number of problems in which imaginative new applications of mathematics are revealed in the context of new engineering problems. This effort is aimed at overcoming the usual instructional problems found in many mathematics and engineering textbooks and at showing both to engineers and mathematicians some new facets of their respective fields. These are in the process of being edited for publication. Another particularly interesting activity of this panel has been a conference on linear algebra, an aspect of mathematics not traditionally included in engineering curricula but now recognized as desirable. The panel has published its recommendations on the undergraduate program for engineers and physicists.

The third panel, on mathematics for the biological, management, and social sciences, includes members of psychology, business administration, statistics, preventive medicine, and sociology departments, as well as mathematicians. It has constructed suitable text materials for recommended courses and has held a number of conferences. Its report on statistics has been completed, and its tentative recommendations for nonstatistical materials for students of biology have been published.

Preparation for Graduate Study

Perhaps the most controversial recommendations are those intended for the pregraduate training of students of mathematics. These have been published, and represent an imaginative restructuring of the material of college mathematics, as seen in the light of modern research. They are not presented as fare for the conventional mathematics major but for the exceptional student who will become a professional research mathematician.

The committee is still struggling with the question of integrating its various recommendations into offerings suitable for small colleges at which separate offerings for different groups of students may not be feasible. The committee has, however, published a library list of basic books recommended for small colleges. In this transition it is clear that the consultants bureau has proved of great help to the colleges that have used it, and that the consultants have aided many colleges in reorienting their offerings to achieve the level of mathematics courses which students must now have available if they are to be able to handle competently modern work in their fields of specialization.

7

National Associations
in Higher Education

National Organization
in Higher Education

RUSSELL I. THACKREY

IT IS A SALUTARY, though frustrating, experience to attempt to explain to a distinguished foreign visitor the pattern of national organization of higher education in the United States. The visitor starts the interview with a small, open notebook and a respectful attitude. Too often the interview concludes with the visitor edging toward the door, as if trying to escape from a madman thus far harmless in the physical sense, but still to be eluded before his obvious derangement takes a violent turn. The point is, of course, that the visitor may be accustomed to a system under which a ministry of education exercises centralized control over higher education and in which all universities are, so to speak, cast in a similar mold and have the same relationships to the national government. If this is the case, he finds it difficult to understand educational organization in a country where the whole tradition has been one of decentralization of control and diversity of support. This diversity in higher education presents difficulties as well for all those who must deal with the colleges and universities in the aggregate.

Diversity and Multiplicity of Associations

But those who complain of the diversity of voices on the national scene in higher education, who ask that higher education "speak with one voice" on the various proposals and policy issues that arise, are asking what is both impossible and undesirable for the forseeable future. The national organization of higher education in the United States is based on voluntary association for common, and varied, purposes, of individual institutions in fifty-one major political jurisdictions—the states and Puerto Rico—and it is as complex as the nature, sources of support, control, origin, and traditions of these institutions. The primary orientation of an association may be national, regional, state-wide, regional within a state, urban, religious, toward the humanities and liberal arts or toward science and technology, toward various professions, or a combination of several of these.

In each of their *institutional* aspects the colleges and universities belong to associations, and their interests as represented by these associations will be diverse and may even compete. In addition, each school, college, or department of the university may have its national organization; nonacademic and academically related administrative units and individual staff members are organized nationally along a variety of lines—as professors, as international specialists, as chemists, as scientists, as humanists, as English teachers, by professions, and by specialists within the professions. One now begins to have a glimmer of understanding why the national organization of American higher education is so complex.

Since World War II the number of educational organizations of national and regional scope has multiplied, and the activities of both the older and new organizations have increased substantially. The latest issue of the U.S. Office of Education *Directory*, Part 4, lists some two thousand educationally related organizations, and its editor assures me there are many more that, for one reason or another, are not on the list.

It is impossible to categorize these on any logical basis as "higher" education or "elementary and secondary" education, since the vast majority cut across all levels. But one may, on the basis of experience and observation, hazard the guess that the organizational birthrate and membership and program expansion rates in higher education have exceeded those at other levels.

This growth is of considerable concern to educational administrators, governmental administrators, organization executives, legislators, and others on the national scene who are involved with educational policy making and program discussion. Many college and university presidents view these developments with considerable alarm. The announcement of the formation of a new national organization, or the expansion of an existing one, and particularly of a new or increased institutional dues assessment, is the occasion of new protest—though in the end few colleges or universities stay out of new organizations or drop out of existing ones. The fear that to drop out is to run the risk of being left out is strong, and so is the sensitivity to the desire of faculty members and administrators to mingle with others with similar problems, to have their place in the national sun.

The multiplication and expansion of organizations in higher education is, however, not an isolated phenomenon in American life. The number of national associations of businessmen, for example, is also something more than 2,000 (an increase of 48 percent since 1940, compared to a population growth of some 37 percent), and these 2,000 associations employ more than 30,000 people.[1] Enrollment in higher education has increased more than 300 percent since the years

[1] L. L. L. Golden, "Trade Associations and How They Grew," *Saturday Review*, June 13, 1964, p. 64.

immediately prior to World War II, but the "national" involvement in higher education, particularly the increase in Federal and major foundation involvement, has increased astronomically. The 100 or so employees of that giant among U.S. higher education organizations, the American Council on Education, may seem large, but it is modest compared to the 1,000-member staff of the U.S. Chamber of Commerce. Even the Manufacturing Chemists' Association maintains a staff of 24, which—by coincidence—is exactly the number of professional staff members listed in the 1963 *Annual Report of the American Council on Education.*

It is easy to argue that higher education is, on the basis of size of the over-all establishment, volume of expenditures, and, above all, importance to the national welfare, underorganized and understaffed. But this kind of justification—although germane to the theme of this discussion—will not help us much in looking at the very real problems which exist and which do not spring from lack of funds, staffs, or organizations.

The multiplication of organizational activity in higher education has had, as a by-product, a strong tendency to fragment the representation of the college or university *as such* in relationship to the legislative and administrative branches of the national government and to the foundations, corporations, and individuals who provide private funds for educational purposes. It has also placed increasingly heavy demands on the time and energy of many individuals who are called on, in various capacities, to participate in these activities.

Impact of Federal Support on Organizations

Major factors behind these developments are the sharp rise since World War II of the Federal Government in financing higher education and the nature of the ways this has been done, the similar rise of foundations as factors in both educational financing and policies, and the increasingly international orientation of U.S. higher education.

The Federal Government has, historically, been an important factor in stimulating the national organization of higher education. Thus, the oldest national organization of institutions of higher education, the present Association of State Universities and Land-Grant Colleges, adopted a constitution and bylaws in 1887, after the Land-Grant Act of 1862 had necessitated a series of meetings of those institutions charged with carrying out common policies in the programs in agriculture, engineering, and national defense. Coincidentally, in 1887 a *second* Federal act granted research funds to these institutions on a continuing basis and it, too, required an organizational structure to deal with the Federal Government.

The American Council on Education was formed as an "emergency council" of existing national organizations in World War I to deal with acute problems arising from the impact of Federal wartime programs on all colleges and universities—a task of representation none of the existing groups was qualified to perform alone. Although the wartime emergency passed, higher education found reasons for continuing the "temporary" consultative group permanently. Federal activity during the depression and during and after World War II emphasized the wisdom of having a common meeting ground for action on at least those problems on which a substantial consensus could be reached.

The Association of American Colleges, which originated in the need of church-related colleges for a forum, has evolved and expanded to become the chief spokesman for liberal arts colleges under whatever auspices, and to become increasingly concerned with both Federal Government and foundation activities related to higher education. The American Association of Junior Colleges, founded to discuss the common problems of a relatively new movement in American higher education, has had a multiple expansion of staff and activity as the major foundations, the Federal Government, the states, and private resources began to see in this development the hope for quick action to make up in part for years of neglect in "gearing up" higher education to meet the sharp rise in the birthrate in the post-1940 years.

The great expansion of Federal support has, in addition to benefiting higher education, also been a primary source of some of the problems of organization today. So long as the Federal impact on higher education was confined to a few institutions or to the college or university as a whole (as during war and depression), most of the national professional, disciplinary, or scholarly organizations were chiefly discussion forums whose members benefited from knowledge of the views of others and from the personal acquaintance engendered. When the national government became a large-scale source of funds—for research, for college housing, for international activities, for fellowships, for a whole range of purposes largely having the character of aid to individuals, or aid by categories, or for narrowly defined purposes—the impact on national organization and representation in higher education was immediate.

Federal support of activities related to higher education took the fragmented character so familiar to all of us for a variety of reasons, some based on a considered philosophy of approach, others on inability to solve the perennial controversies over institutional eligibility to receive aid (church-state) and over the spectre of "Federal control."

Channeling of most Federal support of higher education activities on a discipline-oriented, student-oriented, research-oriented, category-oriented basis brought into being whole new species of administrative officers who have organized nationally, and it has also brought greatly expanded national activity by previously existing groups. University fiscal officers found that policies originating in Washington, as contrasted with those of private donors or state legislatures, might influence fiscal solvency or the reverse dramatically. New emphasis on counseling and guidance, on student loan programs, the discussion of national scholarship programs, caused student personnel groups (there are more than thirty national organizations in the field) to become concerned first as specialists with the drafting and administration of workable programs, and subsequently with the policy issues of whether there should be new or expanded national programs.

As Federal support of research in the natural sciences and the health fields grew to proportions unimagined before World War II, scientists and organizations of scientists became the chief architects of Federal policy of *how* such support should be channeled, and, indeed, to a substantial extent, of *how much*. Since most of these funds flow as grants to individuals or teams of individuals, or for structures or equipment for specific categorical purposes, it has become almost impossible for all but the strongest university administrations—and their trustees—*in fact* to control the amount and nature of involvement in Federal research programs, unless the university happens to be one of those suffering from too little rather than too much involvement. Thus we have the interesting spectacle of a distinguished committee of the National Academy of Sciences–National Research Council recently giving whole-hearted endorsement to a continuance of past emphasis on grants to *individual scientists* and in the same report calling on university administrators (*not* individual scientists and their organizations) to be more vigilant in discharging *their* responsibilities for seeing that the possible conflicts of interests of the individual inherent in present programs don't get out of hand. (In street-corner parlance, this is called the "heads I win, tails you lose" approach.)

Similar examples could be cited over a range of problems and programs. The role of the specialist as specialist, of the administrator of a particular program on campus, in the formation of total college and university policy usually is relatively clear. His views are subjected to the criticism and competition of his opposite numbers, of the faculty as a whole, of the central administration and trustees, and out of this process comes a *university* policy which hopefully takes into account the many factors involved in a decision on expanding this or that department, school, or college, putting more money into scholarships or less, using funds for support of specialized activities or for general institutional support, pushing undergraduate fees up to support graduate and research expansion. On the national scene, however, when the organizations representing all these perfectly legitimate interests and viewpoints choose to establish national offices and press their views vigorously and *independently* in the halls of Congress and before administrative agencies, the general effect is that of a Tower of Babel. The interests of the college or university as a whole institution, and the spokesmen for these interests, tend to be drowned out, and Cabinet members and congressmen cry out, "Who speaks for higher education?"

One result of all this is that some in higher education who have favored the segmented approach to Federal support of activities as contrasted with broad general support, on the ground that it is "less likely to lead to Federal control," are finding that in fighting the shadow of Federal control they have lost the substance of institutional control. A national policy of fragmented support is, after all, still a policy, and its effect is fragmentation. Scores of separate Federal programs are each surrounded by a nexus of laws, regulations, and administrative policies. Hardly anyone, in or out of government, wants Federal control. Any attempt to exercise it through the medium of a broad program of institutional support would be vigorously and successfully resisted by an aroused and united higher education community, with the full support of the public. But the issues posed by regulations, policies, or laws involving a single specific program, relatively small in itself, are rarely sufficiently dramatic to arouse opposition. And there is always a clientele for the program within the university which may urge, both within and without the institution, acceptance of minor harassment rather than loss of the program.

Thus we find conditions attached to categorical and individual programs, even though the funds are channeled through the university, which would be unthinkable if applied to support of the university as a whole. And the capacity of the higher education community to resist the first is weakened by the fragmentation of organizational and individual interests which accrue to specific programs. A classic example is the imposition by Congress of a flat percentage limit on payment for indirect costs of research grants. University administrators have long expressed united opposition to this procedure, and have repeatedly produced detailed support of their contention that the percentage set has caused a substantial drain on institutional funds. They have long enjoyed the support of the national administration in attempting to get the limitation removed. But it is no secret in academic or congressional circles that the chief, and thus far successful, opponents of change have been the ultimate recipients of the research funds, who have taken the attitude that every dollar used for indirect costs—that is, to support the institutional framework essential to their conduct of research—is a dollar "lost to research."

242   Russell I. Thackrey

Washington Headquarters

When the writer moved to Washington to establish a national office for his organization on New Year's Day, 1947, there was no National Science Foundation, no National Defense Education Act, no Fulbright program, no Agency for International Development, no U.S. Information Agency, no College Housing Loan or facilities program, no Cooperative Research program in the U.S. Office of Education, no National Aeronautics and Space Administration, to name a few examples. The U.S. Atomic Energy Commission had been established a year before, but its relationship to higher education remained to be defined, and the Defense Department's wartime research activities were still largely to be converted to a peacetime basis. The Public Health Service had a research budget of about $8.4 millions, and the U.S. Department of Agriculture (aside from the great war-generated research programs) was still the chief furnisher of Federal funds for research. Everyone in higher education is familiar with what has happened since.

In that same year, 1947, the American Council on Education had 56 constituent members, of which 15, or 27 percent, had Washington offices. In 1961 at least 27 of these same 56 constituent members as of 1947, had Washington offices—more than 48 percent of the 1947 total. Meanwhile the Council's constituent membership had more than doubled, and many of the new constituents had established Washington offices. By 1961 the U.S. Office of Education *Directory* listed 116 educational associations, at all levels, with Washington offices. There have been many additions since, and the list grows monthly. Still other organizations, chary of identification with the political atmosphere of Washington, have maintained offices elsewhere and substantially expanded their travel budgets.

Graduate deans, librarians, university women, nurses, veterinarians, historians, political scientists, psychologists, business officers, personnel and guidance administrators, natural scientists of various disciplines, engineers, geographers, book publishers, architects, physical education directors, business officers, alumni, public relations officers, teachers colleges, pharmacists, home economists, psychiatrists, trustees, parents, professors, admissions officers, visual aids specialists, broadcasters, are a few of the groups having Washington offices—or about to have them—with some interest and activity in the national policy area. Many of these groups have long published scholarly and professional journals, and the multiplication of these in recent months may indicate a growing feeling that such activity is indispensable to status and prestige on the national scene.

International Educational Activities

Just as interest in various phases of international educational activity has grown apace since World War II, so have organizations devoted to various international programs. The old-time Institute of International Education has established many regional and international offices, including a notable expansion of its Washington office as liaison point with the Federal Government. Foundations have assisted in greatly strengthening the work of the institute and of the American Council on Education in the international field, and have likewise been instrumental in the establishment of a variety of new organizations, chief among them being Education and World Affairs, headquartered in New York but inevitably heavily involved in activities centering in Washington.

Demands on Individuals

The demands on the time and energy of individuals in higher education by various organizations having a "legitimate" claim on them may be illustrated in the field of graduate education. At present there are 11 national or regional organizations of graduate deans, ranging in membership from seven to 231. Largest is the comprehensive Council of Graduate Schools in the United States. Others are based on university status, on *public* college or university status, on regional groups, on religious lines, or on combinations of the above. Regional groups overlap. For example, the 101 institutions of the "Midwest" Conference on Graduate Study and Research apparently range from the Canadian border to the Gulf, and from the western Continental Divide to the Appalachians, while the Western Association of Graduate Schools also comprehends the areas covered by the Graduate Deans of the Pacific Northwest and of the Pacific Slope. There is scarcely a graduate dean in an institution of substantial size who does not belong to three to four of these groupings, and if he happens to be in an institution which is at the same time Midwestern, Western, or Southern, and reasonably prestigious, he may be involved in as many as six, with five as a minimum. (One of the rare occurrences in higher education happened last December 1, when the Conference of Deans of Southern Graduate Schools voted to disband. Some members are reportedly trying to revive it.)

But this is only one aspect of the story. Graduate deans, as such, are involved in many other organizations: such as the Committee on Institutional Cooperation (of the Big Ten and the University of Chicago); the Mid-America State Universities Association; the Associated Rocky Mountain Universities; and in the councils and committees of the Western, Southern, and New England compact groups. They are sometimes vice-presidents for research, which involves another complex of meetings; they like to retain their connection with their own professional and scholarly groups. Federal research programs, international programs, fellowship programs, foundation-financed programs such as the Woodrow Wilson National Fellowships, the drive for interinstitutional and regional cooperation

—all these have involved them in policy recommending and policy making. And the great expansion of graduate education has brought a new demand for specific accreditation at the graduate level, again with both national and regional policies and mechanisms to be established and work to be done.

On Creation, Expansion, and Functions

The task of sketching the diversity and multiplicity of national organizations in higher education is relatively easy, compared to making constructive suggestions about what, if anything, can or should be done.

Let me start by stating two propositions in the negative:

1. We should give up dreaming about the good old days of relative simplicity in the national organization of education. The most important enterprise of our society needs an organization commensurate with that importance.

2. We should *not* expect higher education to speak with one voice on the national scene in the foreseeable future. Fundamental differences of philosophy, policy, and aspirations exist, and should continue to exist, among different groupings of institutions. The different segments of our universities and colleges, and the varying disciplines within them, have a legitimate interest in national policies relating to higher education, and their voices ought to, and will, be heard through appropriate voluntary organizations. The best we can hope for, and the least we have a right to expect, is an improvement in understanding of the interrelationships of the parts to the whole, of the impact of various plans and proposals on one another and on the college and university community; a consensus on a good many major issues; a reluctance to rush into the creation of new organizations and new national offices until the justification and need have been explored.

SOME SUGGESTIONS

On the affirmative side:

1. *A study of organization*—Despite the plethora of national studies of higher education, I venture to suggest one more. It would be a *factual* study of the organization of American higher education, to show who does what in what fields, how many people are involved, and what it costs. It should be a *technical* study designed to bring out the facts, and without any machinery for involving "distinguished leaders" in education in making a whole series of recommendations for action. Let the facts speak for themselves, and let the results be widely disseminated among university administrators, fiscal officers, foundations, trustees, and faculties. I believe that the setting forth of facts would stimulate constructive action to resolve some of the

duplication and overlapping of effort that exists. If the facts do not do it, no pronouncements by a small group will.

2. *A "look before you leap" attitude*—We need to develop, within our organizations, within university and college faculties and administrations, a more discriminating, reflective, and—if you please— scholarly attitude toward the establishment, expansion, and functions of our organizations. Many administrators tend to react toward new educational organizations, expansion of existing ones, and particularly increases in dues, with a "Heaven help us; Parkinson's Law is working again" approach, an attitude that simply causes an opposite reaction of "Heaven help us; he doesn't understand our problems and importance and the contributions we could make through organized effort." New and promotion-minded staffs of organizations, on the other hand, sometimes "sell" their constituencies on grandiose plans of expansion requiring equally grandiose financing (much of which is to come from unnamed "foundation" sources). In a few years, sometimes one or two, the promoter moves on to other promotions, and his or her successor and his board find themselves with an inflated staff and budget, a cash deficit, and the necessity of sharp retrenchment.

A not uncommon experience among Washington educational bureaucrats such as myself is to be visited by organizations seeking advice and counsel on the establishment of a national headquarters. The questions usually asked are: "Where can we find office space, and how much will it cost?" and "How much will it cost to employ a really top-flight man with national prestige to run it?" *Not:* "Do we really need someone in Washington (or New York) to do what we think we need to do?" or "Is there someone else already doing what we want done, or who could and would do it at half the cost of a wholly new establishment?"

The nature of internal revenue laws and regulations has caused many essentially professional organizations to develop institutional memberships, with the side benefit of having the cost of dues shifted from the individual to the college or university. This is "bad" only when, as noted above, the organization then launches an ambitious program leading to a steadily increasing commitment of institutional funds. One result of all this is that some colleges and universities tend to follow extreme policies with respect to membership in organizations and travel to meetings. One is a policy of "join everything, go to everything," and the other is close to the reverse. Neither is characteristic of an institution devoted to the uses of investigation and knowledge as a basis for action.

Perhaps a first step toward improvement would be the development of a check list for colleges and universities (and separately for educational organizations). The one for colleges and universities might include, in addition to the obvious ones of the nature and purposes of

the organization, such questions as: How many other organizations
are there in this area to which we already belong? What new purpose
will be served by the creation (expansion) proposed? Has the group
examined other ways of meeting the need? What financial commitments are anticipated over the next five years on the part of the institutions? If the organization is institutional in membership, what
procedures do we need to establish to see that the *institutional* view-
point is reflected in its policy decisions and recommendations, particularly with respect to national issues? And so on.

For organizations, the check list might include such items as suggested above with respect to establishment of national offices and
similar matters. Major foundations, too, might think of establishing
a check list, in passing on proposals which involve the creation of
new organizations or major funding of proposals by existing organizations involving implications for the activities of others: Have
other potentially interested organizations been consulted in the development of the proposal? Will their needs be met by it? Does the
proposed new organization have a definite plan and program for
utilizing the experience and organization of other groups, or does it
propose to operate *de novo* as if it alone must establish mailing
lists, consultative groups, meetings, advisory committees—the whole
paraphernalia of communications services needed to reach each of the
two thousand institutions of higher education in the country?

Even these tentative suggestions will not be easy to carry out.
One of the most difficult problems of any institution or organization
is to get people to think about what it is supposed to do. Admittedly,
some of the finest developments in American higher education have
been brought about by people who *didn't* stop to develop a careful
plan for meeting a need but went ahead and did it, and then appointed study committees to clear up the chaos afterward. But a
certain amount of study, inquiry, and planning is called for, I suggest, in the world of today.

3. *A look at the machinery for consultation*—We should pay more
serious attention to the machinery for consultation and coordination
on the national scene, particularly but not exclusively on the Washington scene. Fortunately the situation is not as bad as the recita-
tion would indicate. Washington educational representatives *do* get
together formally through the American Council on Education and
informally in many ways, do inform themselves of the larger issues
as well as those of immediate concern to them. They *are* interested
in the welfare of higher education as a whole, in doing a good job
for the young people of the country, and their mistakes are more
often those of enthusiasm and ignorance rather than those of informed intent.

The constant complaint of members of Congress that they "don't
hear from" educators about the problems of higher education has

caused some organizations, for example, simply to urge their members to "write your congressman what you think about this problem," *without* first having provided the kind of analysis of issues that alone can furnish the basis of intelligent communication. Educators *do* need to communicate more often and more effectively with their elected representatives, but the effect of a flood of mail from educators reflecting complete divergence of opinion from members of the same group, plus lack of information about the issues involved, will hardly advance the cause.

THE AMERICAN COUNCIL ON EDUCATION

The American Council on Education, formed as a consultative body by existing educational organizations, has gone through a gradual but marked and accelerated evolutionary process in the forty-six years of its existence. In the public statements of its officers and in its publications it stresses its role as the "major coordinating body" for American higher education, as represented by its institutional and constituent members. The Council president's 1963 *Annual Report,* for example, notes that "our major concerns have their real locus on the campuses of the nation's colleges and universities and in the programs of other major educational organizations."

That the Council has made a great contribution toward bringing the diversity of viewpoints and interests in American higher education into reasonable focus on many issues no one familiar with the facts will question. Its board and various commissions and committees constitute a reasonable cross-section of the individuals who direct the destinies of the wide variety of institutions in American higher education. Services to institutional members have been greatly improved over the years. Since the first essential to coordination is a common basis of information, of understanding of the facts and their implications, this is all to the good.

However, the American Council on Education, founded as an organization of *constituent* members, is no longer (has not for many years been) the creature of its organizational constituency, is not likely to be their master, and has not yet mastered the techniques of voluntary coordination among equals. As an *institutional* membership organization—the source of most of its financial support aside from foundation assistance—the Council is by this fact, though not by policy, stimulated to become competitive with the constituency which it also wishes to coordinate. The tendency of any able, conscientious staff which sees something to be done is to do it, unless there are well-established guidelines for consultation on whether or not it should be done, who may be doing it already, and, if not, who is best qualified to do it. Coordination among voluntary and independent organizations, to the extent that it is possible, involves a continuous concern for the problems, aspirations, and programs of the coordinated as well as the coordinator.

Among the board, commissions, and committees of the American Council on Education, none is charged with concern for relationships with its constituent members, the services which may be performed for them, ways in which consultation and coordination may be more effective. Of the twenty-four professional staff members as of the close of 1963, one was designated, on a part-time basis, for liaison with constituent members. This is not to suggest that the Council turn back the calendar and become again a constituent-member based or controlled organization. Nor is it to say that the views and interests of constituent members are ever purposely forgotten or ignored. A great deal of consultation goes on, but it is chiefly on a casual and informal basis or dictated by the immediate pressure of events. This kind of interchange is fine. But if the Council wishes indeed to become a coordinator among its major constituent members, it needs to develop a policy and program to this end.

The major constituent members of the Council are equally in need of developing better processes of consultation in formulating and carrying on their own programs. Joint committees and projects between associations, small forums for exploration of fundamental policy issues, would be helpful. Many issues cannot be resolved by discussion, but the process of discovering, in a low-key atmosphere, the areas in which men of good will can agree *only on their differences* may be as useful as the discovery of new *common ground*.

In General

The above modest suggestions offer no panaceas. One of the major strengths of American higher education, one of the interesting things about it, is that there *aren't any panaceas*. There are only problems, constantly changing, which each generation of students, faculty, administrators, donors, legislative bodies, trustees, parents, and the public must meet as best it can. Fundamental issues are rarely "settled" in a fashion that contemporary witnesses can recognize. Some persist and will persist through the foreseeable future; others that once were hotly controversial have virtually disappeared in a slow progress of consensus which only the educational historian can identify. In the first category is the question of the extent to which education is an individual, family, private, personal responsibility or a social, corporate, public responsibility. Among the latter issues is the concern that the equality of opportunity which is fundamental to American democracy shall be inseparable from the actuality of the extent and quality of educational opportunity open to every individual. Differences over means and methods will persist, and the organizational structure of higher education will reflect it in endless variety. The controversy over objectives is so moribund that it persists only in the minds of those who are so far to the right or to the left that they find common ground in the notion that society is best run by a self-chosen elite, and differ violently only on the question of who should constitute the elite.

To make effective the consensus of all but this tiny minority, we need to put more—not less—of our resources into the consideration of national problems relating to higher education, whether the "solutions" to be found are in public or private action, or a combination of the two. We need not apologize for, or be embarrassed by, any probable expansion of the scale of effort on the national scene, or the fact that it is diverse, multiple, and incapable of coordination except as the result of voluntary consultation and agreement. We do need to take more effective action to assure that our organizational means of expression are reasonably effective and efficient, do not duplicate demands on time and thought more than is necessary to reflect the diversity which exists.

Higher education may be compared to a garden in which each individual plant has its own need for food, water, and proper care. Many families, genera, species, individual plants, have their devotees, their enthusiasts, dedicated to their care; some do not. As every gardener knows, this can result in a riot of overgrown giants, competing among themselves for survival, choking out many valuable plants which have not caught the popular fancy. Institutions have their arrangements for head gardeners—and even their garden clubs—to preserve some semblance of a landscape plan, arbitrate between the weeds and flowers, and see that the whole collection gets its due in food and sun. Nationally we distrust head gardeners in the legitimate fear that their weeds of today may be the most sought-after plants of tomorrow. At this point in history, what we need is a better communication among garden clubs, more systematic but sympathetic and probing skepticism about the formation of new ones, and perhaps some sort of Geneva convention—legally unenforceable but morally powerful—against reckless hoe-swinging, the use of sprays that drift on other people's precious specimens, and monopoly of all the hose connections.

Problems of the Professional Associations and Learned Societies

WILLIAM P. FIDLER

IN CONSIDERING the means of improving communication and coordination among the educational organizations, one is faced with the problem of the multiplicity of associations and societies and their great variance in purposes, constituency, activity, and prestige. Also, there is a new giant partner in many facets of higher education—the Federal Government.

Theoretically, all learned societies and educational associations are in favor of collaboration with other groups having common concerns, but even in closely allied fields there are so many organizations that effective contacts can be accomplished only through selective processes. For instance, the 1961 edition of *Scientific and Technical Societies in the United States and Canada* lists 1,597 organizations in the United States and another 239 in Canada. As for the multiplicity of education associations, the directory of the U.S. Office of Education lists over 800 national and regional associations, and another 500 state education associations.

Continuing versus *Ad Hoc* Cooperation

In considering effective relationships among so many groups having such a variety of special interests, one must determine whether additional *formal* contacts would be feasible or whether efficiency in the exchange of information cannot be obtained by means of *ad hoc* arrangements. I grant that there are advantages to some kinds of formal and continuing coalitions, but there is also much to be said for arrangements involving particular and limited purposes, without commitments for continuing relationships. Often a greater virility and spontaneity can be obtained when invitations relate to specific projects. When the need for communications diminishes, a continuing coalition tends to look around for "make work," and few active associations have the resources for merely time-consuming endeavors.

A loose type of formal and continuing collaboration has proved useful to certain groups. For instance, the chief administrative officers of the leading educational associations affiliated with the

250

American Council on Education meet regularly with the president of the American Council to discuss matters of mutual concern. Also, an organization known as M.O.S.S.—Managing Officers of Scientific Societies—established at the suggestion of the American Chemical Society, meets for several days at an annual conference to exchange viewpoints and information on operating procedures and other matters of common interest. The meetings of M.O.S.S. are governed by an agenda so that participants can come prepared for discussion on specific topics. It would be my suggestion that numerous other groups, having closely related interests, might benefit by the examples of the M.O.S.S. and the Washington educational secretariat, but perhaps the major service to be rendered by such informal discussion groups would be the identification of special areas of interest which should be pursued cooperatively on an *ad hoc* basis.

An excellent example of a collaborative enterprise, which brought together some twenty-seven associations and learned societies, is to be seen in the *Report of the Commission on the Humanities*. Three influential education groups—the American Council of Learned Societies, the Council of Graduate Schools in the United States, and the United Chapters of Phi Beta Kappa—served as cosponsors for this provocative study. The commission began its work early in 1963, and its thoughtful report was delivered on April 30, 1964. Twenty-four learned societies collaborated with the three cosponsors and submitted statements for incorporation in the commission's report.[1] It is to be hoped that similar cooperative ventures will be undertaken by interested groups.

Associations of Associations

The most promising media for the improvement of communication and coordination among the various educational groups are the organizations which have as their affiliates a number of educational associations and societies. The one having the broadest representation in higher education is, of course, the American Council on Education. Others with more specialized representation are the American Council of Learned Societies, the American Association for the Advancement of Science, and the Social Science Research Council. Several others could be cited, but these are perhaps the most active educational "holding companies." As you know, these great educational groups sponsor a wide variety of cooperative efforts—through their publications, their joint committees, their annual meetings, and their sponsorship of special conferences. However, some of the most significant problems in American higher education have not been fully explored in recent years by representative groups. It has been proposed by an officer of one of our most

[1] New York: American Council of Learned Societies, 1964. 222 pp.

influential learned societies that an annual meeting of executive secretaries and other officers of the larger educational organizations should be arranged for the discussion of numerous academic problems which might be resolved through special cooperative efforts.

Outline of Issues

In the remaining portion of this brief report, I shall list and comment on a few interesting issues—some limited in scope but others of broad and significant concern—which might serve as subjects for collaborative study; the more important of them could well serve as themes for national conferences.

1. *Extensive reconsideration of curricular needs.* The vast accumulation of knowledge in recent years, some of it demanding new approaches to learning, will necessarily bring confusion into our classrooms if college teachers do not make periodic reviews of course needs, teaching facilities, and appropriate methods of instruction. Several learned societies, particularly in the natural sciences and in the humanities, have already established active education committees which are obtaining the cooperation of related groups in spawning new curricula, developing new ways of training, and in establishing summer institutes for the refurbishing of college teachers. A number of these programs, though managed largely by people at the university level, extend down to the grade school. In spite of these promising efforts, there are fields in which little attention is being given to changing curricular needs and related matters. The learned societies in particular have or should have a special interest in this problem, and coordinated efforts might be the best approach to some phases of it.

2. *A review of current concepts concerning sabbatical leave.* It is possible that the accumulation of knowledge now is so rapid that a teacher needs refreshing more frequently than in the past. Periodic leaves, affording the scholar an opportunity to review the mounting accumulation of new information and techniques, might contribute materially to the over-all efficiency of college teaching, especially in the sciences.

3. *Ethical standards for the academic profession.* My own association, the A.A.U.P., has accepted the obligation to draft a statement on ethical principles, but many groups, particularly those which have administrators as their representatives, should be drawn into this endeavor, for ethical principles in academic life affect the relationships of all groups to each other in higher education. In this connection, I am pleased to announce that the American Council on Education invited the A.A.U.P. to assist in the formulation of a statement on ethical standards in a limited area of academic per-

formance—conduct in relation to contracts for sponsored research.[2]

4. *Continuing defense of academic freedom.* A very effective example of cooperation among educational organizations is the support which has been given to the 1940 Statement on Academic Freedom and Tenure, a document jointly formulated and adopted by the Association of American Colleges and the A.A.U.P., and later endorsed by twenty-six scholarly societies and associations, among which are some of the largest and most influential academic groups in America. A companion document—the 1958 Statement on Procedural Standards in Faculty Dismissal Proceedings—was also jointly formulated by the two associations, and its provisions have likewise been widely accepted. These basic charters, so essential to the well-being of all professors, are in need of continuous support and defense, and I am pleased to report that the vast majority of academic people, both administrative and faculty, recognize their importance even though occasions for defense of them are not always seized upon.

5. *Standards for teaching by educational television.* The body of literature on educational television is becoming almost too extensive for mastery by individuals, and as a consequence numerous educational groups have appointed committees to consider the formulation of standards in particular areas of ETV. The American Council on Education and the A.A.U.P. now have representative groups working jointly on a comprehensive policy statement dealing with standards for the use of ETV. We are hopeful that this statement will be completed during the present academic year. The time will soon be at hand when one of the large educational associations should organize a conference on the important problems being faced by institutions offering instruction by ETV.

6. *Recruitment for the academic profession.* A very useful purpose could be served by an extensive cooperative effort on the part of educational organizations to promote faculty interest in the problem of recruiting our ablest students for service as college teachers. At the present time the A.A.U.P. is attempting to interest its chapters on 850 campuses in establishing faculty committees for the purpose of identifying promising recruits and offering guidance to them with regard to preparation for college teaching, including dissemination of information on available scholarships and fellowships.

7. *Academic concerns in the revision of the copyright law.* During the past five years the Copyright Office of the Library of Congress has held conferences on the proposed revisions in the copyright law

---

[2] *On Preventing Conflicts of Interest in Government-Sponsored Research at Universities: A Joint Statement of the Council of the American Association of University Professors and the American Council on Education* (Washington: American Council on Education, 1964).

and has encouraged all interested parties to submit proposals. In the light of many suggestions, most of which have come from commercial interests which have a financial stake in valuable copyrightable materials, the proposed revisions have undergone numerous changes, and an extensive body of proposals is now ready for congressional consideration. Although individuals and institutions in the academic community do own some copyrights and have a degree of interest in protective measures, the vast majority of academic people are primarily *users* of copyrighted works and, therefore, should make their wishes known concerning the "fair use" provisions of the new law. Certain educational organizations, particularly the American Library Association, have already taken an interest in important aspects of the copyright problem, but other groups should be alert to opportunities to present testimony before congressional committees when the omnibus bill is ready for debate. In view of the highly technical nature of copyright provisions, it would seem advisable for interested associations to identify the copyright specialists from among their constituencies, and to encourage these specialists to get together and determine the most statesmanlike interest which the academic community should take in the forthcoming debates on copyright matters.

The topics presented here are only a few of the issues in higher education which could be promoted effectively by combined efforts of educational associations and learned societies. Perhaps future analyses of these and related concerns will encourage more groups to cooperate with one another in steps to solve many of the problems which span the various disciplines and the interests of educational organizations.

Problems of the Washington Secretariat

THEODORE A. DISTLER

IT IS FAIR to say that communication among the various national associations representing one segment or other of American higher education is good and cooperation extensive. This is so not because of any formal arrangements but largely because the people holding secretariat posts in the Washington area know and respect each other and are more anxious to do a good job economically than to build little empires. Communication with other organizations whose headquarters are elsewhere is not as effective—for lack of similar personal contacts. Increasingly, organizations with a major concern for higher education are moving their national headquarters to Washington, and as this trend continues one can look forward to even more effective cooperation among an increasing number of organizations. Certainly from my observation in the past ten years, I believe that communication, cooperation, and coordination have increased and will continue to do so. There are, however, some problems that go deeper and some questions that remain to be resolved.

The Need for a Plan

There is the question of whether or not, in the multiplicity of organizations representing a great variety of interests in higher education, we are most effectively organized to represent higher education as a whole. We need an objective study of the variety of associations now in existence to answer at least two questions: (*a*) are we presently organized to provide the greatest possible impact nationally, and (*b*) if not, how should we reorganize to provide the maximum impact with a minimum of duplication of time, energy, and effort?

There is a tremendous interest in higher education on the part of the general public and its representatives in Congress. Each year bills are presented regarding aid to education. They are usually considered piecemeal, without any reference to a national pattern or framework. Unless and until we as educators assume responsibility for providing such a pattern or framework, we shall continue to have bits and pieces of legislation not necessarily related to the total problems confronting higher education.

Obviously any grand plan would have to be related to the several states. I realize full well that such a relationship would be extremely difficult to bring about. Nevertheless, if we are unwilling to tackle it and provide such a plan, we may very well have a program that will be less than effective for higher education.

Need for Effective Public Relations

Second, a great vacuum exists in the area of information for the American public. Americans are certainly concerned about higher education, but I doubt seriously whether they are getting the kind of information from which we can expect appropriate reactions in the best interests of higher education. Here again I think we have been remiss. One needs only to read the report prepared by Editorial Projects for Education, Inc., on "Disseminating Information About Higher Education" to see the great deficiency in this area.

It seems obvious to me that we need a national publication for general public consumption which will really provide thinking Americans with the background on which they can base their judgments about higher education. None of the journals published by educational organizations meets this need. They are not strictly scholarly, but neither are they popular. Some degree of compromise is no doubt inevitable, but in any case I often think we would be doing a better job if we joined forces to produce a single national journal of higher education.

Proposal for Further Coordination

Finally, I should like to suggest that every fourth year, instead of holding separate annual meetings at different times and places, all of the major national organizations representing institutions of higher education join in a congress on higher education. During the first two days of the congress, all of the associations could meet together and provide a program with the most distinguished educators in this country and, if necessary, from abroad. The second two days of such a congress could be devoted to the meetings of the several organizations and their constituents. This would give us an opportunity every four years to make a tremendous impact for higher education on our whole nation, as well as provide savings in time and money.

Regardless of how we improve our communication and cooperation with one another, the really important things are for us to (1) make sure that we are not overprogramed and are organized for maximum effectiveness; (2) begin immediately preparing a national plan, and (3) hold a congress every fourth year. We must organize for more effective presentation of the total case for higher education, not only to the Congress but more particularly to the American public.

8

National Policy for Higher Education: Problems and Prospects

Toward a Nationwide System
of Higher Education?

CLARK KERR

THE DISCUSSIONS included in this volume have progressed from internal institutional changes, to the growth of voluntary and compulsory systems for coordination at the state level, to interstate compacts and interinstitutional consortia, to the role of national organizations. It seems logical to conclude by raising the question of whether or not we are moving toward a nationwide system of higher education. If not, where are we going? For certainly we do not stand today where we stood yesterday or where we shall stand tomorrow.

Historical Trends

Viewing the question from an international perspective, we can see a clear trend toward national systems. France, as long ago as Napoleon, established such a system, run from Paris; and Italy and Spain, among other countries, have also given a central role to the national Ministry of Education. The Russian system, patterned in part after the French, is also national in scope and control; and the rest of the Communist world has followed suit.

Even Britain, the home of Oxford and Cambridge, Edinburgh and St. Andrews, has moved toward a national system through the stages of Royal Commission studies, the University Grants Committee with its ever-increasing authority, and now the Robbins Committee Report. And so on around the world.

In the United States, the historical trend is in much the same direction. The first great Federal impact on higher education came a century ago with encouragement of the land-grant universities, a movement which dramatically changed all universities, private and public, in the United States. Agricultural experiment stations and agricultural extension services, under university auspices but with Federal funds and following a national pattern, spread into every state and virtually every county. Military training, whether voluntary or compulsory, was developed with Federal funds and supervision in colleges and universities across the land. A new massive national impact, affecting mainly the universities, came with

World War II as the Federal Government became by all odds the predominant supporter of organized research. More recently, Federal support for scholarships has had its influence on the careers of graduate and undergraduate students alike.

Paralleling this Federal involvement in education has come the growing number and the growing strength of the national associations which represent colleges and universities. A century ago, in contrast to the present situation, nearly all colleges and universities were local, almost isolated, institutions devoted to the service of a small element of the total population and in quite restricted ways. It is inconceivable to us today that the changes of the next century might be as great as those of the century just past; but we all recognize the possibility of further change.

Mutual Dependents: Education and Society

There seems to be an inherent logic at work drawing forth some further change and in the same general direction. Higher education has clearly become an instrument of national policy. Economic growth is dependent in substantial part on the training of highly skilled personnel and the generation of new ideas by institutions of higher education. The health, as well as the wealth, of the nation is closely related to the performance of these same institutions. The security of the nation itself, in the long run, depends on the quality of the work done in university laboratories. The greater the intensity of international conflict and the greater the intensity of needs that can be met only by higher skills and newer discoveries, the more higher education will become an instrument of national policy.

Colleges and universities have always been dependent on resources beyond those assigned to current production and current consumption. These resources were once mainly in private hands and in the hands of state and local agencies. But increasingly in the United States, particularly with progressive income and corporation taxes, these resources have been in the hands of the Federal Government. Federal resources have been rising concomitantly with Federal concern for the products of higher education—increased capacity to support has matched increased Federal interest in higher education.

Higher education has also become so varied in its interests, so expensive in some of its equipment, so complex in its service assignments, that it cannot remain easily in the grasp of a single self-contained campus. Some machines to be well used must be used by several or even many institutions. Library resources, to be adequate, must be shared. Subjects to be taught in all their variety at the graduate level require some specialization and thus coordination of effort. Service projects in foreign lands often require talents beyond the resources of a single institution. Thus there are all sorts of compacts, consortia, master plans, joint projects; many of them sponsored by national foundations or Federal agencies.

Each of these signs—international trends, the course of our own national history, and the inherent logic of the situation in which higher education finds itself—points toward the eventual development of what might be identified as a truly nationwide system of higher education. Yet I strongly doubt its emergence in the foreseeable future.

Forces of Autonomy

The resistances are strong and, I think, increasing. The drive for autonomy by individual institutions is very persistent, and autonomy will be relinquished only under compelling circumstances. Similarly, states and even regions zealously guard their claims for authority and independence in the control of higher education.

Supporting these institutional drives are individual resistance by faculty, students, and alumni, many of whom desire to retain a sense of community, a sense of control, a sense of individuality which would be incompatible with a nationwide system of higher education. There seems to be a growing concern about increasing size, increasing complexity, increasing change within our bigger universities, a concern which meets its counterpart in American society at large. Desire for a smaller, a simpler, a more stable, a more cohesive college or university matches the desire for a smaller, simpler, more stable, more cohesive society. This is not to suggest that all the persons on a campus who hold such views necessarily hold them about the surrounding society—often quite the contrary is true; but the same phenomenon is occurring inside as well as outside the university, and it has its impact.

A truly nationwide system of higher education in a nation as diverse as, and with the traditions of, the United States would be unwieldy. There would be too many levels of authority to be efficient, too much frustration to be effective, too little control to assure compliance. But most important, there is no grand design by the Federal Government to take over higher education, and there is no real need for it to do so, since national requirements can be met far short of a nationwide system. There is no prospect of a Napoleon as there was in France, nor a Communist take-over as in Russia, nor a massive failure to meet the changing needs of the nation as there has been in England in the last few years and in many of the less-developed countries. Rather, I think, we in the United States are drawing to the end of an historic period of rapid administrative changes—a period of increasing organizational interdependence; and entering a more stable period during which the organizational changes of the past two decades will be consolidated and modestly expanded, mechanisms improved, and a more even balance between the competing demands of autonomy and interdependence achieved. I expect, in particular, a growth in voluntary consortia of many sorts and for many purposes.

The Emerging System

The system which will emerge will be neither atomistic nor monolithic. It will be pluralistic, with many centers of power related to each other. The Federal Government and the national foundations will continue to have the most fundamental influence on the general direction of growth. In particular, the Federal Government is likely to penetrate somewhat further into the expansion of medical education, the geographical distribution of strong centers of higher education, the creation of greater equality of opportunity for the ablest young people, and the support of research outside the areas of science. The Federal Government will continue to have the major single impact on how much is spent on higher education, on the distribution of expenditures among different activities and fields of interest, and on the regional location of endeavors.

At the level of administration, the situation will continue to be very mixed. Already, detailed administration is variously shared by the institution itself, by foundations, by Federal agencies, by coordinating councils, by state agencies and legislators, by consortia, and by associations. It is high time that there be some clarification of respective managerial roles. Bureaucracies overlap bureaucracies. A gradual and piecemeal movement toward simplification would seem to be a natural consequence of a period highly creative in developing new mechanisms of coordination and control. But in the end, the administrative arrangements will remain complex because of the complexity of the interests involved.

At the level of individual preferences by faculty members and students, the current degree of freedom of choice will generally be maintained. Students will sometimes not obtain their first choice of institution or course work as conditions become more crowded; and, for the same reason, faculty members will more frequently obtain theirs. But we are a very long way from the central assignment of students to institutions and fields, or the central control of faculty positions and salary levels. Thus faculty and students retain their essential freedom; national authorities have the greatest leverage on new policy directions; and administrators are fractionalized and occasionally fractured at the levels in between.

Conclusion

Our pluralistic system of higher education matches our pluralistic society in the United States. It is rather instructive to note how the organization of systems of higher education around the world tends to parallel the political, social, and economic systems of which they are a part. So also in the United States. Here too the adaptive character of higher education is an essential characteristic —changing as conditions change. A society can see itself reflected in its universities and colleges; and its universities and colleges can see themselves reflected in the society of which they are a part. Neither mirror is perfect; but, imperfections aside, the consistency of image is there. The pluralistic United States has a pluralistic system of higher education. In a pluralistic system there are constant small adjustments, few clarion calls. Neither autonomy nor interdependence has any universal and ultimate claim one over the other. Their respective claims must be accommodated, inconsistent as they sometimes are. The process of accommodation is continual, sometimes faster, sometimes slower, but never ending. This is a great source of confusion in a pluralistic system. It is also the source of our great strength.

Basic Premises for a National Policy in Higher Education

LOGAN WILSON

THERE WAS A TIME in our history when higher education was regarded as an absurdity for the majority, a luxury for those who could afford it, and a necessity only for clergymen. But that time is long since past, and the indispensability of higher education to our whole society is now generally recognized. Only recently, however, has there been much cognizance taken of the need for a national policy in this area. Although the right development of such a policy is a major task confronting us, my purpose is much less presumptuous. It has to do with the basic premises or guidelines which should precede policy formulation. As I see them, there are at least eight such premises to be taken into account in any sensible plan for the long-range development of higher education. What are they?

1. *A strong and viable system of higher education is essential to the national welfare.* Everybody agrees, I am sure, that this is one of the facts of modern life which every nation of consequence must accept. We Americans have benefited immensely from being the first people to sense it, but we ought to be more acutely aware that we no longer monopolize the idea. The Russians, for example, have gone much further than we have in developing some aspects of higher education as an instrument in the service of the state. The emerging nations are currently learning that educational development must precede virtually every other kind of forward movement.

It is no longer necessary to argue the causal connection between trained manpower and productivity, between enlightened leadership and the nation's welfare, or to give other utilitarian justifications for educational adequacy. Nor should we have to remind ourselves that education in a free society is intended to serve individual purposes as well as collective goals. Our growing dependence upon the services of colleges and universities underlines the importance, nevertheless, of a public obligation to make higher education strong enough and viable enough to meet any future contingency.

We accept without question the proposition that our system of defense should be the best we are capable of devising and maintaining. My contention is that a wise national policy for our system of higher education must be based upon the same uncompromising premise.

2. *The need to expand and improve American higher education is urgent.* In recent years the public at large has read and heard much about the plight of our colleges and universities. Madison Avenue has joined educators in advertising the ubiquitous struggle for funds, staffs, and facilities, and today many parents are, indeed, anxiously wondering whether there will be enough colleges ready for their children by the time their children are ready for college. All of these concerns, of course, are emphasized by the knowledge that our college-age population will be doubled in the next decade and that at least 50 percent of the total will expect a post-secondary school education.

Notwithstanding these apprehensions, the willingness of the public to expand higher education in response to widely felt needs seems to me beyond question. Public pressures will brook no alternative to the enlargement of most institutions and to the creation of new ones. How many colleges and universities will be added to the more than 2,100 we already have is anybody's guess, but it hardly seems likely that the American zeal for proliferating campuses will be abated in the critical years ahead.

That our system of higher education will become bigger is almost a foregone conclusion. Whether it will be made better is less certain. Expanding the educational establishment without also bettering it makes no more sense in my opinion, however, than enlarging the military establishment without providing for advances in military technology. In other words, our exigencies are such that we must set our sights for more quality as well as for more quantity in higher education.

The urgency of getting on with the business of expanding and improving our system of higher education is inherent in the lead time required to show results. Academic buildings, for example, normally entail a period of not less than three years from authorization to occupancy. Beginning with freshmen, at least four years are needed to produce engineers, five or more to train scientific workers, seven or so for academicians, and even longer terms for medical specialists. What I am saying, in effect, is that many of the foreseeable problems of higher education in 1970 will be satisfactorily solved only if we start coming to grips with them now.

3. *Expansion and improvement should have national policy guidance.* The mere idea of a national policy for higher education is

something most citizens have not thought about, still others would oppose in principle, and comparatively few would urge as being essential. Considering the nationwide networks in business and industry, communications, and transportation, it is strangely anachronistic that local autonomy continues to characterize most of our institutions of higher learning. Educational diversity and pluralism, of course, are values we have sought to maintain. The challenges confronting us are now such, however, that valued features of our system of higher education must somehow be incorporated into planning which encompasses the entire nation as a unit.

In developing higher education to meet future needs, it seems to me that our emphasis should be less on institutional independence than upon interdependence. The advancement of learning is so important to our general welfare that it must not be left solely to chance or local determination. Illustrative of the concerns which, in my opinion, call for national policy guidance are the following: What kinds, number, and distribution of institutions will best meet the nation's trained manpower needs ten, fifteen, or twenty years hence? Under what circumstances is it better to expand existing institutions and under what circumstances to create new ones?

What are the pros and cons of the junior or community college as a solution to the problem of numbers? When is the conversion of a junior college into a senior college and of the latter into a university justifiable? How many more first-rate centers of graduate study and research does the nation need? Where should they be located and who should be responsible for developing them? How may costly overlapping and unnecessary duplication among institutions be minimized?

What can be done to promote more exchange of information and ideas among the various state-wide boards of higher education? Are there better devices for drawing related institutions, public and private, into closer cooperation? How can quality controls become effective throughout the entire system of higher education?

As a recent brochure has pointed out, the "doers" of American higher education are in local, independent, and state enterprises. Their approaches are inevitably piecemeal, with resultant national and international shortcomings. Yet, the greatly increased importance of higher education to the national welfare and its major role in shaping the future of our society point up the conspicuous need for a policy to guide its development. By tradition and inclination, the 2,100 colleges and universities of this country have tended to go their separate ways. It is increasingly obvious, nonetheless, that the purposes of separate groups and institutions may not add up to the requirements of the nation.

In brief, I believe that we have entered an era in which our colleges and universities must cease to be a mere congeries and become a genuine system characterized by unity no less than by diversity. To be effective, such an enterprise must be based upon a consensus concerning means and ends. It is, therefore, imperative for us to identify, analyze, and place in broad perspective the major problems and policies affecting higher education in the United States in order to move ahead with the conversion of scattered efforts into coordinated endeavor.

4. *National policy and Federal policy need not be one and the same.* Although there may be a few persons who believe that the Federal Government should coordinate higher education, most of us would agree that Federal policy should be a part of, rather than a substitute for, national policy. I am confident of our ability to modify existing arrangements through more joint planning and implementation under a system of free enterprise.

Moreover, it is encouraging to note local, state, and regional developments in the right direction. Many of our institutions have recognized that long-range planning must be something more than campus planning. Similarly, institutional leaders and others are realizing that plans should not be made unilaterally, but in the light of what is being done and contemplated at other places.

Evidence of joint enterprise is to be seen in the Midwest College Council, the Great Lakes College Association, and other voluntary groupings of similar institutions. The arrangements worked out by Mount Holyoke, Amherst, Smith, and the University of Massachusetts demonstrate what can be done in furthering a common policy within a locality. Again, there are the consortia of major universities, exemplified by the Committee on Institutional Cooperation. Within some states, presidents of institutions have formed voluntary associations to engage in joint planning and to agree upon divisions of labor. In still other states, politically appointed commissions or boards have assumed responsibility for interinstitutional policy making and coordination.

Quite comprehensive arrangements are to be noted in the Southern Regional Education Board, the Western Interstate Commission for Higher Education, and the New England Board of Higher Education. These movements all point up a trend toward more collective enterprise intended to serve state, regional, and national, rather than strictly local, needs.

In view of these and other developments I shall mention presently, my judgment is that free enterprise is capable of formulating a national policy for higher education. The problem at hand is largely one of organizing and articulating the decision-making process. My preference for a national, as contrasted to a Federal, policy to shape the growth of all higher education, moreover, is not intended to imply hostility toward the involvement of central government in the concerns of colleges and universities, or vice versa.

One of our pressing needs at the moment is also for a Federal policy in this whole field. Although the relationships between the Federal Government and higher education have on the whole been mutually beneficial, strains have been created inadvertently because there has been no coherent set of principles to guide Congress and the dozens of executive agencies in the actions they have taken. Until recently, furthermore, higher education itself has been unable to formulate any set of priorities regarding Federal aid. When we have both a national and a Federal policy for higher education, I believe that the Federal role can be defined in a way which will strengthen rather than weaken the diversified support and control of American colleges and universities.

5. *A realistic assessment of existing strengths and weaknesses is overdue.* Any national policy intended to aid higher education should take into account that present arrangements have resulted from more than three centuries of development in this country. In addition, they have been influenced by an even longer span of European experience. Our system, with its dispersed support and control, its free play of cooperation and competition, has in general served us well. Not only has educational opportunity been readily accessible at low cost in most parts of the country, but also the quality of that opportunity in our best institutions is now unexcelled elsewhere in the world. In research and public service, our colleges and universities are being widely copied as models.

Unlike their counterparts in many other countries, our institutions of higher education have lay boards of trustees, and this fact alone would lead some outside observers to conclude that academic freedom in the United States must function under continuous restraints. Actually, however, this has been the exception rather than the rule, and the scheme has tended to preserve localized independence in decision making. Furthermore, it should be noted that the freedom of our whole system has never been curbed by the control of any political, religious, or other centralized agency.

The educational assets which we have developed over the years unquestionably must be maintained and strengthened; yet we should not close our minds to the fact that we have also incurred some liabilities. In an era when our national manpower should be brought up to the highest possible point everywhere, the quality of educational opportunity is still poor in some regions. In many institutions, professorial salaries still lag behind the wages of truck drivers and factory laborers. Libraries and laboratories too commonly are inadequate and outmoded—and occasionally, I might add, on campuses where the athletic facilities and marching bands are most impressive! Diploma mills and some accredited institutions are permitted to go on year after year fostering shoddy standards.

Some of our educational ills can be cured by more money, of course, but not all of them. In my opinion, the present scheme of arrangements between and among institutions needs to be modified. We must begin to look more realistically at the increased costs and shortcomings of unilateral action. Institutional independence and interdependence must be more effectively reconciled, and we must be willing to forego autonomies which would raise the price of national adequacy in higher education beyond our ability to pay. More honesty and courage are called for from educational leaders to resist the local opportunism which causes wasteful competition and rivalry between institutions. More thought and effort must be given to working out a sensible division of labor and a mutually beneficial set of relations among colleges and universities.

As we make our plans for the future of American higher education, we shall certainly want to strengthen its best features, but we shall likewise need to correct its known deficiencies. This does not mean that we shall eventually achieve excellence everywhere, to be sure, yet it does imply that nowhere should we be willing to tolerate anything less than adequacy.

6. *Higher education will be financed adequately only when costs are regarded as investments rather than expenditures.* Although there is no consensus concerning the best ways to support our colleges and universities, there can be no disagreement about their pressing needs for greatly increased funds. The inordinate amounts of time and energy educational leaders now have to give to fiscal problems and the consequent neglect of more strictly educational problems are evidences of an already critical situation.

An obvious cause for this unfortunate state of affairs, of course, is that higher education is not getting its proper share of the gross national product. Yet this does not tell us why. In my judgment, the main reason is that money for education is popularly regarded as an expenditure rather than as an investment. Altogether too many alumni, I suspect, give to their alma maters (when they do give) with the same benevolent and charitable feelings that motivate their contributions to Community Chests and United Funds. Likewise, tax-supported institutions often get only what is left over after various public agencies have received their prior allocations. Even such a deliberative body as the United States Congress has traditionally assigned a very low priority to legislation for higher education. In short, our underwriting of higher education is being determined mainly by what we think we can afford rather than by what we ought to allocate in order to achieve those national objectives which can be attained only through higher education.

This situation will not be remedied until it is realized on all sides that educational expansion and improvement must be treated as investments.

Insofar as the average college graduate is concerned, a Harvard economist has recently estimated the material worth of higher education at $200,000 to $250,000 in increased earning power. The values of education to the whole of society are incalculable, of course, but one study has shown that 24 percent of the increase in the GNP from 1929 to 1957 and 44 percent of the heightened productivity per worker can be attributed to the higher educational level of our labor force.

Nearly everybody knows that ordinary capital investments in labor-saving machinery more than pay for themselves. What more people must learn is that the dividends from investments in education are even greater. Aside from the material benefits to be derived, the intellectual and social gains from betterment of the higher learning are inestimable. The higher learning, indeed, not only promotes the common good, but also in its own right represents all that is best in our civilization.

A wise national policy in and for higher education therefore must be founded on the premise that economic and civic self-interest necessitates an increased investment in our colleges and universities —not in terms of what we ought to do to help them, but for what they can do for us and our posterity.

7. *The disjointed organization of higher education must be unified.* As I have stated elsewhere, some of the shortcomings of American higher education are to be found outside rather than inside institutions. That is to say, weaknesses in the whole structure may be in the mortar as well as the bricks. In periods when the load of national responsibilities borne by higher education was relatively light, perhaps this did not matter too much. Since this is no longer the case, however, the total structure needs to be shored up at critical points.

In an effort to offset the inherently loose articulation of our system, a vast multiplicity of agencies, associations, committees, commissions, and boards has come into existence. Some consist of individual scholars, scientists, and educators drawn together by fields of academic specialization. Most of these associations are national in scope, but some are geographically less comprehensive. *Ad hoc* groupings set up to deal with particular problems come and go on the educational scene, yet the plethora of conferences and conventions being held all over the country at any given time suggests that it is easier to add to, than to subtract from, the total roster.

In addition to the individual membership and special purpose organizations, there are also organizations representing the various common divisions and segments of colleges and universities and, still further, the comprehensive associations of entire institutions. Several years ago I remarked that despite the efforts of these various groupings to promote many kinds of unified effort, their sheer number and multifarious functions create further problems in themselves, "so that paradoxically the whole of American higher education is both underorganized and overorganized." As a consequence, collective endeavor is often confused and weakened on the national level by vested-interest group pressures, splinter movements, and fragmented approaches.

Recognizing the need to avoid chaos and to effect a more unified leadership in and for our system of higher education, many institutions, agencies, and associations are joining forces with the American Council on Education. Since the Council has a small professional staff, limited financial resources, and no sanctions at its disposal, it can be no more effective than its constituents and others with whom it deals may want it to be. Like many other educational associations, the Council has to rely mainly upon cooperation to further coherence and unity of endeavor.

Whether voluntary effort can be successfully marshaled for the joint and inseparable task ahead remains to be seen. For our nation to survive and prosper, however, it would seem that we must move either toward more cooperation or toward more coercion in developing the strong and unified system of higher education we must have. In the light of this option, I am confident that our preference will be for cooperation.

8. *The efficiency of freedom should be safeguarded.* Whatever we do to tighten up the loose organization of education, it should be remembered that freedom is more than a mere shibboleth of the academic profession. Far from being an impediment to efficiency, it is an essential condition for the advancement of higher learning. The fact that our leading institutions are also the places where free inquiry and creative thought flourish best is no accident. Accordingly, in the endeavor to strengthen and unify our educational system, we must not sacrifice a main advantage we now have over the more rigid systems of totalitarian nations.

Diversity of support and control has been an influential factor in the past in protecting our entire system against outside interference from any single source. As the public sector of higher education grows larger, the importance of keeping it insulated from direct political control also grows. Furthermore, as both public and private institutions become more involved in Federal relations, it will be necessary to shield the pluralism of our system against the intrusion of bureaucratic controls from a central source.

Finally, I think it should be recognized that institutions of higher education have certain obligations which transcend time and place. Without regard to the pressing demands of the moment or of the society, such institutions are committed by tradition and purpose to advance knowledge for its own sake and to pursue the truth wherever it may lead. To serve our nation and civilization best, they must be free to criticize and to challenge. In the long pull, I suspect, the vigorous performance of this function may prove to be the most useful service they can render in advancing the general welfare.

A Better Partnership for the Federal Government and Higher Education

LOGAN WILSON

MORE THAN FIVE generations have passed since the Federal Government first concerned itself with education, and to many of us it seems absurd that we should still argue whether there should be such a concern. There is nothing absurd, however, about the continuing need to consider the nature and extent of the involvement. My view is that the rapidly growing interdependence of the government and higher education calls for an unending assessment of the partnership.

In the year 1776 there were only nine institutions of higher learning in this country; today there are more than 2,100. Our history attests the critical role colleges and universities have had in this nation's security and progress, and our present circumstances magnify rather than diminish this role. Moreover, since the final responsibility for our collective security and welfare can reside only in the Federal Government, a close partnership between government and education in our kind of society is unavoidable. Our present task, it seems to me, is to make this partnership as effective as possible.

Noting one aspect of the relationship, President Eisenhower's Science Advisory Committee stated in 1960: "The partnership is a fact. It has done much more good than harm. It seems certain to grow in importance unless the American people decide to accept a second-rate standing in terms of power, of comfort, of knowledge." The Committee's report sets forth some guidelines for the advancement of science. It lists broad principles, such as giving Federal support for excellence, increasing the number of first-rate teaching and research centers, attracting more talented students into science, encouraging new fields of knowledge, and so on. It makes pointed recommendations for the nation's further progress in science. Fortunately, many of these guidelines for the development of science are now being used extensively.

Unfortunately, the need for comparable guiding principles for Federal participation in the development of higher education as a whole has not been widely recognized. In some quarters there is still a strong sentiment that the functioning of our colleges and universities should be strictly a local, state, or private concern. This view often reflects ignorance of the heavy commitment the Federal Government already has in certain sectors of higher education. A review of the piecemeal, *ad hoc* pattern of Federal programs in turn suggests that even in Washington there is reluctance to face up to the implications of what is unquestionably a permanent and growing partnership.

To be sure, Congress has evidenced specific concerns. The keen legislative interest in what medical school research can do for the bodies of the elderly is obvious, even though there is apparently less interest in what liberal arts colleges can do for the minds of the young. Various Federal agencies have been explicit about the missions or tasks they have wanted colleges and universities to perform for them. And let us acknowledge also that diverse segments of education have been active in trying to promote Federal aid for their particular objectives.

In commenting on the fragmented nature of Federal participation in higher education, I do not imply that nobody has come forward with a unified approach to a comprehensive problem. This year, and for several recent years, the American Council on Education—to mention but one agency—has set forth such a program. President Kennedy's program was aimed at expanding individual opportunities, improving quality on all levels, and strengthening vocational, special, and continuing education. His plan did not advocate having the Federal Government take over local responsibilities, but contended that in the present era, state, local, and private efforts are not enough. However, the main principle specified regarding Federal participation was that it "should be selective, stimulative and, where possible, transitional."

President Johnson has expressed himself most emphatically regarding the importance of a comprehensive view of the needs of our educational system. Before we decide how the Federal Government can most appropriately and effectively aid in meeting these needs, I strongly believe that we must agree upon basic principles and establish guidelines for future action.

Acknowledging my temerity for getting into what should be a high-level committee or commission task for leading educators and others, I shall venture my own tentative views. They stem in the main from my recent experiences with the American Council on Education, where we are frequently in a mediating role between the Federal Government on the one hand and higher education on the other, but I want to make it clear that the observations are mine and do not necessarily represent the Council's position. The six principles I offer are set forth—not in the expectation that anybody will now endorse my bill of particulars—but in the hope that the educational community will soon reach its own consensus.

However this may be, our future is being shaped *now*. Certainly, it is high time for us to reach a better understanding within our own community and in the nation at large about the ongoing partnership between the Federal Government and higher education.

The National Interest Principle

In assisting higher education, the Federal Government should make national interests rather than local or special needs paramount. I suppose most of us would agree that the Federal Government must concern itself with extending educational opportunity, promoting economic growth, upgrading manpower, undergirding our security, and advancing our collective well-being. Colleges and universities are essential to the achievement of these objectives, as well as their own special and distinctive ends. Likewise, individuals must be educated for useful citizenship as well as for the furtherance of their private purposes.

In my opinion, it is a mistake to assume that all institutional and personal educational objectives are equally important to the national welfare and hence equally deserving of Federal support. Although I favor a concerted effort to increase the number and geographic spread of first-rate teaching and research centers, I doubt that any sensible person would favor taking Federal research and development funds away from such institutions as Harvard, M.I.T., Chicago, Michigan, and California and spreading them thinly among a large number of institutions where aspirations often exceed capabilities.

Aside from the wastage entailed in an indiscriminate, across-the-board doling out of Federal money, even our greatest institutions, which are truly national and even international in their service, render services to special constituencies which seem to me to be inappropriate for Federal support. The Harvard Houses, for example, are a fine environment for undergraduate learning but the expense entailed is certainly beyond what the Federal Government should be expected to underwrite. Or, to consider the curriculum itself, there may be many subjects in addition to theology for which we should not expect financial support from Washington. Of course, I have been in the nation's capital long enough to know that it has no monopoly of wisdom regarding education's best interests, but I have also been on enough campuses to know that provincial judgments sometimes put stadium enlargement ahead of library improvement, and find more pride in a resplendent marching band than in a roster of Woodrow Wilson fellows.

We should remember that few, if any, of the 2,100 or more colleges and universities in this country were founded by communities, states, churches, or private groups with the national interest primarily in view. (In fact, the military academies at West Point and Annapolis are the only long-standing institutions having this original purpose.) In a society as mobile and interdependent as ours is today, however, the Federal Government must promote the national interest by assisting important educational endeavors for which local, state, or private support is either lacking or insufficient. This may mean placing an expensive scientific installation, such as a particle accelerator, on the campus of a single university already possessing great human and material resources. It also may mean special assistance to poor states that pull down the level of our manpower by lagging badly to the rear of the academic procession.

In brief, I maintain that Federal aid should not be ladled out to any segment of the population merely to ease the burden of carrying local or special obligations. When the national interest is not being adequately served, however, I believe that there is no substitute for Federal concern and support.

The Resource Development Principle

Federal assistance should be conceived not as a form of benevolence to institutions and individuals, but as an investment in a national resource. Neither colleges and universities nor students should be aided merely because they are needy, but because of their potential contribution to our collective achievement as a people. Although I doubt that very many members of Congress think of appropriations for education as being in the same category as veterans pensions and old age relief, there manifestly is not a full appreciation of education's importance as an indispensable element in the nation's security and well-being.

An American Council on Education brochure, *Higher Education as a National Resource,* puts it this way in stating the case for Federal concern:

American higher education is a priceless asset fundamental to the national purpose. It cannot be spoken of simply in terms of the value of buildings and equipment, the total number of persons served, the teachers involved, or the research performed. The nation's colleges and junior colleges, universities, research institutes, and professional schools are all of these things, but something more. Broadly conceived, higher education constitutes a precious national resource essential to the achievement of great national goals and to the achievement of worthy aspirations of individual citizens. It is a resource also in the sense that, given favorable conditions, it is as capable of self-renewal as is a properly conserved forest.

This same statement goes on to point out the growing pressures on higher education—the pressures of enrollment increases and of new knowledge. In view of the tax revenue limitations of localities and states, together with the declining proportion of total support from private sources, how can one escape the conclusion that our Federal Government must assume a larger role in the conservation and improvement of higher education?

The potential human resources in all regions of the country are of similar capability, but the means to finance higher education are very unevenly distributed. This latter circumstance makes it especially difficult in some states and regions for institutions to give adequate support to graduate and professional education, and the problem is complicated even further by the siphoning-off of talent to more prosperous sections.

What I am saying is that the expansion and improvement of higher education are too vital to our future to be left entirely in the hands of local and private enterprise. Adequate financial support for the nation's colleges and universities must be regarded as a funding operation rather than a relief measure, and the cost must be treated as an investment in human capital rather than an ordinary expenditure. The investment required is indeed a heavy one, but not nearly so heavy as the penalties we and oncoming generations will have to pay for failure to conserve and strengthen a critical national resource.

The Selective Principle

If the Federal Government is not to assume the whole burden of support for higher education, its decisions of necessity imply priorities. Colleges and universities are accustomed to getting their funds with strings attached, to be sure, but this does not lessen the desire of some to have substantial Federal grants to spend as they please. To spread decision making, there are also those who would prefer to have Congress dole out funds to the fifty states for internal allocations, or else resort to simple formulae for spreading them everywhere.

Since it is neither possible nor desirable for the Federal Government to take over the entire support of higher education, it is evident that there must be some selectivity by levels, institutions, programs, and projects. This being so, I believe a more suitable pattern can be found than the one now resulting from our piecemeal approach. To move more systematically, however, there should be a meeting of minds between government and education about priorities of importance and urgency.

For example, I think a better case can be made for Federal aid on higher than on lower levels. I am not arguing that higher education is more directly related to the national interest, or that its needs are more urgent. Admittedly, more dollars are needed to bolster primary and secondary education, but these are the levels where local concern, understanding, and support are strongest. We pride ourselves on the fact that our common schools are community-centered enterprises. Our colleges and universities, on the other hand, have always had a different structure of support and control. Their constituencies are more widely dispersed; political and geographic boundary lines are less relevant to the services they perform; their policies are much less susceptible to uniformization.

In principle I advocate appropriate Federal aid for all levels of education and see no necessity for an either/or alternative, but in fact I want to point out that the private-public schism is far less serious on the higher level and that lesser sums of money are required to produce stimulative or multiplier effects in response to changing national needs.

Even in higher education, as I said earlier, I do not believe in Federal assistance to disciplines across the board. From the point of view of liberal education, art and philosophy may be more essential than astronomy and engineering, but is this a valid reason for expecting the Department of Defense or any other Federal agency to give support to all aspects of the curriculum? In my opinion it is the responsibility of individual institutions rather than of the central government to maintain balance in education, and to resist or countervail influences to the contrary.

The other side of the coin, however, is that institutions can maintain this balance successfully only if the government underwrites fully the costs of Federal projects undertaken by colleges and universities. Not only is the government falling short of meeting institutional indirect costs on research projects, but also it is not reimbursing out-of-pocket local costs for ROTC, international education programs, and various other services institutions perform for Federal agencies.

Working through the American Council on Education and other voluntary associations, colleges and universities are getting together about their own priorities of importance and urgency. There is still a need, nonetheless, for more agreement on all sides about the ordering of events. More persons must become aware that the expansion and improvement of faculties and facilities should precede any massive program of scholarships and other student aids. Or, to give another example, the development of graduate and professional education is perhaps less popular, but its continued encouragement is hardly less urgent than the multiplication of junior colleges and other undergraduate institutions.

In summary, I believe that our only real choice is to step up Federal assistance to education. As we implement this decision, I hope that we shall choose to do those things which will be of maximum benefit to both government and education.

The Complementary Principle

Federal aid should strengthen rather than weaken diversity of support and control, and should complement rather than supplant local effort. Alongside its shortcomings in an era of rapid social change, the American system of higher education has some great strengths which should be maintained. The dualism of public and private institutions, for instance, upholds the pluralism of our culture, and varied sources of financial support keep higher education as a whole from being subservient to extraneous influences. Likewise, the tradition of autonomous governance and the wide variation in aim and scope foster a free competition in the advancement of knowledge which is of inestimable value to a dynamic society.

Despite the protests of those who oppose Federal aid on the grounds that it weakens the diversity of support and control, my contention is that it has had and can continue to have an opposite result. Wisely and fairly distributed, government funds further a mixed pattern of support which is beneficial to all institutions, both public and private. Although I favor outright grants for certain kinds of aid and am cognizant of the difficulties inherent in matching requirements, I do feel that in most situations Federal aid should be linked to incentives for increased local and private support.

Paradoxical as it may seem, I believe that many institutions could safeguard their autonomy and freedom more effectively by tightening their internal organization. Often without either faculty or administrative authorization from their own campuses, too many different voices are speaking in Washington for their segmented interests and even, in some cases, for education as a whole. This not only confuses Congress and the Federal agencies but also tends to block a unified approach to interrelated problems.

Over and beyond the need for more internal cohesion, colleges and universities will stand a better chance of upholding their integrity through voluntary joint agreements among themselves than by going their separate ways. Collectively, they can resist distorting influences which only the strongest of them can resist individually. Of course, this implies a common code of ethics in some new areas of relationships where no such code now exists, and perhaps even the necessity for self-policing.

To borrow a phrase from a Carnegie *Quarterly*, there is a growing "inseparability of politics and education," and it is for us to make the most of this fact of modern life. Past experience alone should remove the fear many persons still have that Federal support necessarily carries with it Federal control. Speaking as one who has dealt with state legislatures, private donors, and the Federal Government, I would agree with McGeorge Bundy that support from Washington has been and can continue to be "a reinforcement of the freedom of the higher learning." Our common task is to see that Federal aid offsets the shortcomings and builds upon the strengths of the American system of higher education.

The Merit Principle

Although Federal assistance will be needed to increase the availability of higher education, it will be needed even more to improve quality. Quantity and quality are not conflicting objectives, but we may be sure that expansion and improvement will compete with each other for whatever funds are available. My guess is that the heaviest local pressures will be for throwing all possible resources into expansion, and hence I want to stress the critical need for Federal funds to keep qualitative improvement moving forward. This is my main argument for the merit principle as a guideline for allocating a considerable proportion of moneys from Washington.

One reason I am apprehensive about the neglect of quality in higher education is the great magnitude of the funding operation which will be necessary to underwrite expansion between now and 1980. Everybody knows about the "tidal wave" of students, of course, but few persons are vividly aware of just what it signifies. The problem is more readily grasped when we realize that to cope with it we hypothetically would have to double the size of all existing colleges and universities, *and* establish a thousand more institutions with an average enrollment of 2,500.

Since egalitarian sentiments will probably be on the side of expansion at the expense of improvement, I would favor a discriminating use of Federal allocations to make certain that standards are maintained and strengthened. This means that government money will produce the best results if it is distributed according to the merit principle instead of being scattered everywhere with a dead-leveling effect.

Despite occasional charges of bias and favoritism against government agencies and the panels of experts used by them to determine which individuals, projects, programs, and institutions are worthy of assistance, the procedures they usually employ seem to me to be the only appropriate ones for many kinds of undertakings. National Science Foundation procedures, for example, utilizing advisory panels drawn from the academic community itself, much more closely approximate those used on most college and university campuses to allocate funds than do across-the-board schemes.

Conversely, I think that Federal funds should not be given as subsidies for budget-balancing purposes to institutions perennially on the verge of bankruptcy nor to institutions with overly ambitious ventures.

In many states we can already observe the unfortunate consequences of what someone has aptly called the "university syndrome."
By this is meant the overweening desires of altogether too many
institutions to become full-fledged universities in name and scope.
There is nothing wrong per se with such aspirations, but in the
process of change, unfortunately, some of them are transmogrified
rather than transmuted. The nation has no need for more second-
and third-rate institutions at any level, but it does have a desperate
need for more first-rate centers on all levels. In short, we cannot
afford to lose sight of the importance of quality in higher education.

The Coordinated Plan Principle

Federal assistance should be guided by a long-range plan for
the most logical development of the American system of higher
education as an entity. As I have said elsewhere, there is now
too much unplanned diversification among our colleges and universities. We really have no system of higher education in the strict
sense of the term, but merely a congeries of institutions. Some
regions have too many indiscriminately established and inadequately
maintained institutions, and elsewhere there is a dearth of colleges
and universities. The presence of diploma mills in many states
demonstrates the ease with which almost anybody can get into
the business of higher education.

To be sure, decentralization has its virtues, but these often have
their own reverse defects. Disparate educational endeavors, for instance, do not always produce the total endeavor required to meet
our national needs, and the unevenness of educational opportunity
limits the entire nation's manpower potential.

Just as we can no longer afford to behave as a mere federation
of states in international affairs, so can we ill afford to continue
educational policies and practices which do not make sense in an
era of increased interdependence within the nation. The costs of
unilateral action have become too high, and the penalties of wasteful
competition too great. In the past it may not have made much
difference that we were relatively oblivious to national objectives
in higher education, but we have reached a time when all of our
colleges and universities must participate in those purposes essential to our common survival and well-being.

In view of our changed circumstances, we in higher education
should not expect the Federal Government merely to underwrite
the *status quo*. Both our institutions and our government must aim
for higher and better things.

There simply must be more institutional cooperation and unity
of effort, and these must be guided by a sense of common purpose.
Other than meeting the need to expand our system of higher educa-

tion, what other objectives do we have in view for 1980? From my point of view we are fortunate in being one of the few modern nations not having a ministry of education which supports and controls the educational establishment. Lacking this central direction of enterprise, however, we are under the necessity of demonstrating that cooperation, no less than coercion, can bring us together to accomplish national objectives. Patterns of state, regional, and national cooperation have already emerged. Some of our states and regions now have long-range plans. It remains for us to develop some plan for the nation as a whole.

The American Council on Education is moving in this direction. Our Commission on Federal Relations and our Commission on Plans and Objectives for Higher Education are addressing themselves to the kinds of questions which must be answered. We are calling upon the most knowledgeable persons we can bring together, for example, to promote a better partnership between the Federal Government and higher education. Since the Council is the major organization of colleges, universities, and other associations in the field of higher education, we are making every effort to formulate proper guidelines and get widespread acceptance of them.

We are moving ahead as promptly as we can in the full knowledge that the actions of Congress and more than forty executive agencies of the Federal Government are already making policies and setting direction which affect the future of American higher education. In our view, there is no longer any option in educational circles between institutional *laissez faire* on the one hand and coordinated enterprise on the other. Each institution should have its own sense of public mission, of course, but my own conviction is that the educational community has a right and a responsibility to share with the government in the determination of policies and directions that will, as much as any other factors, shape our whole future.

State and Federal Legislative Relations

STANLEY J. WENBERG

DISCUSSION OF the role of the Federal Government in higher education almost invariably centers on the role of Federal funds in aiding states and collegiate institutions to get certain work done.

In my own legislative relations, the pivot point of misunderstanding has all too frequently been the concept of Federal "aid." We don't speak of "state aid," "alumni aid," "endowment aid," or "church aid." Yet we seem to insist on describing funds received from the Federal Government as "federal aid." The fact is higher education has failed to develop a clear differentiation between a Federal role or "Federal responsibility for higher education" and the concept of "Federal aid."

Discussion of the role Federal funds will play in the deployment of higher educational resources within a state puts us on almost totally uncharted waters. Robert D. Calkins, in his paper, "Government Support of Higher Education," published in connection with the McGraw-Hill symposium on *Financing Higher Education, 1960–1970*, states:

> The power of the federal government to support higher education is no longer seriously questioned. Yet it is an overstatement to assert that a positive policy of assisting higher educational institutions now exists, except in special and limited areas. The present policy has been aptly described as one of using and even exploiting the unique services of these institutions as essential to the national interest, but without contributing more than incidentally to their solvency, their perpetuation, or their improvement.

Federal Funds as a Basis for Growth

Whether one considers the flow of any particular Federal dollar into higher education a distortion of a state's picture depends obviously on the vantage point from which one views that dollar. As a member of a North Central Association accrediting team, I visited "Aspiring University," a modest, emerging, former state college. This visit was in connection with a request that four new doctoral programs be accredited by the association. Two of these programs were in physical sciences. My responsibility related to the administrative rather than the academic soundness of such programs at the institution and in the state involved. In this context it was interesting to observe that the availability of Federal fellowships was given as one of the prime reasons for the initiation of the doctoral level science programs. It is an understatement to say that staff members at "State University" of that state looked upon the development at the emerging college "less favorably" than did the staff members at Aspiring University. Indeed, one dean at State University observed that Federal funds had made it possible for the institution to move into very costly doctoral programs "through the back door," with no insurance of quality or even of continuing state support.

Such illustrations are legion. They lend credibility to Dr. Calkins' statement. They also raise the question, "How did we get here?"

On another tack, there are such spokesmen as John A. Perkins, who argues that "the critical problem in the next ten years is not so much one of research but one of teaching larger numbers of students. The present pattern of Federal aid is not generally directed toward instruction." The question Dr. Perkins deals with in his paper, "The Federal Government and Higher Education," does not depreciate the need for research funds—it merely supports the point that Dr. Calkins made that, by and large, the Federal Government has tended not to help build higher education with a sense of responsibility for its total success, but rather to tap narrow segments of it as one more available national resource.

Before we press too hard on Washington, one question we need to settle with ourselves is whether or not we are ready to change our feelings about the large bulk of Federal relationships with higher education. A change in language, if it is to occur, should reflect a change in attitude.

Resource or Recipient?

In an oversimplified analysis, funds coming to universities can be broken into two major classes: (1) universities being tapped as a resource (research training grants, etc.); (2) universities being recipients under programs logically classified as Federal aid (the National Defense Education Act Loan Fund, academic facilities grants, the GI bill, etc.).

Our universities, in most of these programs, are less the masters of their own fate than grateful recipients of funds from the Federal Government. Increasingly it is being argued that we should shift from selling services and accepting aid to positive recognition of the Federal Government's responsibility for certain kinds of activities in our institutions, a responsibility that covers both adequate and continuing support for these activities.

Consideration of an environmental health center which taps the resources of many departments of the university, but principally those of the department of public health, has more regional and national implications than it does state. There are only twelve graduate-level public health departments in the higher educational structure of the United States. If this area of research and learning is thought of as a national-level responsibility, provision of facilities, the maintenance of these facilities, and provision of continuing staff and research funds become a Federal responsibility.

Federal and State Support

The illustration is meant only to make the point that, if broad areas of Federal responsibility can be identified, numerous specific activities within a complex university could be and ought to be supported totally with Federal funds. Other funds available to these universities might then be deployed in a pattern more appropriate to each state's needs.

For any of our public institutions it does not seem unreasonable to expect that ultimately there would be no more control over the Federal funds than there is over the state funds once the general areas being supported are defined. It would seem reasonable and consistent that neither level of government would have any more right to abdicate general responsibility for the funds than it would have to control their precise use. For our state universities, what is called for here is a transfer of the pattern of relationships that exists at the state level to relationships at the Federal level.

The new academic facilities bill literally challenges all of us to work toward this new conception. Up to now most of us have isolated Federal dollars from state dollars. The meshing of Federal money and state money for the first time is requiring us to work out our own state house relationships on the role of Federal dollars in our state-financed construction programs.

Whether we will be wise enough or persuasive enough to sell the concept of a new kind of state-federal partnership in higher education remains to be seen. Can we strike a balance between the tremendous pride many of our states feel for the progress we have made thus far with public higher education, on the one hand, and the factors that define a new broad role of Federal responsibility, on the other?

Partnership for the Future

Can we bring our individual congressmen from an almost over-zealous programmatic commitment to a new sense of higher educational responsibility? With the need for less exploitation of specific talent, there is need for a more abstract understanding by the administration, the Congress, and the agencies of the Federal Government of responsibility in depth for areas which have a higher level of national relevance than of state relevance. It would require governors and legislators to identify a partnership role in getting the job done. Acceptance of Federal support of educational agriculture reflects our ability to achieve this understanding.

The same pattern can develop in other quarters of our universities. It can be argued that, if the health of the nation warrants major investments of Federal dollars in facilities and research, justification is not related to the ability of the Federal Government to command matching funds in any particular state. If the Federal Government is making a grant on a basis of recognized investigator competence, it could be argued that its responsibility is complete and that facilities, staffing, and maintenance become components of that responsibility.

Up to now such funds have been thought of as aid. We in higher education, to our increasing disadvantage, have helped entrench that concept of aid. By treating such matching funds as Federal aid, and therefore as bait in favored areas of our institutions, rather than as part of deliberately planned expansion and development programs, we have allowed them to literally warp the deployment of our state provided resources.

If we are again to become masters in our own households, we must, to our individual legislators and congressmen, appear to be less the beggars for each morsel and more the leaders in planning for a three-way partnership in getting the job done.

In the process some of our staffs and programs already under way may be disadvantaged. In the process we will need to identify the political leaders both at the state and Federal level who have the vision of and the commitment to what is at stake in our mission. In the process we will offend others less sensitive or realistic about our problems. But in the end we will have the partnership that is the promise of the full support our higher educational enterprise requires and deserves.

Government and the Universities

JOHN W. GARDNER

IN THE PAST few years, the government-university relationship has been studied almost to death, and as one who is partly responsible for that fact, I'd like to offer a few comments.

It is not easy to view the present large-scale relationship between government and the universities in any kind of meaningful perspective, perhaps because it has developed too recently for us to have grasped its implications. In order to see the problem in the broadest terms, let us begin with three fairly large generalizations:

1. Present government-university dealings are only a part of a far-reaching and profoundly significant trend in the relationship between the government and nongovernmental sectors of our society.

2. Both government and the universities are being changed by the relationship. Neither will ever be the same again.

3. University people should concern themselves not only with what this means for their own institutions, but with what it means for the government. It is their government too.

New Trends in Relationships

When I say that the government-university relationship is part of a larger trend I refer chiefly to the fact that the Federal Government's contractual relationships with industry have expanded as dramatically as its relationships with the universities. The Federal Government's changing fiscal relationships with state governments, as reflected in the phrase "the New Federalism," are also relevant in this connection.

Do the emerging relationships with the universities and with industry represent an increase in government power or a decrease; a centralizing trend or a decentralizing trend? When one considers that many industrial companies and universities are now in some measure dependent on government support, one is inclined to see the trend as a growth in government power. But to the old-line Federal official, used to a world in which government funds were spent for purposes defined by government and administered by hierarchically organized departments under complete government control, the new trend looks like a grievous *loss* of government power. He can't appraise what it is doing to industry and the uni-

286

versities, but he knows that it is having a profound effect on government. Wherever he looks, he sees lay advisory bodies recommending how government money shall be spent, and he sees nongovernmental organizations spending it. Both industry and the universities spend their contract money to outbid government in the hiring of scarce personnel. The universities assert that both contract and grant money should be spent in ways that they themselves define, and they do not welcome the advice of well-meaning government servants. It is difficult for the Federal official to observe all this and feel that his power is growing. His feeling is better expressed, perhaps, in a letter I received recently from a distinguished civil servant. He wrote: "When those mild academic fellows say the meek shall inherit the earth, it's not a pious expression, it's a plan of action."

In short, the new partnerships cut across the old public-private categories as well as the old centralization-decentralization categories. A new sort of relationship has been created, and we are going to have to judge it by new criteria. Fortunately, it is a relationship that is still evolving, so we still have a chance to shape its future course.

Defining Conditions of Relationships

When government agencies and universities work together there are predictable sources of difficulty. Surely we know those difficulties by heart now. I shall mention only two or three of the most salient problems. The government agency tends to surround the relationship with more and more defining conditions, to the point where the university feels that its freedom of decision is undermined. This does not reflect a sinister desire to diminish anyone's freedom. It stems from the nature of government responsibilities and habits of mind. The remarkable thing is not that all agencies show these tendencies, which they do, but that some agencies have had the wisdom to curb them.

Just as the government agency tends to tighten the defining conditions of the relationship, so university people seek to loosen them. They tend to push all contracts and grants in the direction of the general support grant—fewer conditions, more freedom to define objectives, and greater continuity of support. The ideal relationship as far as the university man is concerned would be one entirely without any complicating context, which is to say without any context at all, money passed in the dead of night from a donor who would never know the object of his largesse to a recipient who would never know who gave the money or why. Some government observers refer to this as the "leave it on a stump" approach.

Underlying these differing approaches is a fundamental difference of outlook on the issue of accountability. The accountability of the university varies of course with the various kinds of contracts and grants. In basic research grants it may be limited to the barest minimum of fiscal reporting, but in contracts it may be more complicated. It is not easy for university people to understand that the government lives by accountability (and no one would wish it otherwise)—accountability to the taxpayer, to Congress, to the General Accounting Office, and to the White House. In most contract procedures, the government agency has delegated some of its powers to a private organization. Naturally it tends to want to impose on that organization the same accountability it requires of itself. What it fails to understand, of course, is that excessive zeal in demanding accountability may create intolerable conditions for the universities with which it is dealing.

Just as the government agency is often too rigid in demanding accountability, so the university is sometimes too cavalier. The university should sympathize with the government's basic problem and should focus its criticism on those forms of accountability that are clearly inappropriate to a university. When it can serve the government's requirements without damaging its own position, it should do so.

Lack of Understanding between the Partners

Dealings between government and university people are marred by other kinds of misunderstanding. The failure on the part of government to understand what a university is about is still with us. It is not universal among government agencies—there are some immensely gratifying exceptions—but misunderstanding is still so frequently encountered as to be deeply disturbing.

Unfortunately this failure on the part of government has its counterpart in the academic world. University people feel little or no need to understand what government is about. And as long as that is true it will be a source of trouble.

Universities may also be criticized for bringing to the relationship a sense of intellectual and moral superiority that is extremely irritating when conflicts of purpose arise. The irritation is heightened by the fact that the university representatives are usually more articulate than those of government.

Professors tend to manifest the sense of moral superiority more aggravatingly than do deans or presidents. (A faculty friend of mine says, "Naturally! They have more to feel superior about!" He didn't intend it as a joke.) There exists among many faculty people (and indeed among professional men everywhere) a widely accepted myth concerning the purity of the professional and the corruptness of the administrator. On the one side, the myth asserts, there are scholars and professionals—pure and selfless spirits who think only of the high requirements of their callings; and on the other side, there are the administrators, organization men and politicians— seekers of power and status, who achieve their aims by a willingness to compromise their convictions. The myth is sustained by frequent repetition of Lord Acton's aphorism. It is hardly surprising that these attitudes nourish a certain paranoia in the academic man who holds them: In every encounter with decision makers he sees himself as the potential victim.

But it is ironic that faculty people place government representatives in that category, because the faculty man and the government servant are in many ways alike. Both think of themselves as dedicated to ideals of service. Both see themselves as having chosen careers that do not involve great expectation of material gain. And in fact the government servant may be making a more serious financial sacrifice than the faculty man with whom he is dealing.

Separate Missions, Separate Identities

When I say that we must have greater understanding between government agencies and universities, I do not mean that the relationship should be more intimate than it is. Actually, there is some advantage to the public interest in keeping a certain adversary quality in the relationship. Under such conditions, the agency is continually alert to the requirements of its mission, its accountability to the taxpayer, and its constitutional responsibility. And the university never forgets that it was born free and should remain so, never forgets that its purposes are not identical with (indeed sometimes at odds with) the purposes of the government agency. Neither of the participants loses its keen sense of separate missions and separate identities.

We all know of situations both in industry and in the educational field in which strong ties exist between middle-level government executives, congressmen, and outside interest groups. There is nothing inherently wrong in such ties. People who are trying to get something accomplished through government channels inevitably come to know a good many government officials; in fact they may help with the recruitment of such officials. They also come to know members of Congress. If the relationships between all of these people are characterized by mutual trust and teamwork, much may be accomplished in the public interest. But there is some danger that each of the various participants may become less sensitive to his own special responsibilities. All concerned may compromise themselves a bit for the sake of stability in the relationship and the predictable success of their joint efforts. Furthermore, such an interlock of interests tends to include all the people who know enough about the subject to criticize it effectively. Really stringent criticism does not arise, because "members of the club" are not inclined to attack one another.

The government-university relationship will work well only if each of the parties to the relationship is strong enough to play its role effectively, and if the terms of the relationship are such as to permit each to retain its integrity.

It is not easy for us to think of government as a victim in any relationship involving the world of education, but James Conant points out that in many states the official agencies for dealing with elementary and secondary education are too weak to function effectively and are at the mercy of the professional educators who maintain lobbies in state capitals. At the Federal level, groups from the educational world have on more than one occasion pursued policies that have tended to weaken certain government agencies. They have rarely pursued policies deliberately designed to strengthen them. In the case of the Office of Education, it is well known that some educational leaders believe that their professional associations will be best served if the Office is weak.

I would assert this as a general principle: *In their dealings with government agencies, the universities should worry almost as much about the health and competence of the agencies with which they are dealing as they do about their own autonomy.* The relationship cannot be a healthy one if the government agency involved is weak, poorly staffed, or disorganized. The evils flowing from that condition will impair the whole relationship.

Just as every government agency needs informed critics, so it needs discriminating and intelligent friends. On the whole, the university world has shown little concern for the health of the government service.

Extent of Institutional Dependence

Just as the soundness of the relationship requires that the government agency be healthy and competent, so it requires that the nongovernmental institution (whether industrial or academic) never lose its essential independence. That sounds obvious to the point of comedy, but it bears repeating. The Bell Report on government contracting found in reviewing the aircraft industry that the percentage of total sales attributable to government business ranged from a low of 67 percent for one company to 99.2 percent for another company. And this led the authors of the report to ask: "In what sense is a business corporation doing nearly 100 percent of its business with the government engaged in free enterprise?" I would reply, "In no sense that makes any sense."

A number of universities today receive amounts from the Federal Government that represent a large percentage of their annual budgets. In some cases most of the Federal funds go to support laboratories that are essentially separate from the university. The extent to which the university itself is actually dependent on government funds must be examined for each particular institution.

Many universities are more dependent on the Federal Government today than they care to admit. But that assertion is not only not original, it is no longer even helpful. What we need now is a more analytical scrutiny of the *ways* in which universities become dependent upon government funds. Clearly, some kinds of government support carry little or no danger of dependence, while others are very dangerous indeed. The formula one usually hears is that the more the university allows government money to get into the core of its budget and its operations, the more heavy is the dependence. The more it keeps government funds insulated from the main operation of the university and confined to projects that can be jettisoned at will, the more it preserves its independence.

But every one knows that it really isn't that simple. If projects are very large, there is almost no way of insulating them. When a substantial number of gifted scientists are brought onto a campus for a government project, they become a significant factor in the life of the institution, whether or not anyone intended that outcome. The funds at their disposal attract graduate students. They command laboratory facilities that university personnel are eager to share. Some accept part-time teaching responsibilities.

The universities, in their contract and grant relationships with government, have not yet had to face the problem of retrenchment on a large scale. If and when that issue arises, the government may find that it simply cannot pull out of certain major activities. There is little likelihood of retrenchment across the board in the government's relationship with the universities, not in the near future and not in the far future. But it is quite possible that the government might decide, for example, that one of the giant laboratories it supports through the universities has outlived its usefulness. And it might then discover that it was politically unfeasible to close that laboratory.

Obviously, if it becomes recognized throughout the university world that the government cannot in fact accomplish major retrenchments, the relationship from that point on will be on a markedly different basis.

Conclusions

Far from a general retrenchment, I foresee a steady growth in the government-university involvement. In the light of that prediction, my advice to the universities is this:

1. They must understand the relationship in the largest terms—what it means for them, what it means for the government, and what it means for the whole society. And they must care about the health and integrity of their government and the whole society almost as ardently as they care about themselves.

2. The universities must become exceedingly knowing in the art of preserving their own autonomy. The issue of university autonomy will never be finally solved. It can only be lived with. But the more fully one understands the direction in which our society is moving, the more clearly one sees how vitally important it is that the universities continue as independent centers of thought, criticism, and initiative.

3. Finally, the universities must make one last effort to regain some measure of control over their own destiny. Clark Kerr was everlastingly right when he said, in his excellent book *The Uses of the University*, that the main things that have happened to the universities in recent years have happened as a result of initiative from outside the universities. There can be no doubt that this is true. And perhaps it must always be true. But I cannot really accept that notion. I believe that the best chance for the universities to play a role of genuine leadership in determining their own future is through the more effective operation of their associations, such as the American Council on Education. But it will also require a level of awareness and a quality of statesmanship throughout the academic world that has not existed to date. A number of college and university presidents, deans, and professors have staunchly faced the larger issues, and we all owe them a debt of gratitude; but they cannot do the job alone. They must be able to count on an informed and active constituency that knows very well what is at stake. If such a constituency emerges, then these very able leaders will receive the backing they deserve and their effectiveness will be multiplied. And then the universities will be not only magnificent resources, as they are now, but masters of their own fate, which now they are not.

AMERICAN COUNCIL ON EDUCATION

LOGAN WILSON, *President*

The American Council on Education, founded in 1918, is a *council* of educational organizations and institutions. Its purpose is to advance education and educational methods through comprehensive voluntary and cooperative action on the part of American educational associations, organizations, and institutions.